Infinite Variety

DAN LOWREY'S MUSIC HALL 1879–97

Eugene Watters
Matthew Murtagh

Infinite Variety

DAN LOWREY'S MUSIC HALL 1879–97

GILL AND MACMILLAN

First published in 1975

GILL AND MACMILLAN LIMITED
2 Belvedere Place
Dublin 1
and internationally through
association with the
Macmillan Publishers Group

Jacket and text designed by
JARLATH HAYES

7171 0711 6
Printing history 54321

Printed in Great Britain by
Fletcher & Son Ltd, Norwich

Contents

Acknowledgments

Acknowledgments are due to the Trustees of the British Museum, to the librarians of the National Library of Ireland and of the Library of Trinity College, Dublin, and to the authorities of the Bibliothèque de Genève and of the Deutsches Museum, Munich, for the use of information and illustrations from their collections; to the staff of the Public Libraries at Leeds, Liverpool, Belfast and Cork for their generous help in the research; to the Codman Company, the Tiller Company, and the Superintendent of the Zoological Gardens, Dublin, for specialist information and items supplied; to Dr J. F. Larchet for valuable help in the search for Paganini Redivivus; to the host of people who ransacked their files and their memories; and to Rita E. Kelly who re-created some of the faded old prints as black-and-white drawings.

Sources

THE BOURKE COLLECTION OF THEATRE PROGRAMMES. Library of Trinity College, Dublin.

THE HOLLOWAY COLLECTION OF DIARIES, PLAYBILLS, PROGRAMMES, ETC. National Library of Ireland.

THE LAWRENCE COLLECTION OF MSS AND SCRAPBOOKS. National Library of Ireland.

PARISH CHURCH RECORDS, Leeds and Liverpool.

RECORDS IN THE PUBLIC LIBRARIES of Leeds, Liverpool, Belfast and Cork.

MRS SARGEANT'S RECOLLECTIONS. Information given, in conversation and correspondence, by Mrs Norah Sargeant (1882–1967), a daughter of Dan Lowrey's. Filed in the Murtagh Collection.

THE STAR ENGAGEMENT BOOK (1894–97); in the possession of the Sargeant family.

THE MURTAGH COLLECTION. The result of over thirty years' research by Matthew Murtagh; comprises items of London and Dublin Theatre History in general; London and Dublin Music Hall History; books, magazines, photographs, prints, posters, programmes, gramophone records, song-sheets, advertisements and critiques; copies of interviews and special articles in newspapers and periodicals; a Register of Artistes and Items with extensive notes on each; an Annual List, compiled by the Collector, of all Stage Acts appearing at Dan Lowrey's and other Theatres and Music Halls; and a detailed Bibliography. Kept at his home and available to scholars.

To the Memory of NORAH SARGEANT

CHAPTER ONE

1829–78 Out of the Wreck

In the year 1829 disaster struck the town of Roscrea in County Tipperary.

A Traveller of the time, coming upon Roscrea in the fertile valley surrounded by a grace of hills, saw it as 'old and Irish' and charming at a distance; but close up, it was a pathetic mixture of elegant private gateways, trim lawns and doorways with colonnades, shops with diamond-paned windows, mouldering hovels, cobbles, ruts, dungheaps and duckpuddles, the chimneys of woollen and whiskey mills, a round tower from Celtic days, cholera morbus and rotting thatch, where about nine thousand people lived in an uneasy pattern of solid wealth, unskilled drudgery and sheer degradation.

Ancient Tower at Roscrea

All round the town, in shielings and mud huts on the rich lands, on the bogs, on the hills, swarmed the serfs, politely called the peasantry, a people whom history seemed to have uprooted and reduced – in the Traveller's phrase – to lounging lookers-on, subsisting on potatoes and Irish airs, on the brink of the Great Starvation.

The town had its music. The harp was coming into vogue, and the piano; Tom Moore was all the rage, and the ringletted daughters of the gentry and of the professional and the new commercial class played 'The Harp That Once Through Tara's Halls' with a nice touch of sentiment for the departed glories of a Celtic Neverneverland. Outside in the mud and sheepdirt of the street, the music was not quite so refined. The frequent fair-days brought itinerant balladsingers, fluters, pipers and chest-fiddlers whose songs were the news-sheets of the times, celebrating shootings and jailbreaks, the anarchy, massacres, riots, faction fights and the hurley matches for which Tipperary was famous. The language of the songs was as coloured as the neckerchiefs of the singers – a kind of English, which had retained the accent and some stray speech habits of the rich and subtle language of the Irish past. Such as it was, this raw stuff was the People's music, affording them, along with their fierce religious loyalties, some glimpse of a reason to live.

Roscrea, set in sheep country, possessed Buckley's thriving woollen mills. Among the hundred or so (fortunate) workers in Buckley's, there was a man named Patrick Lowrey. In the misty past, his surname had been the name of kings, and meant 'the Wellspoken One', but he was unaware of it. There is a theory that his father or some of the Lowrey family had escaped the Massacre on Vinegar Hill in the last fierce uprising, but instead of nursing this bitterness among the feckless hordes on the roads, the Lowreys had come into the Town, put the past and the language of the past behind them, and faced the new reality. So we find this Patrick Lowrey, undistinguished from the rest of the millworkers, eking out a small and uncertain existence for his young wife and himself.

In 1823 their first child was born and named Daniel, perhaps after the uncrowned King of the People, the great O'Connell: like all mothers, Mrs Pat Lowrey nursed the secret faith in her firstborn. When the child was six, disaster struck the town.

In a hard time, under the stress of competition in the English common market, Buckley's Mills were forced to shut down. There was an ominous silence in the town. Crowds gathered to stare in stupefaction at the closed gates, knowing they had only one choice; they must either go back to the mud huts of their tribe to swell the death-rate in the impending famine (it came in 1847), or emigrate.

From Roscrea, as from all over Ireland, the first tricklings of the Great Exodus began. O'Briens, Flynns, Sullivans, joined the stream of the displaced and the deracinated – Irish, English, Scots, Italians, Negroes, Poles – that were rushing into those fungoid industrial growths, Liverpool, Leeds, Birmingham, the breeding-places of the New People. From his comfortable lodging in the Valley House Inn, the Traveller noted that the most attractive posters on the walls of Roscrea were the notices of rival Companies offering passage to Emigrants.

Realist as always, Patrick Lowrey set his face to the future and joined in the flight. He sold what little he possessed, took his wife and the child Daniel, went to the Company Office and bought tickets for the Van and the Boat. The covered horse-drawn cars left Roscrea daily for Dublin.

The Traveller describes the scene, the ragged throng in the roadway, the fiddle music, the lighted windows in the dark of dawn, the drinks, the wild unnatural laughter, the grey frieze, the babies and bundles, girls stupid with weeping, the old people kissing the hands of the exiles till the whip cracked and jerked them asunder.

The Caravan left Roscrea at six o'clock in the morning, travelled the seventy-five miles with relays of horses through the teeming and miserable Midlands, came into Dublin by the Great Western Road at Kilmainham on the ancient Hill of the City, and reined to a halt at Number 8 Cornmarket at six o'clock in the evening. On foot then down Cork Hill and the cobbles of Dame Street to the Quays, joining the grey swarm, stunned with shock and home-sickness. Torn between the consuming hatred of the Irishman for his native land and his terrible love of it. The Boat slips down the estuary, they smell for the first time the salt air.

Writing now nearly one-hundred-and-fifty years later, it seems unlikely that even one frieze-clad figure in that anonymous crowd could be picked up and pinpointed; yet, searching through directories, reference libraries and parish church records, we pick up the trail. Patrick Lowrey with his wife and child got as far as Leeds.

The Irish population of Leeds was by then already larger than that of most Irish towns, and, like thousands of native English workers who had been driven by hunger and spoilation from the Yorkshire countryside, they lived in dismal and unwholesome dens of brick and flint. The Lowreys got accommodation in Wheeler Street, since demolished, and Patrick, a weaver by trade, found work in the mills, probably in the Steander Flax Mills not far off. The linen industry in Leeds was at its peak and employed more than ten thousand workers. And here, in the atmosphere of country craftsmanship reduced to the state of an industrial slum, the boy Daniel grew up.

Dan Lowrey's Marriage Certificate, August 1840. Dan is described as a Dyer, his father as a Weaver, his father-in-law as a a Miner. The four X's show that bridegroom, bride and both witnesses were illiterate

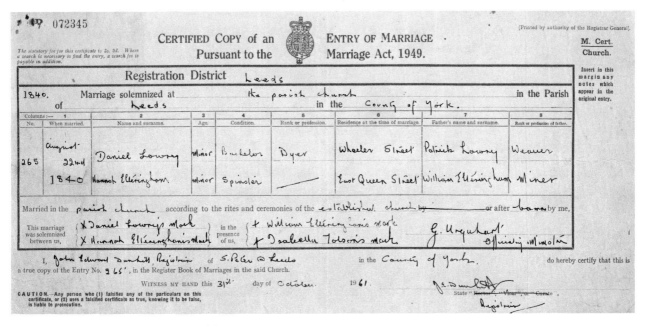

072345

The statutory fee for this certificate is 3s. 9d. Where a search is necessary to find the entry, a search fee is payable in addition.

[Printed by authority of the Registrar General].

CERTIFIED COPY of an ENTRY OF MARRIAGE
Pursuant to the Marriage Act, 1949.

M. Cert.
Church.

Insert in this margin any notes which appear in the original entry.

Registration District Leeds

1840. Marriage solemnized at the parish church in the Parish of Leeds in the County of York.

No.	When married.	Name and surname.	Age.	Condition.	Rank or profession.	Residence at the time of marriage.	Father's name and surname.	Rank or profession of father.
265	August 22nd 1840	Daniel Lowrey	Minor	Bachelor	Dyer	Wheeler Street	Patrick Lowrey	Weaver
		Hannah Ellerington	Minor	Spinster	—	East Queen Street	William Ellerington	Miner

Married in the parish church according to the rites and ceremonies of the established church ~~by~~ or after banns by me,

This marriage was solemnized between us, X Daniel Lowrey's Mark, X Hannah Ellerington's Mark; in the presence of us, + William Ellerington's mark, + Isabella Tolson's mark. G. Urquhart Officiating Minister

I, John Edward Dunhill, Registrar of S. Peter @ Leeds in the County of York. do hereby certify that this is a true copy of the Entry No. 265, in the Register Book of Marriages in the said Church.

WITNESS MY HAND this 31st day of October 1961. J. E. Dunhill State "~~Rector~~", "~~Vicar~~", or "~~Curate~~". Registrar

CAUTION.—Any person who (1) falsifies any of the particulars on this certificate, or (2) uses a falsified certificate as true, knowing it to be false, is liable to prosecution.

At seventeen, on 20 August 1840, he married a native girl. The bride, Hannah, was twenty, daughter of a local miner, William Elteringham. The marriage took place at the Parish (Established) Church, Leeds, and Daniel on this occasion is described as a dyer. There is a family tradition that he had some schooling – later when he was established as a Comedian he featured a piece called 'The Irish Schoolboy' being taught by 'The English Schoolmaster' – but much as he learned from the Englishman, it hardly extended to writing; the evidence is he was in the last degree illiterate, for he signed the marriage register 'X (his mark)'.

The couple set up house at Mercy Street, off Wellington Street on the west side of the City, and there their first child, Thomas, was born on 28 March 1841.

By this time, with steam-ships in the offing, the linen boom was over in Leeds, and once again many of the Irish population were on the move. There is now a gap in the records. Daniel Lowrey, last heard of in Leeds as a dyer in the textile industry, next turns up in Liverpool, surprisingly, as a professional comic singer, doing the rounds of the taverns and the back-street song-and-a-drink rooms, and cannily putting a few pounds together to go into the innkeeping business on his own account.

The Port of Liverpool

Since Samuel Lover created the Stage Irishman in the person of Handy Andy, much has been written on the subject, most of it, in Joyce's phrase, the purest kidooleyoon. Among the critics who have cocked the walk on the Anglo-Irish literary scene, the tradition of the Comic Irishman, like everything else that smacks of the bog or of the back street, is faintly sickening; and they repudiate him as an insult to Irish national self-esteem. Yet it was the Irish exiles themselves who created this character in the beerhalls and singing taverns of industrial boomtowns like Leeds and Liverpool. The character answered a need in the Audience as well as in the Singer; the exiles found themselves at home in the Figure, in the tone of the Irish voice that sounds through any number of overlays of London or Yorkshire, in the sidelong wit which is a heritage from the older tongue, and in that kind of humorous democracy which will talk to Queen Victoria in the same way as it will ask a barmaid for a pint of porter. In the comic resilience of the Figure whom no amount of buffetting will down, they found relief from the long crucifixion of their culture and the wreck of their tribal life. The academic term is 'catharsis' – a nice word for the cleaning out of poisonous matter repressed in the bowels of a nervous system. And not only the Irish, but the exiles of many lands – Germans, Italians, Coloured People, Slavs, the English themselves exiles in their own land – found brief moments of self-understanding under the spell of the Comic Irishman, the Comic Yorkshireman, the Cockney, the Coon.

It may be said, too, that the Singing Comics, as they clowned their way through the Century, played a prime part in the democratisation of the Theatre, and in the slow process of social anarchy which led to the break-up of the old world and the uncertain emergence of the new.

It is impossible to say when or in what circumstances Daniel Lowrey first set up as a Comic Singer. Extensive research in Leeds has failed to unearth his name in the entertainment business there. In Liverpool, the Directory for 1851 lists: 'Lowrey, Daniel, vocalist, 12 Ashfield Street', which shows that he must have been singing for a living from the previous year at least. The 1852 Directory does not list him, but he appears in 1853 as: 'Lowrey, Daniel, musician, 16 Great Oxford Street'. In 1857 he has reached his goal, and is described as a 'Victualler', at 22 Cleveland Square, a Tavern.

This 'Tavern' is interesting, for at that time 'tavern' and 'music hall' were almost identical terms. At Cleveland Square, Lowrey as 'victualler' supplied food and drink to his customers, with a bit of song and dance and comic patter thrown in. Show business was not then quite the rat-race which it later came to be, yet it was still a test of grit and endurance in which many fell drunk by the wayside while the weak went to the Poorhouse. Daniel had nothing to give him a hand up but his own brawn and brain, a Yorkshire–Irish voice and the nerve to survive, and he began at the bottom, doing his song-and-patter for a couple of shillings a night in what you might call the Celtic Twilight of the Liverpool Workingman. The entry for 1857 shows that, at the age of thirty-four, he had pushed himself as far as ownership of a Tavern.

By all accounts, he was a good solid type of Comic rather than a

Dan as 'Pat of Mullingar'

brilliant Clown; he lacked the slick insouciance of the later Irish Comics, many of whom had the advantage of not being Irish anyway. A surviving picture taken in his prime shows him as a stocky figure, heavily built, with large jowls, an incipient double chin, wide-set eyes under heavy lids, and a shock of short stiff hair. He is dressed in the skirted frock-coat of the traditional Irish jarvey, with a double-breasted waistcoat over a comfortable stomach, a pair of 'smallclothes' or kneebreeches unbuttoned below the knee, while in one hand he holds a dented coachman's hat, in the other a whip. The picture is entitled: 'Dan Lowrey as Pat of Mullingar Conversing with her Majesty'. The heavy eyes are half-shut, the big mouth is drooped open, and one can almost hear the sloother of words let gently fall – 'Shapers, yuhr Maggisty, the sofferin bame in yuhr eye is as good as a kiss to me harse'.

In that age of sprawling industry and rootless populations, the musical drinking-house was a business booming as never before. Already in the larger English centres it had passed from the Tavern stage to the Music Hall proper, and was well on the way to becoming the Variety Theatre which in turn gave way to the enormous structures and huge financial corporations of the end of the Century. But it is to be noted that the small place, such as Dan Lowrey's Tavern, where songs and somersaults were simply sideshows to the main business of the bar, formed the basis of the whole movement, and to the very end the drink and the bars were a prime element in the uninhibited enjoyment expressed in the Music Hall ritual. And in their best days both Music Hall and Variety Theatre retained that folk tradition of intimate relation between the Stage and the Audience which was part and parcel of the singing Tavern.

Dan's Tavern did so well that he bought the shop next door and threw the two premises into one. He remodelled the interior, with living quarters for himself and family overhead, and refreshment rooms and variety area downstairs, and had the exterior re-done in a very chaste style, with roundhead windows, a few stucco plaques and a shop-front window in quite elegant taste. Clearly, his new Tavern was designed to give uplift to his clientele. He then set about choosing a name. On 23 July 1858 the Duke of Malakoff paid a civic visit to Liverpool. He was Jean-Jacques Pelissier, a Marshal of France and a hero of the Crimean War; he had taken the fort of Malakoff before the storming of Sebastopol, and he was given a riotous welcome in the streets of Liverpool. Dan, always alive to popular sentiment, styled his new premises 'The Duke of Malakoff' and set up an effigy carved from bog-oak over the door – an effigy not of the Duke, in fact, but of himself.

The uncertainty as to whether the place was a Tavern with singing on the premises, or a small Variety Theatre with drink consumed, is reflected in the official accounts given of The Malakoff. The Liverpool Directory lists it as a Tavern, while Broadbent's *Annals of the Stage* sets it down as a Music Hall. The same authority gives a picture of the elegant façade of The Malakoff set neatly into its cosy corner in Cleveland Square, and shows the famous bog-oak effigy of Dan in the traditional garb of the Irish Comic, wearing knee-breeches and caubeen hat.

Dan, now more well-to-do than any of his people had ever been since the time they were kings, settled down to life as an artiste, innkeeper and family man, all in one. His son Thomas was aged seventeen; two further children, both girls, were born in Liverpool; his wife, Hannah, died soon after the birth of the second and Dan married again, this time a Liverpool girl, Charlotte Summers, a quiet person who has left no mark on the story although she must have been an immense help to the Comedian in creating the home, managing the refreshment business and caring for the three motherless children.

As soon as The Malakoff was under way, Dan bought a smaller place at 1 Ellenborough Street and opened it as a musical tavern called The Nightingale. He also acquired a victualling business at 37 Virgil Street. One sees him feeling his way, plotting his destiny. Like many illiterates he had a solid head for business, and he continued to thrive in his triple capacity of innkeeper, theatrical manager and Irish Comedian. Again like many illiterates, he found himself at a loss in the matter of book-keeping as soon as his business grew beyond the slate and chalk stage, and was at the mercy of strangers employed to do his accounting for him. He ensured, therefore, that his son Thomas got the best schooling which that time and place afforded, and in or about 1860, before Thomas was yet twenty, his father put him in charge of the business management of The Malakoff and The Nightingale.

When Dan was in his forties he grew restless again. He felt there was something yet to be done, some shine to be put on the story. He had been born in Ireland, reared on the songs of Ireland, and remembered how his mother had carried him that grey day down to the Boat. He began to have a hankering to return, successful and well-to-do, to that legendary land and do something for his people, as he had done in Liverpool, in the way of a well-managed singing Tavern; and so he decided to look for an opening in an Irish city. His friendship with the American–Irish Comic, W. J. Ashcroft, who had Ulster connections, may have directed him towards Belfast, and certainly Belfast seemed to offer scope, for the Music Hall idea was as yet new to the North of Ireland. He left his son Thomas in charge of all his Liverpool business, and that there might be no break in the tradition, he made the young man change his name to Dan. Then he sailed for Belfast Lough, searched for a site, found one in North Street and opened his new house in 1871. Always sensitive to theatrical fashion and wishing to bring to the shipyard smoke and icy Sabbath of the City on the Lagan something of the houri quality of Liverpool–Moorish Spain, he called his Music Hall The Alhambra. English Charlotte, uncomplaining, packed for the two girls and herself, and sailed for Belfast to join him.

The Malakoff Music Hall, from Broadbent's *Annals of the Stage*, 1908

He did fairly well, but he was never quite at home in Belfast. The climate was a bit sharp for his chest, and the Northern wit was sharper and more ironic than his own softer form of drollery. He began to think of Dublin. A few professional visits showed him the extent and style of the City, the variety of population, and that curious critical friendliness of the Dublin Audience which has always been a charm and a challenge to visiting Artistes. So when his friend Ashcroft expressed a sentimental wish to own a Music Hall in Belfast, because his parents had emigrated from that City, Dan offered to sell him The Alhambra if he could find a site in Dublin.

In July 1878, the site was found.

CHAPTER TWO

1878–9 The Star of Erin

Crampton Court lies between the River Liffey and Dame Street; it is one of a series of ancient streets, courts and bottlenecks which run from that broad and fashionable thoroughfare down towards the River. In College Green, the façade of Trinity College and the colonnade of the Old Irish Parliament form the heart of classical Dublin; passing the colonnade to go up Dame Street towards the Castle, the third of these narrow streetlings on the right is Sycamore Street, and the fourth, twenty yards farther on, is Crampton Court.

From Dame Street, one enters by an archway and a tunnel under the buildings, and emerges unexpectedly into a little open courtyard. The thrum of the City hardly enters here; one is alone with prowling cats, crumbling brick, dusty glass, old mildewed books in the cobwebbed windows of abandoned businesses, an immense blank wall along one side with barred doors, posters, and the indefinable smell of Theatre.

Underfoot flows the River Poddle, long since gone underground,

The Dame Street entrance to Crampton Court as it is today

emerging into the Liffey not far away, its outlet guarded by a strong grating designed to prevent Fenians from crawling up the Poddle tunnel in order to plant dynamite under Dublin Castle.

To this particular spot Dan Lowrey came.

Crampton Court from the interior

The Court had once been the site of a military barracks, occupied until about 1720 by the Horse Guards. The Dragoons were not without some fun in their enclosure, for the Court housed a Singing Tavern in which Peg Woffington is said to have done her piece as a little girl. Madame Violante the Rope Dancer had set up a booth in Fownes Court nearby, and tried to steal a dramatic march on the Royal Theatre patentees (then at Smock Alley, quite close) by producing a Lilliput version of Gay's *Beggar's Opera* with child actors, and the little Peg as Polly Peachum (1729). This was an early episode in the War of Theatre versus Music Hall which the Lowreys, in their turn, had yet to fight.

When the Horse Guards vacated the barracks, the property was bought by Philip Crampton, a bookseller, who had his own house there and developed the Court as a business centre. The tavern was rented to a variety of Managers but it would never have passed beyond the Singing Tavern stage had it not come into the possession of one Henry Connell, a man alive to its possibilities. He had an eye on the London development of Tavern into Music Hall, and had a strong touch of the showman in his make-up.

In 1855, entering the dark days of Christmas, he splashed an advertisement in the *Freeman's Journal*: 'Henry Connell begs to inform his numerous Patrons that this Monday evening he will open the MONSTER SALOON. Two spacious Rooms have been erected for the accommodation of Gentlemen who wish to partake of chops, steaks, kidneys, oysters, etc. and at the same time commanding an uninterrupted view of the Entertainment in the Saloon at this now popular and fashionable Resort, decidedly the most elegant Saloon in Ireland.'

Connell's Monster may be claimed as the first Dublin Music Hall properly so called, though as yet there was no charge for admission, and Men Only seems to have been the rule.

The Entertainments show how far the Song-and-Supper idea had been superseded. The Saloon had a proper Stage with proscenium arch, and scene-painters were employed. Connell showed Ceiling Walkers, Comic & Sentimental Singers, Danseuses, Duettists, a Baritone, an Irish Character Actor, an American Magician, a Clogdancer, a Child of the Air. On New Year's Eve the candles shone amid hollyberry decorations on the good cheer of chops, beer, wines and spirits, with Kirk the Baritone singing his own composition, 'The Battle of Alma', and Dempsey the Comedian performing *Richard the Third* – a potted version in the form of comic song and monologue, since Connell had no Drama Licence.

The enclosed Court, beyond its dark tunnel entrance, acquired a certain naughty kind of glamour from the Nightlife of music and smoke, the grubsteaks, the raffish company and the 'shewing of limbs'. Connell is said to have brought over an expert from Richard Morton's Canterbury to deal with the problems of appealing to the 'popular' without offending the 'fashionable', and fuse both into a new kind of atmosphere which would have both class and spice – the recipe, in short, for Music Hall.

On Connell's death in 1865, the Tavern and Saloon passed to his wife Mary. The pervasive personality of the showman which had held all the conflicting elements of the Enchantment together was missed. An attempt in the Seventies to give a Wild West touch to the place by calling it The Buffalo did nothing to help, and it degenerated into a Free-and-Easy of the boozy and disreputable kind called, simply, The Widow Connell's.

In July 1878 the business was put up for sale. Dan Lowrey hurried down from Belfast, went among the horse-trams and curricles on the cobbles of Dame Street where fifty years before his father and mother had taken him down the Hill into exile, entered the Court, looked from under his heavy lids at the complex of Rooms, Bars, Stage and floor-spaces, went to the solicitors and bought the lease.

Lowrey showed Dublin that he meant business. His plan was to demolish The Widow Connell's and the adjacent premises, and to erect a fully equipped Music Hall on the site. The premises he acquired at the time comprised No. 8 (The Monster), No. 7 beside it, both fronting onto the Court, as well as two premises at the back of these, fronting onto Sycamore Street. This would allow his new building a width of sixty feet and a depth (from the Court back to Sycamore Street) of about seventy feet. Dublin Theatremen were alert, sensing a threat to their dramatic monopoly; but they could see from these modest dimensions that there was no question (as yet) of a monster Palace of Enchantment.

For the planning, construction and decoration of his new enterprise, the old Comedian was determined to get the best value in Dublin for his money. He dreamed of something more elegant even than his Malakoff. To design the building he engaged the fashionable and famous John J. O'Callaghan, Fellow of the Institute, 'a man of rare and commanding genius'.

O'Callaghan was a native of County Cork and had served his apprenticeship in the offices of Deane & Woodward when that noble partnership was in its heyday, specialising in a particular type of 'Venetian Gothic' which was warmly praised by Ruskin, at that time the arbiter of European elegance. As a pupil in Sir Thomas Deane's office, O'Callaghan had worked on the designs of the Kildare Street Club, and he was sent over as clerk of works to the Oxford Union Building, for which Deane & Woodward's design had won an international award. He took the opportunity of studying the wealth of Oxford University buildings, and came home a lifelong convert to the Mystery of the Middle Ages. He then set up on his own account with an office in Harcourt Street, and soon, by his painstaking attention to Gothic detail and a detestation of the fruity style of the Renaissance, he became the ecclesiastical architect *par excellence*. His buildings were spread over Ireland and included St Mary's, Haddington Road; the Convent and Schools of the Irish Sisters of Charity, Ballaghadereen; the Catholic Church, Clifden; Messrs Mooney's Licensed Premises, Harry Street; the Italian Building at All Hallows; the Hospital of the Holy Ghost, Waterford; and Dan Lowrey's Music Hall in Crampton Court.

O'Callaghan may well have been puzzled by the demands of the stout

The old walls designed by O'Callaghan which have survived to the present day

man with the Yorkshire–Irish accent who had the backing of the banks to show, as well as a respectable weight of watch-chain. It appeared that he wanted neither a Theatre, nor a Licensed Premises, nor a Private Dwelling, nor an Eating-House, but a happy combination of all four. The Architect, a genius in his own line, rose to the occasion. He envisaged a medieval interior, a Great Hall, Galleries, Gothic beams and vaultings, a procession of piers along the side-walls having the spaces between them hung with oil paintings and a dramatic disposal of lights – not hundreds of candles as in the Middle Ages, since these unfortunately would not be allowed, but the latest in gasaliers, not now to light the surplices of altarboys and the coifs of nuns in choir, but pretty barmaids and the limbs of acrobats in flight. There was nothing he could do about the façade – that would merely be jobwork, sandwiched between old buildings and fronting on the ill-lit Court – but for the interior he had a clear space to work with. He got down to the drawings and, in the event, not only satisfied his client but produced a little masterpiece.

The building contract went to T. & C. Martin Ltd of the North Wall; the labour was hired directly by Lowrey himself and paid on a day's work basis, under the direction of a foreman, a Mr Lavary. The various sections of the work were given to different sets of contractors: painting and decoration were done by Dockrell's of South Great George's Street; the gas-fittings and carpets were by Arnott's of Henry Street; and every stage of the work came under the personal supervision of O'Callaghan.

In 1879, when the construction was well under way, Lowrey sold The Belfast Alhambra to Ashcroft for £2,000 and transferred The Malakoff, The Nightingale and his other Liverpool properties to his son Thomas. He now had his wish of a lifetime, and intended to devote his money, his art and his entire attention to the Dublin venture.

Christmas was coming. There was a last-minute rush to get the Music Hall finished in time for the opening night. Very few were allowed in to see the shape of things to come – friends of O'Callaghan mostly, interested in architecture and the arts, and Lowrey's friends in the Theatre, Ashcroft in particular and Pat Kinsella, the Dublin Comic.

The Hall was orientated from west to east, from Crampton Court to Sycamore Street, with the offices, ticket-booths and Bars at the Crampton Court end and the Stage and upstairs living-rooms at the other. The groundfloor contained the Pit, the large Bar and the Smokingroom. A flight of stairs, six feet wide, led by easy treads to the First Gallery, which ran round three sides. Here the Promenade extended all round, at the back of the seats – long oak benches with leather cushions. Above, a space remained for the Top Gallery, on which work had not yet begun. There

Interior of Dan Lowrey's, from a Programme Cover

were seats for 365 people; add a further 300 – thronging the Bars, chatting in the Smokingroom, standing or strolling in the Promenade – and a figure of six to seven hundred would fill the house.

The Stage at the Sycamore Street end was remarkably large. The proscenium arch, resting on piers with curved bases and capitals, stood thirty-four feet above the floor of the Stage. The tympanum (within the curve of the arch) was incised with light woodland relief, and held a large central medallion on which Dockrell's man was painting a portrait of Tom Moore whose centenary was at hand. There was plenty of off-stage space, with dressing-rooms, scene-bays and toilets, and the vaults of the original premises, still intact, gave good room for storing apparatus and stage properties.

A low balustrade and railing cut off a generous area for the Orchestra. Within this area, on each side, were the private boxes with sliding curtains, abutting onto the apron of the Stage itself so that the occupants would be in on the scene.

There were three entrances, all from the Court, all leading to the passage which gave onto the Pit, the large Bar and the stairway. A fourth entrance, which would lead to the Stage and the Pit direct, was in the course of construction at the Sycamore Street end.

Connoisseurs were intrigued by the medieval treatment in the construction, designed to emphasise and lay bare the structural lines. The sidewalls were divided by rows of piers carrying moulded arches, these piers running the whole way up – floor to Gallery to ceiling – as if showing the skeleton upon which the body of the house was contrived. The ceiling over the Hall was lightly curved, with the effect of an awning, and segmented by moulded ribs, intersecting, leaving a series of panels between; each of the centre panels had a perforated diaper opening to the louvred ventilator which ran the whole length of the roof. The underfloors of the Galleries had their bearing timbers exposed and decorated, so that the whole effect was one of elegant realism. Between them, Lowrey and O'Callaghan had created a new image: the Music Hall.

The Hall was provided with men's lavatories and retiring-rooms for the ladies. Bars and Refreshment counters were separated from the Entertainment area, as was the Smokingroom: Lowrey meant to attract the ladies by keeping the show-space clear of tobacco smoke and ash, and he was also anxious to acquire 'theatre status' under the Law, which he could not do if drinking were allowed in the Auditorium.

As winter came on and the work neared completion, he began to think what his dream should be called. Remembering the poverty of his childhood, his parents' flight, the rising star of hope for his class and countrymen, he composed the name, got someone who could spell to write it out, and had it carved in the stonework above the door:

DAN LOWREY'S STAR OF ERIN MUSIC HALL

On Monday 22 December 1879, Dan Lowrey's opened for the first time. The Court was thronged an hour before opening time so that the crowd overflowed through the tunnel and onto Dame Street. Among the invited guests were the Architect and members of the contracting firms, with artisans and labourers who had worked on the building, representatives of

Theatre managements, writers and journalists. Also present was Lowrey's son Thomas (now known as Dan) from Liverpool, dapper and distinguished. The crowd pressing for admission included Trinity College students, soldiers of the Dublin garrison in their red coats and regimentals, dockers, draymen, railwaymen, clerks, shopboys – Dubliners of all kinds – some few with their wives or sweethearts, all spruced up for the night and looking forward to a drink, a song and a bit of amusement under the same roof as the tophats and the solid-money members of society.

The doors opened at 8.00 p.m. and the money jingled. Body of the Hall, 6*d*; Gallery, 1*s*; Reserved Seats, 1*s* 6*d*. Every inch of standing room was taken.

Coming in from the murk of the Court, they were charmed with the lighting. The very best in gasaliers illuminated all parts of the House, and the Hall itself was lit by three large Sun-lamps and six Star-lamps. People gazed about in delight, exclaiming. Both architecture and light gave the impression of an enchanted world.

Music filled the air. The Orchestra consisted of four violins, viola, double bass, clarionette, flute and piccolo (doubled), trombone, two cornets and drums. It was under the baton of William Henry Lowrey, son of Thomas and grandson of Dan, who had flair, a fine masculine moustache and a brilliant musical talent, and who, at twenty-one, was already leader of a danceband for balls in private houses, and a Professor of the Violin. He had been helped by R. M. Levey, Musical Director of The Theatre Royal, to form Dan Lowrey's Orchestra, recruiting experienced musicians, mainly Dublin men. William Henry himself had whipped them into Music Hall shape. They played Irish melodies and popular tunes and airs from light Opera. 'Singularly effective', said the Press.

Between the items of entertainment the crowd wandered, swayed to the music, drank, chatted, admired the features. There was the delightful

A Dublin Hebe, from *Zoz*

Professor Codman on the Bill of the Opening Night

feeling that everything was new. The Bars were sparkling, spacious, got up in an attractive style and 'blessed with barmaidens'. First-class wines and spirits were on sale at the ordinary prices, as well as the workingman's pint of Guinness and 'O'Connell's Famous Old Dublin Ale'. Lowrey had himself engaged the barmaids, picked for good looks and character, skilled at once to provoke the good humour of the drinking males and check familiarity; wearing long dark gowns with a touch of lace at the throat and wrist, hair braided and bottoms padded with horsehair, they were 'the Hebes' to the comic pen.

The Stage impressed everybody. There is no mention of tableau curtains (tabs), although they appear in later drawings. A dropscene, twenty-four feet by twenty-two, had been painted by Charles Wood, and it was reported that 'Mr Lowrey has a new scene in preparation representing Sackville Street and the new Carlisle Bridge'. Another notable feature was the Picture Gallery of oil paintings which hung along the wall of the Promenade. These portraits were mainly of Dan Lowrey, one in evening dress and two in the dress of his favourite comic characters: *Pat of Mullingar* and *The Whistlin' Thief*. The artist is unknown, but the pictures appear to have been part of Dockrell's contract for the decoration.

Apart from the Orchestra, the Entertainment that night was modest, planned to provide something for all tastes, and was well received. Serio-comic singing and dancing were provided by Little Nelly. Mademoiselle Miaco the Boneless Wonder performed contortions in the air. The rage for blacked-up acts was reflected in the Mad Minstrels Blanquin & Hurst, and in Craven & Cowley the Ethiopians. Signor Zula swung by his feet from a high trapeze, carrying two half-hundredweights hung from a piece of leather in his teeth, and afterwards hung from the trapeze by his teeth swinging in a shower of fireworks. To cater for family audiences over the Christmas season, Lowrey billed Professor Codman with his celebrated Punch & Judy Show; generations of the Codmans have specialised in Punch and Judy and the tradition survives in this Liverpool family to the present day. Another family touch was provided when Master Thomas Lowrey, another grandson, took the Stage as 'the youngest Irish representative comedian'. The Lowreys had arrived.

The Star opening received an excellent press. The comic paper *Pat*, wrote: 'This hall which is the brightest and airiest place of entertainment in Dublin, is well deserving of a visit.' The *Freeman's Journal* remarked: 'Mr Lowrey has spared no expense to make his new venture comfortable and popular, and we believe that he has framed rules for the conduct of the theatre which leaves nothing to be desired.' A polite hint here: 'we believe Mr Lowrey will not offend our Moralities in his Music Hall.'

The night after the opening, 23 December, when the waltz airs and the clink of glasses were in full swing and the crowd was gazing at Mademoiselle writhing under the bright green light of the gasaliers, the dark blue helmets and truncheons of the Dublin Metropolitan Police were seen entering. Swiftly they pushed through the merrymakers and arrested Dan. At the Police Station he was charged with selling liquor upon a portion of his premises which had not an alcohol licence. It was Dublin's Christmas-box to him.

CHAPTER THREE

1880 Early Bills

With the New Year Dan took off his evening dress and reverted to his Character Costume, with flopbrim hat which was a cross between the headpiece of his Mullingar Jarvey and a Wild West sombrero; thus attired he was to be seen leaning on the Orchestra rail, chairing the Entertainment, supervising the sixpenny Pit and the twelvepenny Gallery, or in the Refreshment Rooms cracking drolleries with the dockers below or the doctors above, subduing the Trinity students and keeping an eye on the Barmaidens.

His Venetian–Gothic Music Hall was a Family affair. With his two girls and their stepmother Charlotte, Dan lived in the rooms above the Stage. Of the grandsons, handsome William Henry led the Orchestra and young Tommy continued to appear in Irish Songs & Characters.

He hired Richard Delarue Lloyd as Manager to handle the accounts, wage-bills and Engagement Books. As Stage Manager he had old William Summerfield of Liverpool, gentle and whitehaired, who had been 'reared on the planks' and had a fine flair for designing scenes, ensembles, Circus acts, illusions and limes. His Stage Carpenter was Jack White, a Dublin man. He himself was Chairman and Artiste in this creative team. He was licensed as 'Victualler', but he certainly intended 'Theatre'.

Dan's particular brand of Irishry was tinged with the memory of the peasant Pikemen of the past and the wearing of the Green, a sentiment nursed in exile and not quite in line with the emerging social realism of the Irish City, where the new Shop and Artisan Class had evolved and were now prospering through the medium of English. As for the wage-slaves swarming in tenements, they were beginning to see that the Dublin Masters of Industry were as much their enemy as was the Imperial Raj. The air was tinged with the first touch of social revolution, but Dan was more at home with 'The Harp that Once'.

On 12 July, the traditional date for the Drums and Sashes of the Orange Parades celebrating the victory of Free Conscience at the Boyne, he planned a counter-demonstration entitled *Shamus O'Brien, a Tale of the Ninety-Eight Rebellion.* The script was based on a poem by Sheridan Le Fanu; sets were designed and built by Summerfield and Jack White; the story was presented in a series of Dramatic Tableaux in which the whole Company then at the Star took part, with Irish melodies and patriot ballads and sprightly jig-and-reel gyrations by the Chorus Girls.

Another Green Night was had in October when the performance was under the Patronage of the Ancient Order of Foresters. The Foresters were mainly professional and business men, often in the greybeard stage, finding a relaxation from the humdrum of life in the myth of the native pine, the ash and the oak, and dressing up in a half-military half-woodland style. Their quaint and romantic kind of racialism gives colour to the Cyclops Episode in *Ulysses*, and it is caricatured by O'Casey in the character of Uncle Pether in *The Plough and The Stars*. That night their splendid Band was on the Stage; all floors and Bars were bright with the green uniforms and cocked hats of the Foresters and the swords and moustachios of their Officers. Drink flowed and all were heroes and happy.

On these Hibernian Nights Old Dan was in his element as 'Pat of Mullingar'. Dublin jarveys were famed for their colourful style in language and driving and few visitors to the City left without having had a taste of the rip-roaring joys of a wild ride through the streets in a jaunting-car. It was Dan's favourite Character:

Then should ye want a car sirs
I hope ye'll not forget
Poor Pat of Mullingar sirs
And his darlin' little pet,
She's as gentle as the dove sirs
Her speed ye can't deny
There's no blind side about her
Though she only has one eye!

The same light and lilting humour pervades his 'Whistlin' Thief':

'Pat of Mullingar', words and music

PAT OF MULLINGAR

ALLEGRETTO

Sym

Voice

They may talk of Flying Childers And the speed of Hark a-way Till the fan-cy it be-wilders As you list to what they say,

Sym.

But for *rale* style and beauty tho' you Travel near and far The fastest mare you'll find belongs to Pat of Mullin-gar

CHORUS.

She can trot a-long

When Pat came over the hill
His colleen fair to see
His whistle low but shrill
The signal was to be.
Mary, the mother said,
Someone is whistlin' sure.
Says Mary, it's only the wind
Is whistlin' through the dure –
(*Dan whistles 'Garryowen', Audience joins in*)
Mary, I hear the pig
Unaisy in his mind
But mother you know they say
That pigs can see the wind!
(*Pig grunts. Pit, Gallery, Bars, all grunt*)
And mother, you know the fiddle
Hangs close beside the chink
And the wind upon the strings
Is playing a tune I think –
(*Violins perkily pick out the tune, Audience hums*)
That's true enough in the day
But I think you may remark
That pigs no more nor us
Can see anything in the dark!
(*Dog barks. Barks from all over the House . . .*)

And so on until the whistling, grunting, barking and the whole pothering 'deludhery' is consummated 'in the arms of her Lover'.

In due course Daniel Lowrey, Vintner, appeared before the Court charged on two counts: 1. that he did offer for sale and did sell intoxicating liquors upon that portion of The Star of Erin Music Hall which formerly had been No. 8 Crampton Court; 2. upon that portion which had formerly been No. 7.

Mrs Mary Connell for the defence deposed that during her ownership of the said No. 8 the Bar there had been properly licensed, and that the licence had been in the proper form transferred to Mr Lowrey. But the Inspector of Police pointed out that the Bar on the second floor, adjoining the Gallery, had not existed in the Widow Connell's time, and could not be said to be licensed. Counsel for the defence cited just such a case in Liverpool, which had been found in favour of the defendants. Court agreed, and dismissed the charge on this count.

On the second count, the Inspector gave evidence that he himself had seen intoxicating drink being sold on the opening night of the Music Hall upon that part of the large Bar on the groundfloor which protruded into the old No. 7 area. Mr Lowrey should not have extended his Bar in that direction without first having notified the Authorities. Court agreed, found Mr Lowrey guilty on this count and fined him £2 with costs.

One thing was clear to Mr Lowrey as he unloosed his wallet; the attack had been so sudden, the charge so precise and technical that clearly there was some Power in Dublin that did not like his Theatre enterprise.

In the stress of it all Dan was ageing before his time, and already he was losing touch a little with the changing age. Typical of the figures of an older day which appeared in the opening year of the Star was the Character-Actor, Valentine Vousden.

His real name was Carney. Born in 1825 of Irish–German parents in Hawkins Street where his father kept a shop, he was given a good education in literature, music and dancing. Isolated, dreamy, brilliant, he could find no place for himself in the middle-class Dublin scene, so he went to England and became Professor Vousden, Dancing Master. He married an English girl and returned to Dublin at the age of twenty-one to dance Harlequin in the Queen's Theatre Pantomime. He stayed on, playing a medley of song, dance and character parts on the Dublin Stage, and at last he hit upon an act in which he could use all his many talents in one: Valentine Vousden the Polynational Character Actor. His first one-man show of this kind was called *The Unity of Nations*; Vousden sang compositions on the theme, danced folk-dances, played the violin, ventriloquised, gave readings, lectured, delivered verse-monologues, made quick character changes and played all the leading brands of Humanity – Irish, German, English, French, Italian, Scots, African, Asian, American – enacting himself the age-old dream of the United Nations of the World.

He toured far and wide with this Protean act and others like it and became a legendary name in the small Towns and Cities of the land.

When Dan Lowrey billed him at The Star in June 1880 he was sixty-five, grey and cultured in tone and manner. Many of his songs were serious and had moral overtones – 'Man Know Thyself', 'Pulling hard Against the Stream'. But his Character-parts were gems of stagecraft, his humour was racy, and all the old magic remained in the most famous of all his songs, 'The Irish Jaunting Car'.

Afterwards he plodded for years the round of the Halls, appearing in Pat Kinsella's little Harp as late as 1891. But the strain was telling. His mind became affected; he carried into real life the illusion of the Stage – once he tried to pay a jarvey with a biscuit, insisting it was a sovereign – and in the end he disappeared into the Dublin Poorhouse. Eventually his son came from England to rescue him, and brought the old Proteus to live at Bexhill-on-Sea in Sussex where he died in March 1907, leaving a name which more than one Actor has taken for himself and which lingers in Dublin still.

Even in those early days the range of artistes featured was dazzling. 1880 saw Monsieur Zampi the Gymnast with One Leg Only; the American Crack Shot George Warriner assisted by Miss Tony Sinclair, Singer and Sand-dancer; 'another of the burnt-cork brigade'; Jim Keefe Banjoist and Negro Minstrel, *The Cruise of the Calabar*; First Appearance of Ferguson & Mack American Speciality Artistes, the Rage of London; First Appearance of Mlle Milano and her Ballet Troupe of nine Ladies; First Star Appearance of Peter Johnson who has held the Championship for Swimming Underwater for over Fifteen Years, with his Two Beautiful Daughters, winners of Gold Watch for Ladies Championship in '77 and Silver Cup in

’79, they eat, drink, smoke, turn somersaults, gather eggs into a basket, talk, write, play, swim and prove themselves to be Mermaids in a great Glass Tank of Water on the Stage . . .

Among the Irish Characters in this opening year at Dan’s the finest was undoubtedly W. J. Ashcroft. There was a touch of the Northern bite in his humour, a kind of salt breeze blew onto the Stage when he entered.

His parents had emigrated from Belfast in 1840, and he was born at Pawntucket, Rhode Island. He ran away and joined a Troupe of Minstrels touring the Saloons at the farthest extremes of log-built civilisation, in Newfoundland, Nova Scotia, Prince Edward Island. Having survived ‘the fists, frost, firewater and fornication’, he went up in the ranks, joining many other Drama and Circus Troupes travelling the rails and the trails, and eventually, with the Sands itinerant Group, he played the planks through Upper and Lower Canada, California, Virginia, Nevada, Mexico, until his eyes grew accustomed to vast horizons.

In 1870 he went into management in New York, opened the Theatre Comique, with himself as the principal Comic, and gained an enormous reputation. But homeless and homesick, Ashcroft could never settle; he took to the road again, received a cordial reception in the great Cities of New England, but remained unhappy. He married an English Actress, Kitty Brooks, with whom he made several visits to England; his Irish Song-and-Dance Characterisations from the raw New World went well in London, and he played leading Halls to crowded Houses.

In 1876 he had a huge success with ‘Muldoon the Solid Man’. The song had an old Irish air and the lyric was based on words by Ed Harrigan with verses added. Ashcroft did Muldoon in tophat and tailcoat, the poor Irishman who had ‘elevated’, flamboyantly prodigal, but with a hard core of commercial know-how – typical of Ashcroft himself, for he could never make up his mind whether he wanted to be a Big Businessman in Theatre or a droll upon the boards.

Dan Lowrey, another exile, was in his own way of much the same divided nature (Vintner and Comedian) and the two became fast friends. As we have seen, Ashcroft bought The Belfast Alhambra from Lowrey and he came frequently to The Star, where all classes responded to ‘The Solid Man’:

I am a man of great influence
And eddicated to a high degree,
Came here when small from Donegal
With my cousin Tim I crossed the sea.
In the Alton Road we were situated
In a lodging-house with my brother Dan:
By perseverance I elevated
And came to the front like a solid man!
All together now –
Come with me and I’ll treat you dacent
I’ll set you down and fill your can.
As I walk the street each friend I meet
Says, there goes Muldoon the Solid Man!

In a different vein from Ashcroft was Pat Kinsella. Pat was Dublin-born, jovial, wholly at home by the Liffeyside where he rapidly became Dublin's Comic Character number one. It was a hard life, no worldwide fame, no security, but he seemed to thrive on it, playing comedy roles in Melodrama at The Queen's, dancing and singing solo acts all over Town, and playing Clown in the Christmas Pantomimes from year to year at the little Royal, at The Queen's and in Michael Gunn's great lavish Gaiety. He knew the temper of the Dublin street, quick, humorous, cynical; his solos sung with gusto burlesqued alike the marching Red Military and the dream of the Green Men marching, and got home to the hearts of Pit and Gallery with the extravagant verve of 'The Ballybough Brigade', 'The Mud Island Fusiliers' or 'Ballyhooley'.

Pat Kinsella as 'Conn the Shaughran', from the comic paper *Pat*

Resting, from *Pick-Me-Up*

All three were written by Robert Martin of Ross. Martin was an odd fellow, one of the landowning class, a Justice of the Peace, owner of Ross House in the Lake Country of County Galway, a Unionist in politics, a scholar and a wit. But he had a Lady Gregory kind of relation to the People, appreciated their extravagant irony which had as much anger in it as humour and, using that quality, made many song-hits in Fashionable Burlesque at The London Gaiety, until half that City was singing:

We don't care what we ate
If we get our whiskey nate
In the Ballyhooley Blue Ribbon Army

Ever after, even on the Bench, he was called 'Ballyhooley Bob'.

Pat Kinsella, on breezy terms with everyone, became a close friend of Dan's. He was 'Dublin's Own', plump, light as a feather on his feet, rosy-cheeked with a shock of chestnut hair, and as he came on the Stage of The Star brass, drums, brogues, boots, all hearts went marching *à la militaire*:

We are no soldier spoonies
When fighting in campaign
We march like men to Mooney's

And back to camp again.
We lay a tax on travellers,
We beg, we borrow, we bone,
And we're such blockheads that another man's pockets
We just take for our own.
(Full House now, the rousing chorus –)
We're the boys to drink and fight
Batterin' skulls is our delight,
Which is the left foot from the right
Divil soul does know.
As soon as one of the Corpse appears
Mothers to childer shout, My dears
There's the Royal Mud Island Fusiliers,
They're doin' the Sintry-Go!
(Zip, zip on the drums and buglecall –)
They call us chicken-stealers,
That isn't right y'know
For it's well known to the Peelers
We love a Poultry Show;
And the Jury finds us guilty,
The verdict soon appears –
That a love for chickens has played the dickens
With the Mud Island Fusiliers!

In April, when the birds sang in the trees of Sackville Street, the limbs of Dancing Girls were first glimpsed in Crampton Court. Mlle Milano arrived with her well-trained Troupe of Nine. The effect was electric. Bars emptied on both floors; drinks unfinished, patrons surged into Pit, Gallery and Promenade when, under the baton of William Henry, strings, wind and cornets glided into the Girl-number and the legs came twinkling on the Stage. Design and costumes were in bright hues; the emphasis was on figure and footwork – the waltz, the schottische, polka, minuet and evolutions *à la militaire* performed with verve and precision. The name 'Milano' brought a hint of the warm South and grapes ripening, but the style was 'English' – open-air girlishness, pranksome, frolicsome, full of breeze.

Lowrey now saw that Troupes of Dancing Girls were essential. Ballet had the advantage of having an air of respectability from its long association with Grand Opera and Opera Bouffe, and even the stricter souls in Victoria's Dublin could – in the divine name of Culture – enjoy a glimpse of limb in a foaming froth of underclothes.

This sense of peep-show was enriched by the invention of 'limelight'. Gurney, a chemist, had discovered that if a piece of lime was heated in a flame of burning hydrogen it became white-hot and gave out a brilliant light. The idea was seized on by the Theatre. It was found that a platinum wire coated with lime or even a piece of blotting-paper soaked in a lime solution could be used: the paper burned away but a glowing skeleton of lime remained. Summerfield and Jack White had learned to control this luminous lime without setting fire to The Star; with the gasaliers dimmed and the flashing figures limelit from below, the Girls were moulded in

Arthur Lloyd in 'The German Band'

three glowing dimensions, while their dancing shadows on backdrop and set drew the spectators farther into the naughty trance, and the Night concluded with an Eruption of Mount Vesuvius.

Troupe followed Troupe, and in time *les Girls* danced their way into Dublin Legend as 'Dan Lowrey's Chicks'.

10

Top of the Year's Bill was Arthur Lloyd (December). He was a Music-Hall man in a way that was new to Lowrey. He waved no flags. The speech and the attitudes of the common man everywhere, brilliantly delineated, were the themes of his art. He was expensive, taking a nice slice out of the fortnight's takings; but he did entice a little of Dublin's *bon ton*, and many who had never before ventured down the tunnel to Crampton Court now flocked to see the Face that had launched a thousand Song-Sheets. Lloyd sang in evening-dress, a Scots voice with London overtones:

I loved her, and she might have been
The happiest in the land,
But she fancied a foreigner who played the flageolet
In the middle of a German Band.

He had been trained from childhood as an Actor in an Edinburgh Company in which his father was Comedian at £5 a week. Young Arthur discovered a gift for writing songs to be sung before the curtain while the scenery was being changed and, though he hankered to be a Great Actor, he went into Music Hall because, cannily enough, he felt there was more money in it. Having tried himself out at The Whitebait Tavern in Glasgow, he felt he was ripe for London.

An unknown Scots boy doing the round of the Saloons and the Penny Gaffs, he was on the starvation list and to make ends meet he took a job with a hatter in the Strand. There he learned to shake off the trappings of the fustian Stage and to listen to how people really talked. In the streets he came alive to attitudes and speech habits; he picked up catch-phrases, spotted a comic sense of pathos, a vocal delight in sheer nonsense, a knack of cutting pretension down to size; and he distilled something of all this into the songs he composed and presented. In his time he published more than two hundred of these ditties, all of them of considerable popular appeal.

He rode every day into town on an omnibus driven by a chatty Cockney named Joe. Joe's caustic criticism of everything under the sun was, 'No thankyer. Not for Joseph!' The Scotsman's quick ear caught the tone of the phrase and enshrined it in a song entitled 'Not for Joseph!' It was an immediate success. 'Not for Joseph!' became a cant phrase on the lips of all classes, in all circumstances. The song sold 80,000 copies, a record for the time and for a long time after, and on a wave of acclaim young Lloyd came to The London Pavilion.

The Pavilion was a new venture, recently renovated as a refreshment-cum-variety premises by a pair of Jewish restaurateurs, Loibl and Sonnenhammer. An air of champagne and the glitter of diamonds lingered there from the earlier establishment, The Argyll Rooms, while at the same time it had the aura of a tavern from its days as The Blackhorse Inn. Shrewd Lloyd seized the essential: combine the Argyll air with the Blackhorse aura, the diamonds with the beer, a place on the stage and in the bars and balconies for both the *bon ton* cravat and the New Cut coat of the fish-monger. Lloyd could in his own style combine both, and he engaged and trained artistes to do the same. He made a fortune and a name, and The 'Pav' became the Centre of the World.

The face that came into the light at Dan's was heavy, homely and dimpled when he smiled. The voice was of a rich timbre with a wealth of comic tone. He was a bigger draw than the Chicks even, and with Ashcroft, Pat Kinsella and Old Dan himself, he established the Male Comic as the heart of the Night Rite.

CHAPTER FOUR

1881 (January to June) The Dublin Scene

In January 1881 things looked uncertain in Crampton Court. Business was not brisk. Lowrey's main enemy was the Puritan climate and the bad odour that clung to Nightlife from ages past.

To Respectable Dublin, Music Hall meant 'The Shades' and caused a shudder. There had been a real 'Shades'. Early in the Century a hardheaded Scotsman, George Homes, having made a fortune selling cakes in Sackville Street (now O'Connell Street), put up a large building called the Royal Arcade in College Green, housing various shops and offices. Later he added a Hotel-cum-Tavern which he called The Royal Shades, and here he engaged an Italian Band and Tyrolean Yodellers to enliven the place and add zest to the chops and drink in the London song-and-supper-room style.

The Shades was astutely named, hinting at Hades, the witching hour, and an escape into the Natural Life in a mist of whiskey-punch at fourpence a tumbler. The Ghosts that haunted the Shades were mostly down-at-heel poets, failures of one kind or another, threadbare academics nursing their long churchwarden pipes, hackwriters and starveling reporters begging the loan of a bottle of ink from the Proprietor and scribbling off their stories at the drinking-tables. Clarence Mangan knew it well, and Carolan, the Harpist, played there as a youth.

The Shades disappeared in the great fire which gutted the Arcade on 25 April 1837. But the name was remembered and the fashion spread. Singing Taverns blossomed all over Town. Meetings usually began after dark, sometimes with a Resident Chairman to sit at the high-table and preside over the Revels, sometimes with a new Chairman elected every week. Props were primitive: at The Straggler Tavern in Capel Street the Artistes performed on planks laid across barrels. In some spots the performers were the drinkers themselves, but mostly they were poor Players who strutted and fretted their lives through the Three Kingdoms and literally sang, danced or stood on their heads for their supper. And all were liable, whenever the Law felt like it, to be taken up as Vagabonds, Jugglers, Japes and Trulls, under the Moll Flanders Act of 1747.

Such Caverns were at first called Free-and-Easies. The most select of them was Henry Jude's at 12–13 Grafton Street. It was here in the Spring of 1873 that the Sisters Fulton kicked themselves into immortality in the new French form of an ancient fertility dance, the Can Can. Frequent habitués were the Students of Trinity College and of the Medical Schools – the spoons were nearly all flat in Jude's, for the Students rapped them on the tables in applause, or beat time to their roaring chorus, 'On the Back of Daddy-O!'

Early High Kicks, from *Pick-Me-Up*

Most notorious of the Free-and-Easies was John Bull's Albion Tavern in Dame Court, the scene of the lurid Judge and Jury Shows.

These uninhibited Mock Trials were conducted by Renton Nicholson, author of *The Autobiography of a Fast Man*. He was an unstable fellow, living on his wits which were not many. For years he had tried his hand at flash journalism, dabbled in show business of the spicier sort, and after a few spells in the King's Bench Prison for debt, came as Manager to The Garrick's Head Tavern in Bow Street. In his one and only stroke of genius he revived the old game of 'The Court' and set up mock trials in the Tavern to attract custom; the idea caught on and crowds came to his 'Court' to eat, drink, royster and take part in the 'Jury'. Flush with success, he was engaged as Manager of both The Coal Hole Tavern and The Cider Cellars in London and before long he brought the 'Court' on tour to Dublin.

On 1 February 1855, The Albion announced: 'They have arrived! The learned Judge will light his cigar at eight o'clock.' Chief Baron Nicholson on the Bench, assisted by Actors from The Coal Hole as Accused, Police, Counsel, eccentric Witnesses, with the drinkers acting as Jury, tried and decided cases quite unfit for publication. This parody of the Law in liquor was more than mere fun; in Dublin especially, where the Hanging Judge was a grim reality and where Speeches from the Dock were best-sellers, to guy the Law Courts was a dangerous delight.

The Trials at The Albion were a roaring success. They seized on topical murders, breaches of promise, adulteries and other notorious cases of the day; most of the proceedings were *ex tempore* and grew wilder as the small hours drew on, and patrons could release plenty of libido through the medium of the make-believe. Naturalism was the rule; one of the professionals generally played The Prostitute, with dialogue and stage business to match – so much so that the Judge and Jury Company were hauled before a real Court to answer a charge of obscenity.

All these elements, The Shades, Jude's, the Free-and-Easies, the Jury Shows, had tinged the Dublin notion of Nightlife with a hellfire hue. The well-bred, the uppercrust and the decent poor would as soon go to the Devil as to Dan's.

It was becoming plain to Lowrey that Music Hall in the sense and on the scale he was attempting it would have a hard battle to fight in Dublin. More than one attempt had been made to push the Singing Saloon in the direction of Theatre, but almost all had failed, or had like The Widow Connell's degenerated into frowsy Free-and-Easies. The sole survivors were The Mechanics, The Harp and The Grafton.

The quaint little Mechanics in Abbey Street had arisen on the site of a Minor Theatre burned down in 1839. It was rebuilt and taken over by the Dublin Mechanics Institute – 'for the scientific and literary improvement of the Dublin Operative Classes'. The amenities included a reading room, a lending library and a small hall for lectures and concerts. This hall was taken by a succession of lessees and run as something more than a Tavern and something less than a Theatre. Its name was frequently changed, but Dubliners always called it The Mechanics. It was 'illegitimate' (that is, it had no licence to stage Plays or Pantomime), had a touch of the daft Dublin poetic atmosphere since its end-wall abutted on the City Morgue, and was poor and ill-constructed in comparison with Lowrey's Gothic Venetian Star.

The Harp was tiny. Opened in the Seventies by Moses Nolan in his Tavern at Adam Court, it was well-run but remained primitive and rather a Free-and-Easy until the end.

The Grafton in South Anne Street was a shade larger, was vigorously managed by George West and was a great success. Smoking was allowed, but it was never a Free-and-Easy for its Bar was separated from its Auditorium, and those who had not come to wine and dine had an uninterrupted view of the Stage. It was sited just off fashionable Grafton

An East End
Theatre
Saturday night
Jack B Yeats /5/91

LEFT 'Hellfire' Drawing of a People's Theatre, by Jack B. Yeats, from *Ariel*

Street, and by keeping its interior bright and colourful and by engaging the best Artistes available, George West had managed to do the impossible – appeal at once to the workingman and to the more raffish of the *bon ton*.

Fashion was beginning to follow the raffish into The Grafton, but it was not yet ready to venture into the shadows of Crampton Court.

Dan Lowrey's, The Grafton, The Harp – these were the three 'Music Halls' in the new meaning of the name. There were other halls, many of them large and well fitted up, which might be hired on occasion for Concerts, Variety Acts, Prize Fights, Circuses – The Rotunda, the Ancient Concert Rooms, The Metropolitan, The Molesworth, the Earlsfort Terrace Skating Rink – but none of these was offering the kind of intimate entertainment which had developed out of the Singing Saloon.

Oddly enough, Lowrey's chief antagonist turned out to be neither The Grafton nor The Harp, but the great Gaiety Theatre itself.

Finding the highbrow and *décolleté* Gaiety against him, Lowrey was somewhat at sea, and no wonder. For Theatre like everything else in Dublin is bedevilled by history, and the Proprietor of the Gaiety had a Royal Patent going back to the time of Charles II.

Cromwell's Puritan Republic had shut down all Theatres by Law. Charles II had not repealed the Law, but had granted a Patent to his friends to operate two Theatres in London and one in Dublin. The first Dublin House set up under the monopoly was at Smock Alley, and this Royal Patent passed from Theatre Royal to Theatre Royal and from Proprietor to Proprietor down the years.

Meanwhile the Law had more or less lapsed. Illegal Theatres and Singing Saloons had sprung up everywhere. The Law at last accepted the fact and decided to grant licences to creditable houses to produce Drama, Opera and Pantomime, provided that drinking and smoking were not permitted in the Auditorium. This meant, in Dublin, that as well as the Royal Patentee the Proprietors of the few 'Minor Theatres' could now produce Stage Plays while the Song-Saloons and the Free-and-Easies could not. Hence came the cleavage between the Legitimate (licensed for Plays) and the Illegitimate Stage.

Prosecutions were frequent. The Illegitimates tried every kind of dodge to introduce Dramatic Skits, Sketches, Opera items, Harlequinades and even full-length Pantomime into their Saloons and Free-and-Easies. Such competition did not much worry the Royal Patentee; but with the emergence of the Music Halls, The Grafton and The Star of Erin, with their large and cheerful Refreshment Rooms kept back from the Auditorium, and their fully equipped Stage – Taverns as far as the Law was concerned, but Theatres in actual fact – the war between the Legits and the Illegits took a sharper turn.

The Royal Patentee at this time, and self-appointed guardian of the Legitimate Theatre, was Michael Gunn. The Gunns were of Scots extraction, and did business as pianoforte and harmonium importers, publishers and sellers of sheet music, at 61 Grafton Street. The Brothers John and Michael took over when their father was accidentally drowned in 1861. Enterprising men, the pair built The Gaiety Theatre in King Street. It was a lavish affair, Italianate style, gilt and stucco interior, immense Opera

Emily Soldene as 'Chilperic', from her *Recollections*, 1897

Stage, frescoes by O'Hea. On the opening night, 27 November 1871, the piece was Goldsmith's *She Stoops to Conquer* by an English Company, prologue spoken by Mrs Scott Siddons to a glittering Audience of the Notabilities, including the Lord and Lady Mayoress.

The Gaiety became the leading Playhouse. Under the inspiring and vigorous management of the Gunns the finest Actors and Troupes in Theatreland were attracted to Dublin in season after season of Shakespeare and the Classics, Italian and English Opera, and that hilarious cross between Opera, Leg Show and Pantomime called Opera Bouffe. Here appeared the divine Madame Ristori and Sarah Bernhardt; and it was here that Emily Soldene rode a circus horse onto the Stage, in tights, with a succulent display of thigh which had caught the roving eye of the Prince of Wales when he saw her on a poster at a pig show.

In 1874 John and Michael acquired the old Theatre Royal, then at Hawkins Street, and with it they acquired the famous Royal Patent of Charles II.

They were cousins of George Edwardes, Manager of The Gaiety Theatre in London, and were well aware of the dangerous development of Music Hall there. If this new kind of People's fun were to develop in Dublin it could very well close every Legitimate Theatre in the City. So from the moment that Lowrey arrived in Crampton Court the eye of the Royal Patentee was on his every move; and Michael Gunn in particular was determined to see that this newcomer, offering an attractive Nightlife composed of both Tavern and Stage, kept strictly to the limits of his non-dramatic licence and observed – in respect of the Bars, seating, doors, stairs, fire regulations, drinks and Stage performances – the last iota of the Law both ancient and modern. It was not known for certain, but there was a strong suspicion in the Lowrey Family as to whose was the hidden hand behind the Police raid on The Star of Erin the night after it opened.

John Gunn died in 1877. Three years later the old Theatre Royal was burned down. Michael Gunn transferred his Royal Patent to The Gaiety, now the supreme light in Dublin Theatre, and he meant it to remain so.

Despite these difficulties, the year 1881 got off to a good start. The comic paper *Pat* published a page of drawings showing the Artistes currently at The Star, and Old Dan himself leaning on the rail, heavy-featured, wearing his character caubeen. Comment:

> I and my friend, whose picture you behold, dropped into Dan's on Saturday night last and found it packed from floor to ceiling. Being rather late we had no chance of getting seats, so remained in the Promenade. We could hear what was being sung and even got a peep at the Stage now and then, as you can see from the accompanying sketches. When we were not able to see the performers we sketched the backs of the people before us. We also had the pleasure of seeing Dan himself in all his glory, not to speak of getting a glance at the courteous and efficient Manager, Mr Lloyd. And then those charming Hebes behind the bar! Ladies, I offer you my sincere respects and only wish that all ladies attending in bars were as civil and attentive.

RIGHT Sketches from *Pat*, January 1881. Note the two soldiers in out-town uniform among the crowd standing in the Promenade. Old Dan (*bottom left*) keeps an eye on things and 'Hebe' (*right*) stands at the beer-pull

Dan-ites.

Very much above bar

A Great Hunter.

A jest-of-drawers.

DAN LOWREY'S.

I and my friend—whose sketches you behold—dropped into Dan's on Saturday night, and found it packed from floor to ceiling. Being rather late, we had no chance of getting seats, so remained in the promenade We could hear what was being sung, and even get a peep at the stage now and then, as you can see by one or two accompanying sketches. When we were not able to see the performers, we looked at the *backs* of the people before us. We also had the pleasure of seeing Dan himself in all his glory, not to speak of getting a glance at the "courteous and efficient" manager, Mr. Lloyd. And then those charming Hebes behind the bar! who have a word and a smile for everybody, and so leave no heart aching. Ladies, I offer you my most sincere respects, and only wish that all ladies attending in bars were as civil and attentive. We managed to get a peep at Austin, "the Royal Lightning Cartoonist," who is really very clever. The rapidity with which he sketches well-known faces is truly wonderful. We also saw Mr. Hunter, an "American-Irish Comedian and Dancer," with a decidedly North of Ireland brogue. He is a fine dancer, and one of his songs, "Muldoon's Cousin," is rather good. Professor Beaumont, who seems to have got hold of all Professor's Anderson's famous tricks, is also worth seeing. The next time I visit Dan, I must go a little earlier, and see more of the show.

That's Himself!

Hebe.

Coburn as 'Tommy Atkins', from the *Sketch*

Still, the ageing man faced the future with foreboding. Night after night, week after week, the unending effort went on to keep the Refreshments flowing and item after item moving across the phantasmagoria of the Stage – Clowns, Coons, Lady Serio-Comics, Chicks. A Lightning Cartoonist. A Ventriloquist with his Woodenheaded Lilliputians. Pongo the Man Monkey. Tom Allen Bareknuckle Champion of England in a Grand Assault. Troupes of Dogs. Girls on the High Wire. Japs. A Statue Artiste, most powerfully formed Specimen of her Sex, presents in Figure and Limb the Gods of Ancient Greece and Scenes from the Bible. Castellotto on his Ladder of Life. Louisiana Troubadour Quartette. The King of Cannon Balls and the Queen of Clubs . . . an unending stream.

For Baldoyle Race Week (May) he ventured beyond his licence and produced a Racing Sketch, *Neck or Nothing*. And, topping the Bill, he presented Charles Coburn. Coburn, of the London Pavilion School, was like Arthur Lloyd a man of some culture, bringing a refinement to comic singing. He gave a moving portrayal of an old man with the song 'Another Kind Love', and impersonated a Parisian singer delivering a chansonette in French, encored from all parts of the House. In Dublin Coburn had been a Grafton Artiste, appearing there regularly and drawing large crowds; George West cannot have been too happy to see him engaged at The Star. But he was expensive. Lowrey had sunk his last shilling in creating the Music Hall, and to compete for such Artistes as Coburn and Arthur Lloyd called for more money than he could afford just then.

Expensive also were the Dancing Girls. As a fillip to the fun of the Race Week he engaged the Gunness Troupe of Eight. With these the old haphazard days of the Dancing Girls were over. Tessie and Louise Gunness had been *premières danseuses* at Drury Lane and had then trained their own Troupe of Ballet Girls; costumes and choreography were brilliant, the limbwork sprightly and intoxicating. But Tessie and Louise were business girls; travelling expenses and proper lodgings for the Chicks had to be cared for, and Dan could not afford to provide such a bevy every week of the year.

To add to his troubles his health was failing. For years the drain on his vitality had been heavy: the Comedian's life is enough to call on all the energy of a man, but he also had to attend to the Tavern and to the Theatre, for although he had a Manager it was still the personal Lowrey presence in the House that restrained the rowdyism and kept 'Dan's' from degenerating into a 'free-and-easy'.

He bowed to the inevitable. He sent to Liverpool for his son, and in mid-June closed The Star for a rethink.

CHAPTER FIVE

1881 (June to December) Dan the Second

Back in Liverpool Dan Lowrey the Second was in his fortieth year, tireless, affable, well-to-do. He had his share of the Lowrey imagination, disciplined by the social sense of his English mother and stepmother, but from childhood he had a pronounced stammer in his speech.

He had been well schooled; his youth had been leisurely and well-fed. This divided him from the typical emigrant Irish (of whom there were more than 100,000 in Lancashire alone), and from the equal desperation of the English working-class, serfs of the Commercial Power, crowded into the streets of the makeshift City. There was little Wearing of the Green, or of any other colour, about Dan the Second.

He never overcame his stammer and was quite hopeless on the Stage. But he became expert in the management of his father's Tavern Theatres, The Malakoff and The Nightingale, developed a style and a good-natured wit of his own, grew adaptable, quick to catch the tone of the House and of the times. This produced the Showman.

In Christian Street a few doors down from the Lowrey's there lived one William Henry Maguire, a portrait painter. Young Dan fell in love with the painter's daughter, Annie. They were married in the Church of St Nicholas on 23 June 1858 and set up house at 71 Paradise Street, Dan being seventeen years of age, Annie twenty. The following April their first child was born and christened William Henry.

So the years went on and Tavern Theatre became the whole of the young man's life. Both the Lowrey Houses were small and intimate, smelling of beer, sawdust and tobacco smoke, and run on similar lines, admission 3*d*, 4*d*, 6*d*. Dockers, coalmen, men from the workyards of the great Port, mill-hands, mixed Irish and English, coloured men, sailors from overseas – these formed the bulk of his clientele. He mixed among them, knew their wants, their dialects and their jokes; but he always kept a certain reserve, and by his stocky presence, head lifted with jutting underjaw, found he could control even the rowdiest gathering on a Saturday night.

When his father left for Belfast and he acquired full control of all the Lowrey interests in Liverpool, he threw himself into the competitive struggle of Entertainment in that teeming City. Apart from scores of night haunts and sing-song Taverns, there were then about half a dozen fully fledged Music Halls in Merseyside (one, The Parthenon, run by Mrs Stoll, mother of the Music Hall tycoon to be, Sir Oswald) and competition was razor keen. Young Dan studied advertisement, developed his own style in publicity and posters. He travelled, studied Nightlife fashions in London, Paris, Brussels, and in the provincial Towns of England. He followed Stage news, read the Stage magazines, and made himself expert in this new form of People's Theatre. He took financial chances, engaged expensive Artistes and Novelty Troupes in order to draw custom and to raise the level of his Stage. And he took chances with the Law, offering Playlets and mini-Pantomimes to his audiences.

He became a figure in the neighbourhood. His generosity behind the scenes – and there were seamy and ill-lit scenes enough in Victorian Liverpool – became proverbial. The Malakoff was known simply as 'Dan's' where the people, rootless, churchless, white, coloured or black, married woman or girl of the streets, were met with the same smile and word of welcome by 'The Guv'nor'.

Dan Lowrey the Second

Dame Street, looking towards Trinity. Note the horse-drawn trams

Dan and Annie had five children now. William Henry was twenty-one, double-chinned, moustached, musical; in build and temper he had taken after his grandfather, and led the Orchestra in The Star of Erin. The next boy, Daniel, was beginning to be of help in the management of The Malakoff, while the third boy, Tommy, at sixteen was trying his hand on the Stage as the Boy Comedian. The girls, Hannah and Mary Jane (Jeannie), were at boarding-school being taught the polite arts which – fortunately as it turned out – included French.

In 1881 the call came: to come over to Ireland and manage The Star of Erin. He saw it as a chance and a challenge. He sold off The Malakoff, The Nightingale and the other victualling businesses – he and the Old Man would need every halfpenny to finance the new adventure. He gathered Annie and the children, collected his sister Hannah and her husband (Dunbar, a photographer) and shepherded the whole tribe aboard the steam-packet for Dublin.

The Malakoff in time ceased to be a Music Hall and became a warehouse and storage vaults. For long years after, the famous bog-oak effigy of Old

Dan in caubeen and kneebreeches remained above the door. At length it found its way to The Sefton Arms in Ouse Street and was preserved there as a memorial to the Old Comedian and his son who had made a place for themselves in the affections of the City. The effigy perished in 1941 when The Sefton Arms was destroyed in an air-raid, and the old Malakoff building disappeared in the same holocaust.

The Industrial Revolution had all but missed Dublin and the City spread out before Dan Lowrey in that summertime of 1881 was fair to see. It was a distributing and shipping centre rather than a manufacturing town; trees were fresh and green in the streets and parks and the marvellous sunsets down the length of the Liffey were unclouded by industrial smoke. But in its splendid setting at the foot of the mountains it housed the most spectacular slum in the world.

Of a population of some 250,000, about 17,000 belonged to the Nobility, the Vice-Regal Court, the Governing Class. At the other end of the scale there were 150,000 of the humble sort – artisans, small shopkeepers, dockers, porters, workers in breweries and biscuit-factories, railwaymen, tramway and canalmen, hawkers, casual labourers, inmates of the immense Workhouses and the beggarly hordes. The bulk of these had been swarming into the City ever since the Great Hunger of the Forties, sleeping on straw in the big decaying rooms abandoned by the Georgian gentry when Ireland lost its Parliament in 1800. More than one-third of all the families in Dublin had only a single room to live in; often there were two families to a room plus a couple of lodgers. Rent ran to half-a-crown per room, wages averaged from fifteen shillings to eighteen shillings for a seventy-hour week and families were reared on potatoes, blue milk and cheap American bacon at fivepence a pound. Hawking and prostitution apart, there were few opportunities for girls. Lice and rats infested the crowded rooms, and the death-rate (27 per thousand) was the highest in Europe.

The contrast was extreme. Outwardly the scene was dominated by the Victorian Ascendancy, the Vice-Regal cavalcades, the massed march of colour, the lances, helms and trombones of a glorious Empire; while behind the scene there proliferated this slum of an underfed people, paralysed by a Celtic pessimism, dumb to all kinds of politics, nursing in their cups a kind of Robert Emmet romanticism over-ripe and gone rotten, their traditional Irish humour turned in upon themselves, cave-dwellers, the prototypes of O'Casey's joxers, fluthers, paycocks, coveys and uncle pethers.

In between these two extremes stood the solid Middle Class, about 80,000 of them, of Irish, English, Scots, Danish and Dutch descent – the Solid Muldoons, men who had made the grade, the big merchants, the employers in trade and commerce, with their aspiring womenfolk. These were mostly families on the way up, aping the fashions and the moral attitudes of the ruling class, philistines in the Arts, sold on 'Culture' if only it was gilt enough. Being for the most part holier-than-thou, they shuddered at anything to do with the 'lower orders', and at Tavern Life in particular.

This middle-class attitude towards the emergent idea of a People's

The painting of Old Dan which hung in The Star

Theatre is well exemplified by Jack B. Yeats, brother of the Poet. In a pen-and-ink drawing published in 1881 in the fashionable *Bric-à-Brac*, he brutally caricatured the mass Audience which crowded the London East End Halls on Saturday nights: uncouth forms, rags of military uniforms, hats knocked off, grinning prostitutes, waiters fighting their way through the pandemonium with drinks and baskets of bread – the detail is masterly. But his bourgeois upbringing has blinded the artist to the fact that these are real people (rough and rowdy though they may have been), victims of the Industrial Empire, slowly coming to recognise themselves in this new form of People's art, a vitalising force which in time would help to give these Cockney folk a standing of their own.

Arriving in Dublin in the prime of life, sanguine and full of energy, Dan Lowrey the Second had hopes of one day bringing all these classes under his roof.

Old Dan and Charlotte moved out to Terenure, a pleasant little suburb about two miles from Town at the foot of the Dublin Hills. R. J. Lloyd (Arthur's brother) who had managed The Star now returned to the Stage. Dan Lowrey moved in determined to live, eat and sleep on the job. With wife and family he went to live in The Star itself, in the apartments above the Stage. The Dunbars took a house in Crampton Court and continued in the photographic business.

Dan sank his own capital in the enterprise, and with the Lowrey penchant for acquiring property he began to buy up leases in the Court with an eye to eventual expansion of both Tavern and Theatre.

Renovations began in June and took about ten weeks. His son Daniel supervised the construction of the Top Gallery and, taking off his coat, gave his days to this difficult work. The pillaring and bearing timbers of the Gallery had to comply with stringent by-laws; every item of the work demanded the strictest personal supervision, for enemies were vigilant and Dan had no intention of having The Star fall foul of the Police again.

This part of the work alone cost £1,000. It was money well spent for this 'top shelf', running round three sides of the Hall and having no Promenade for standing and strollers, almost doubled the seating accommodation of the House. The overall capacity, including Auditorium, Bars, Lounge and Smoking Room, was now close on 1,000. George West began to fear for his Grafton; Michael Gunn had fears for his Gaiety.

Theatre and Bars were repainted and redecorated. The oil paintings were now hung on the Gallery landings; they were mainly of Old Dan in his Comic Characters – one showed him in evening dress, and one was of Barry Sullivan the Tragic Actor. The Lowrey connection with Barry Sullivan dated from their Liverpool days; his portrait added a touch of class to The Star, asserted the Lowrey claim to Dramatic rights, and brooded over the scene in the costume of Hamlet, an ironic undertone.

Crampton Court had been paved and channelled by the Corporation in the Seventies but the entrance to it from Dame Street was still dark and uninviting. Dan applied to the Corporation to have one of the new electric lamps set up nearby. The lamp was not allowed on the grounds of expense. Nothing daunted he applied for permission to have the light set up at his

The painting of Barry Sullivan as 'Hamlet' which hung in The Star

own expense. No reply. Dan was having his first taste of the Powers that Be.

Sanguine and resilient, Dan Lowrey the Second sat down in his Office above the Stage to draft his posters and newspaper advertisements. He meant business. Notices of the Re-Opening appeared in all the leading Dublin dailies and weeklies, and coloured posters were displayed on hoardings throughout the Town. He bought two high cars, horse-drawn, to be driven through the streets, bells jingling, carrying huge placards of the current Bill of fare.

In order to banish some of the ill repute which clung to the Court since The Widow Connell's free-and-easy days, and to publicise the image of the kind of Nightlife he meant to create, he had a drawing made of The Star, showing O'Callaghan's chaste interior. Stalls and Gallery tiers are seen crowded and comfortable, people are leaning at ease against the Promenade rails, figures lean from the little boxes which are up on the apron of the Stage beyond the Orchestra, divided into curtained compartments neat and rectilinear like railway carriages. Front curtains are draped against the jambs of the proscenium. On the Stage a bevy of Chicks dance in a semicircle about the Première Danseuse against a backcloth of forest, mountain and waterfall; their skirts are light and puffed like thistledown – the only Italianate curves to be seen in that strict Gothic interior.

He had the drawing printed in light colours on the cover of the Programme, with the title inscrolled along the top about an eight-point star: DAN LOWREY'S MUSIC HALL.

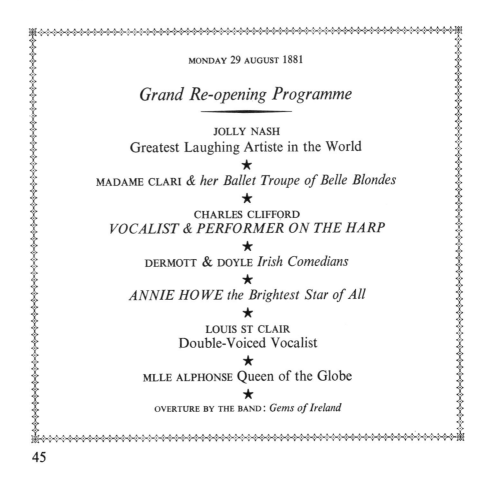

MONDAY 29 AUGUST 1881

Grand Re-opening Programme

JOLLY NASH
Greatest Laughing Artiste in the World

★

MADAME CLARI *& her Ballet Troupe of Belle Blondes*

★

CHARLES CLIFFORD
VOCALIST & PERFORMER ON THE HARP

★

DERMOTT & DOYLE *Irish Comedians*

★

ANNIE HOWE the Brightest Star of All

★

LOUIS ST CLAIR
Double-Voiced Vocalist

★

MLLE ALPHONSE Queen of the Globe

★

OVERTURE BY THE BAND: *Gems of Ireland*

House full. A sprinkling of ladies present. Students of course, and a few professional men. Scribes of the Press and figures from the sporting world. All under the one roof with crowds of the common people. Everybody happy, constant applause in a lively atmosphere of music, the clink of glasses, limelit enchantments and the rhythm of entrancing limbs.

After Nash, who topped the Bill, the great attraction was the Clari Troupe of Blondes. In a variety of costumes they danced Italian style with grace and precision, to a selection of dance-music by the Orchestra – waltzes, polkas, the cotillion (or petticoat dance), and set-dances, Lancers and quadrilles. The Orchestra was rated excellent by the Dublin critics. Between Stage items its renderings charmed the crowded House; strings, brass, woodwind and percussion were used artistically in creating each item of the Show, and the fetching airs lingered in the ears of the people going out into the dark.

Nash stayed for a fortnight. He attracted a considerable following, but belonged in fact to the earlier day of the Song-and-Supper Room. He had been a prosperous ironmaster in the English Midlands, a bluff and hearty fellow with a fine physique, and his jolly songs had enlivened many a midnight party in his wealthy days. Neglecting his iron foundries he went bankrupt, and making the rounds of the Taverns sang for his supper. He had his own style, his ditties were full of belly-laughter, huge chuckles that infected the whole House into fits of helpless mirth. Special songs were written to give him scope for his hysterical attacks – 'The Little Fat Grey Man', 'See Me Dance the Polka', 'I'm Happy-go-lucky Never-say-die'. He also played the concertina and the cornet while tears of laughter streamed from his eyes and his great frame shook.

The principal Artistes featured by Lowrey during the rest of the season were: J. H. Milburn the Man of Many Faces. Dutch Daly Dialect Comedian. Sam Redfern a song-and-patter merchant rattling off comments on the events of the day in a dismal voice to suit his blacked-up face. Joe Lawrence the Two-Headed Nondescript from Leeds, later famous as the father of Vesta Victoria. Dour Donald Dinnie a rock-like Scot in his Highland kilts who had floored all the doughtiest wrestlers of the world. W. J. Ashcroft the Solid Man himself, and the evergreen Pat Kinsella. During October there were bloody riots in Dublin following the arrest of Parnell, Irish Party Leader at Westminster, so Pat's prime number, 'The Mud Island Fusiliers', had to be left out of the Programme: 'batterin' skulls' came a bit too close to the political bone of the moment.

That Autumn the dazzling parade across the stage of The Star continued: Kennetti makes his Great Lightning Leap from the Roof; Herman & Elston, Storm & Richmond, Christy Minstrels, strum their banjos; Witty Watty Walton runs his Excursion Train; Dr Austral and the glamorous

"All among the hay, lads, all among the hay,
Talking to a pretty girl upon a summers day,
All among the hay, lads, all among the hay,
Can't you have a jolly spree, all among the hay."

J. H. Milburn, 'The Man of Many Faces'

Zobéide perform the ancient witchcraft of the Second Sight; Mr & Mrs Mark Johnson unclothe in the flickering limelight of La Studio; Hello! Hello! Hello! return of the Tycoon Troupe of Real Japanese; Professor Hotine's Dogs perform a steeplechase round the stage, ridden by his Monkeys in jockey caps and colours; Professor Maurice and his Two Charming Sisters ride their bicycles backwards, forwards, stand on their heads on the saddle or upon one leg, weaving patterns of motion with glittering wheels; Jessie Mayland Soprano sings arias from Opera and hits from Opera Bouffe; Sara Beryl, famous for her Robinson Crusoe in

Gunn's Gaiety Pantomime, in tights and goatskin, does her comic song and dance; Nat Emmett's Performing Goats are booked, but refused permission to land for fear of foot-and-mouth disease.

Christmas came. The Theatres of Dublin dramatised this Midwinter Festival in their usual style, producing pantomimes of slapstick, spectacle and lavish colour. Dan Lowrey was forbidden to produce pantomime, but he had a bright idea.

Irish trade and commerce were in the doldrums. To help their revival, and to do for Industry what the Land League had done for agriculture, a Great Exhibition of Irish Crafts and Manufactures was planned in Dublin for 1882, so for his Christmas Show Dan designed a 'preview' entitled *Erin's Awakening, or An Exhibition Rehearsed.* All materials used were to be Irish and all costumes to be made by Irish firms; thus it was ensured that the show was topical and public-spirited, and attracted the attention of Big Business to Crampton Court.

Lighting, limes and tableaux sets were designed by Summerfield and White, William Henry planned the musical suite, and all the Artistes currently playing at The Star were catered for in the scenario. The Show opened on St Stephen's Night. It had been a harsh day and the crowd waited in the frozen slush for the doors to open. Inside the Tavern Theatre was brightly lit and decorated with greenery; fires of coal and logs blazed in the Bars and glittered on the polished wood and glassware. The cheapest tickets cost twopence each; it was dear – about the price of a family dinner – yet it was worth it for this was the Midwinter Feast in a way most of these people had never before experienced it.

The Band broke into the Overture, the Curtain went back, and Irish Manufacturers were summoned to appear by warrant of the Fairy Queen. Then green-capped Heralds waltzed, tumbled and wire-walked across the Stage, their svelte figures flattered in Mahony woollens and Lucan tweeds. Weavers mixed into the fun, puppets and ventriloquist's dolls, flaunting Irish flannels among a bevy of Pretty Maidens resplendent in Tuskar serge, Belfast linen, Atkinson's poplin and Balbriggan stockings. Up pops a Comic dressed as a big box of Dublin Matches, up pops another dressed as a Roll of Limerick Tobacco, and the slapstick smacks and sizzles between them. Clogdancers dressed as Guinness Bargemen and Barrels go clattering in jigtime and the Tale is enlivened by a constant stream of Irish Flour, Candles, Clocks, Fruit, Flowers. The Chicks of course dance their delightful ensembles in Limerick Lace.

It was a huge success. 'The Citizens of Dublin owe Mr Lowrey a great debt of gratitude for his wonderful pluck and enterprise' – *Pat.* Theatreland was aware of a new force in the City.

RIGHT Sketches from *Pat* of the Christmas Show, 1881–2. Among the characters are Irish Commercial Magnates, a Fashion Model, a Small Farmer and his Wife, Makers of Matches, Beer, Clocks, Candles and Candlesticks

PAT, 21st JANUARY, 1882.
AT DAN LOWREY'S.
The Boycotted Commercials
a small farmer & his wife
the Star of Erin
D.McE.
Tobacco and Matches
Stout, with a good head on it.
A clock going slow.
A light headed boy.

CHAPTER SIX

1882 The Lions Comiques

1

Lowrey's *Erin's Awakening* showed what he could do in the way of giving dramatic unity to a whole night's Show and still remain within the letter of the Law. In the New Year he carried on the attack and billed The Four Aubreys – an American team specialising in a kind of Acrobat Drama. Through the medium of gymnastics enlivened by clowning and comic surprise they enacted a story with subtitles – The Hotel, The Stranger, The Second Stranger, The Unwelcome Visitor, Imagination, The Dénouement – much as the Ballet tells a story through the medium of the Dance. The Audience not only enjoyed the story but at the same time enjoyed the clever, comic and unexpected manner in which it was retailed to them. To the Law Dan could plead that the Aubreys were merely Acrobats, but their act was Drama in a very real sense; they commanded the highest salary yet paid by The Star for a single act and were 'enormously successful' – *Pat*.

He next had a crack at the Opera monopoly by engaging Tom Maglagan in his *Musical Scrapbook*. Maglagan was in the top rank, a Scotsman whose pronounced accent gave a homely flavour to the exotic part of his performance. He had begun at The Canterbury under Morton and was later the chief attraction at The Britannia, but his talent was not of Music Hall proper and he could never equal the glory of his appearance in *Faust*. Emilyn Soldene, who had brought the lavish Opera Bouffe musical leg-shows of *Chilperic* and *Genevieve* to Gunn's Gaiety, did not think much of him:

> He looked lovely in a kilt and was simply perfect as a Geordie or a Sandy, but in *tights* . . . he was unaesthetic and awful. He had a lovely tenor voice, but was no musician, and would always come in in the wrong place – a bar too soon or a bar too late.

As well as his Opera airs he had a fund of kilty melodies and high-society skits; he mimicked, played the violin and danced the Highland Fling. Essentially an Actor, he specialised in lightning changes of face and costume through all the items of his *Scrapbook*. After a tenor aria from *Faust* he would quick-change into the old frock-coat and floppy pants of the down-at-heel, whip on a limp white tie with long black funereal streamers, dab some blood-red greasepaint on his nose and wail into 'The Ratcatcher's Daughter' or 'Villikins and his Dinah'.

Some of these demotic bits came from Sam Cowell's repertoire in the Song-and-Supper days. One of them featured by Maglagan illustrates the dodges invented by the Illegitimates to put Drama on their programme; it was a potted version of *Hamlet* sung in doggerel rhyme:

> *A Hero's life I'll sing; his story shall my pen mark.*
> *He was not the King, but Hamlet Prince of Denmark.*
> *His Mammy she was young, the Crown she'd set her eyes on,*
> *Her Husband stopped her tongue – she stopped his ears with pi-zon!*

All this caused Michael Gunn to keep an uneasy eye on Crampton Court.

March brought the strangest of all Springs to Dan Lowrey's. First there was Chirgwin the White-Eyed Kaffir. Unexpected, surprising the Audience, Chirgwin leaped onto the scene in skintight black costume, face blacked up, whitewashed hat absurdly tall and cocked at an acute angle over his eyebrow, and cried to the Bandmaster: 'Arf a mo, cocky!' When the laughter died the Kaffir in a strange voice that shifted from a high falsetto to deep barrel-notes of pathos sang:

I am but a poor blind boy
Still my heart is full of jòy
Though I never saw the light
Or the flowers they call so bright.

It was his celebrated 'Blind Boy' – sheer unsophisticated sentiment. The raucous voice reverberated in the nerves of the audience and struck the essential chord of sadness at the heart of life. The Kaffir's fiddle, a one-stringed bazomba made from an old cigar box, echoed in tremolo – 'bl-i-i-i-ndd!' The effect was electrifying. The weirdest element of the act was that there was one dramatic gap in the Black Mask, a diamond of white through which the right eye looked out, a peep of the underlying reality, the common human face hid behind the Tragic Mask. The last note of the bazomba lingered, the packed tiers were gripped in the pathos of the song, the Black Devil cocked one white eye up to the gods, drew a hand across dry lips and, breaking the tension, squawked: 'Could do wiv a drink!'

There followed the Ghost of Paganini. Niccolo Paganini, the Genoese violinist, had been a colourful figure in his day. With long dark hair, saturnine features and flashing eyes, and dressed in rich dark velvet with silver *appliqué*, as he appears in the painting by Maclise, he had cast the spell of his personality and musical bravura upon the capitals of Europe. At the first Dublin Musical Festival in 1831 he had appeared at The Rotunda, composing for the occasion his Variations on a Theme, called 'St Patrick's Day'. He died in 1840. Some fifteen years later his 'Redivivus' or 'Ghost', wearing the remembered costume of the Maestro, appeared playing at Musano's Concerts in Paris. In the early Sixties the Ghost appeared in London. Then in 1868 he was to be found in Dublin, advertising 'Céad Míle Fáilte Concerts, for the introduction and début of Unknown Celtic Talent'.

St Patrick's Day was at hand. The Ghost came into the gaslight at Dan Lowrey's, a gaunt figure with hanks of dark hair, garbed in the black and silver costume as if the Maclise painting had come to life. He played the 'St Patrick's Day Variations' lying on his back. Then followed Irish melodies and traditional reels, all delightfully executed. Music lovers and connoisseurs who had come to Dan's in large numbers found the playing sublime and were amazed as piece after piece came flowing from the strings with a brilliancy never equalled since the fingers of the old Maestro were chilled in death. It was unnerving. Like a spirit in pain the Ghost lay squirming on his back, impelling himself upon his shoulderblades, while he made the violin absolutely speak the tune. His physical anguish increased and, insinuating his body serpentlike between the legs of tables and chairs, he played the 'Carneval de Venice' in the purest tone to a House fallen silent and still. Struggling at last to his feet he played the 'Overture to William Tell' upon a single string.

That strange Spring, Dan's first in Dublin, when the White-Eyed Kaffir and Paganini Redivivus held all breathless at The Star, a daughter was born to Annie Lowrey in the bedroom above the Stage. They christened her Norah. This little girl grew up in the very air of the Theatre. She had free run of Stage and dressing-rooms, played with the Artistes, made friends with famous people – Vesta Tilley, Vesta Victoria, Harriet Vernon – chattered with Wirewalkers, Ventriloquists, Swordswallowers, took rides on Performing Elephants, and had 'the childhood of a lifetime'.

She was only a week old and in her cot when down below, on the Stage, Artois was killed.

Ever since Blondin had crossed the Niagara Falls on a tightrope, aerial acrobatics had caught the imagination of the world. Lowrey's posters advertising Artois were read with interest: this man was going to 'fly'.

On Tuesday 21 March the Auditorium looked like a Circus tent with trapezes and rope ladders dangling on the Stage and out in the body of the Hall. The House was packed and Dan Lowrey watching from the rail saw many faces returned from the night before. When his turn came, Monsieur Artois – he was John Lilly of Leeds – clad in white tights entered to a flourish of trumpets and swung into his act. He went through feat after feat of aerial daring on rope and trapeze in a tense silence broken by rounds of applause. The climax came: it was announced that Monsieur Artois would now perform his unprecedented Leap for Life. He would fly twenty-five feet through the air. The Band ceased to play and in a dramatic silence he began to swing on the bar of a trapeze out in the Auditorium. Having gained momentum he gave a sharp laugh, took off, and shot through the air, graceful as a great white gull, above the upturned faces. His flight took him headfirst over the footlights, across the Stage and through a second trapeze which was hanging there. Instead of perching safely on this trapeze, his body seemed to brush it awkwardly, he hooked the bar with the hollow of a leg, squirmed in a frantic effort to grasp the rope, missed and crashed to the floor. Lowrey, appalled, called for the Curtain.

Several people, including a medical student, climbed onto the Stage.

The Aerialist, from *Pick-Me-Up*

The Aerialist's skull appeared to be fractured. Lowrey came before the Curtain stammering that Monsieur Artois had been very gravely injured and the audience would agree that the Show should not continue. Dazed, they moved towards the exits.

Artois was taken from the Theatre on a stretcher improvised of laths and canvas and carried in a cab to Mercer's Hospital. His wife was sent for. Half an hour later he died.

At the Inquest the gist of the evidence was that Artois had shot from the first trapeze a fraction too soon, without having gained sufficient height and momentum to carry him clean through the second trapeze before leg-hooking the bar.

Mrs Lilly cut a pathetic figure; she told the Coroner that in spite of her husband's earnings she was left in very poor circumstances with no means of support for her children, a girl of ten and two boys. Lowrey was very much affected. Ill with the shock, he came forward in aid of the widow. Not only did he pay her the current week's salary, £7, purchase a burial plot in Mount Jerome and take all the funeral expenses upon himself; on the Friday he reopened The Star with a Benefit Night for Mrs Lilly, and set up a Committee to raise funds out of which he bought and furnished premises for her, giving her enough stock to set up as Confectioner and Newsagent, while she could also let lodgings in the house to visiting Artistes. He never forgot this Death on his Stage.

The Show must go on. In addition to his impudent sallies into Drama and Opera, Lowrey was at pains to get the best in Male Comics, the mainstay of Music Hall. His list this year includes many names in the top flight and some who were only just short of it – Nash, Chirgwin, Harry Rickards, Joe Cheevers, Ashcroft, Pat Kinsella, Harry Melville, J. H. Milburn, Charles Coburn, Henri Clarke, Leybourne and the Great Macdermott.

The Male Comic had developed as something distinct from the Singing Actor. He might make many impersonations in the course of a night, but through all of them it was his own vivid and hypnotic personality which held the Audience. Mocking, pathetic, satiric, highfalutin', down-at-heel, topical, wildly absurd, he was the Joker in the Rite.

He took many forms, many incarnations. Harry Rickards was Jewish, born Ben Leete, bullnecked, with a waxed moustache, and evoked the comic pathos of the eternal Clown, let down always by the Lady, singing:

Cerulea was beautiful, Cerulea was fair,
She lived with her Grandmother in Gooseberry Square.
She was my unkeydoodlum but now, alas, she
Plays kissy-kissy with an Officer in the Artill-er-ee.

J. H. Milburn went through a variety of facial expressions; he was a 'low comedian', that is, he presented song-characters from the lower walks of life, often with their pathetic and too-loud attempts at finery. Harry Melville the Dublin Daisy set the House rollicking in a wild burst of the Absurd:

There was plums and prunes and cherries
And citrons and raisins and cinnamon too,
There was nutmegs, cloves and berries

And the crust it was nailed on with glue.
There was carraway seeds in abundance –
'Twould build up a fine stomach-ache –
You would kill a man twice after eating a slice
Of Miss Hooligan's Christmas Cake.

The topical was always dangerous, for the Dublin Audience was complex and liable to fly out of their dumb frustration at the drop of a political brick. Yet even in the thick of the Home Rule agitation Henri Clarke, through the sheer zest of his comic lunacy, could make them all chorus:

A man may jump upon his mother,
Sister, uncle, cousin, brother,
And they can murder one another
When Parnell's the King of Old Ireland!

May Day. 'George Leybourne has Arrived!'

The Band broke into the famous Chorus, the lithe figure stalked elegantly onto the Stage. And there he was at last, the Lion Comique. There was the celebrated Masher costume they had for years been reading of – bright green jacket, checked waistcoat, primrose scarf, white kid gloves, fawn and faultless pantaloons, and under a sleek topper the handsome half-Semitic visage was enriched with silken sidewhiskers. The personality was charming, the voice was as fine and rollicking as the tune:

Champagne Charlie is my name,
Champagne Charlie is my name,
Good for any game at night, my boys!
Who'll come and join me in a spree?

George Champagne Charlie Leybourne had spent his young years as a hammer-man with a firm of marine engineers, but having the urge to mask and sing he did the Free-and-Easies of the English Midlands for a few shillings a night, eventually rising to £4 a week in Manchester. He adopted the broad check suits, the bright jackets and the wide-striped trousers of the Racecourse Swell – costume was always part of the Leybourne *persona* – and from the first he carried an aura of flash life, titillating the respectable poor with a whiff of fast Society sins, gambling, horse-racing, the lush crib, the Night Club and the Prize Ring.

Coming to London he was engaged at The Canterbury, then managed by Arthur Holland. In those days there arrived in London one Alfred Lee, with nothing in his pocket but the manuscript of a song, music and words, for which a hesitant publisher parted with £20. The song got to Leybourne, Holland dressed him for the part, and 'Champagne Charlie' circled the world.

By the time he came to Lowrey's Leybourne had long been legendary. Champagne flowed like water at his shows and his weekly wage climbed from £30 a week up into three figures, to the wonder of Stageland. Holland, great impresario, equipped him with a carriage, four white horses and a coachman in livery to drive the Dandy Clown in ducal style from Hall to Hall. A rival burlesqued this act by appearing in the streets in a cart drawn

RIGHT Leybourne as 'Champagne Charlie'

by four off-white donkeys, but no mockery could upset the reign of King George; in his gentlemanly splendour, fur-collar coat and flower in the buttonhole, he brought elegance to the profession and more than any other was responsible for bringing Society into the Music Hall. He was first among the Lions Comiques.

This term was coined by J. J. Poole of the South London Hall. It suggested the lionisation of the man, the unprovincial, cosmopolitan quality of his act and of the set he mimicked, as much at home in the bar of a Parisian Night Circus as in a London Club. While the working man laughed at the mimickry he rejoiced in it, for the elegant Jester incarnated the dandy hidden in every man – shopboy, coalman, scrivener's clerk – they were all Champagne Charlies in their dreaming hours and Rollicking Rams at heart. The Music Hall became their temple of worship, their idol the Lion Comique. Many claimed the title, but the five truly great Lions Comiques were Leybourne, Arthur Lloyd, Vance, Leno and the Great Macdermott.

At Lowrey's Leybourne gave a cocktail mixture of his dude-songs, ditties and Society-buck personations. Most were by his chief lyricist G. W. Hunt, sparkling and infectious, taking many a hint from current waltz tunes or even from Church hymns, full of repetition and of phrases that ran trippingly off the tongue:

Captain Cuff, Captain Cuff, you can tell me by my collar.
Captain Cuff, Captain Cuff, tho' I'm not worth half a dollar
I'm mighty stiff in style as my cigarette I puff,
They cry, – Hi! Clear the w'y! Here comes Captain Cuff!

Leybourne in his Masher style

or the everlasting:

He flies thro' the air with the greatest of ease
The daring young man on the Flying Trapeze.
His movements are graceful, all the girls he can please –
But my love he has stolen away.

Then in a romantic ditty, composed by himself, he transposed to a deep and surprisingly rich tone of voice:

May sheeps' heads grow on appletrees
If ever I cease to love,
May the moon be turned to a green cheese
If ever I cease to love!

Having charmed the House to such a whimsical mood he twirled his cane and romped into the daft dude chorus:

For I'm a member of the Rollicking Rams.
Come and be a member of the Rollicking Rams,
The only boys to make a noise
From now till day is dawning.
We scorn such drinks as lemonade,
Soda, seltzer, beer:
The tipple of our Club I'll tell you –
But I can't, for there's ladies here!

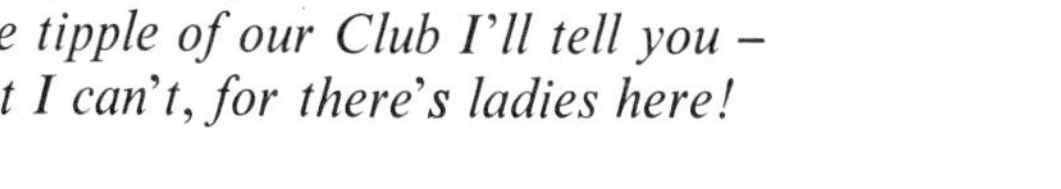

In those days of the long gown and layers of protective petticoat, a glimpse of female flesh belonged to the essence of the Music Hall. This year sultry dancing made its first appearance at Dan's. The Emile Giraud Troupe of Four were billed: 'The only Original Leg Mania Artistes. The Lady Member of this Troupe is the most extraordinary High Kicker in the World, she must be seen to be believed.' The High Kick had come to London about ten years earlier with the French male dancer Clodoche in the dynamic dance he had invented and named the Can Can. It was a wild leg exercise done to a fast four-four time, and when the ladies took it up, giving a glimpse of their dark declivities through a dazzle of underclothes, it raised puritan eyebrows, so much so that when Wiry Sal danced it at The London Alhambra the Middlesex Magistrates stepped in and The Alhambra lost its licence for fourteen years.

Lowrey took a chance with the High Kick, for the fast was becoming the fashionable while the Law on the matter remained obscure. The three males of the Giraud group were costumed as black demons with moustachios and pointed goatees, stiff collars with upturned spikes and long pointed dancing-shoes. The Lady Member's dress in contrast was fluent and floating; she danced in and out among the brisk and bristling Leg-maniacs, was tossed and tumbled, and she kicked displaying her *tout-en-l'air* in hairbreadth escapes from total indecency.

Less torrid than these, troupes of Ballet Chicks were frequently billed. Ballet which had been in danger of dying out had been given a home in the Music Halls and now, revitalised by its touch with the common man, was making its way back into the Legitimate Theatre. Under the influence of the High Kick and the more earthy culture of the Halls, the style of the Chicks that came to Dan's was changing, as *Pat* noted in an article, 'How to Dance':

> If female, wear a very short skirt and assume heterodox notions with regard to the centre of gravity. Let the tips of your toes do duty for the soles of your feet, and do your best to emulate Catherine Wheel convulsions. Go away very tired, take off abbreviated skirt and don a somewhat shabby dress, a somewhat battered bonnet, and a somewhat threadbare ulster, and walk two or three miles home in the rain. Receive nine shillings per week and be satisfied to be considered a Shameless Thing by some half-naked women in the Circle who have several times escaped the Divorce Court by the skin of their teeth.

A clever combination of forbidden fruit and culture was provided by Mr & Mrs Mark Johnson, with Miss Mattie Mitchell, in Poses Plastiques. Dan billed: 'They will introduce nightly their Classical Entertainment "La Studio", presenting with limelight and other effects groups of Living Statuary from the Great Masters.'

Poses Plastiques had a long history among the delights of Nightlife; they had been part of the *risqué* attractions of The Coal Hole in the Fifties. In these Exhibitions, under the aegis of the Greek and Italian Masters of painting and sculpture, the masculine, feminine and hermaphrodite nature of the human form divine could be experienced to a degree not normal in the rigidity of the Victorian whalebone corset and Sunday suit. 'Living pictures became a mania,' writes Hibbert, 'the comic opera choruses were ranged for beauty, and some of the best-known actresses of the day could, if they would, confess to having aired their charms in these circumstances.'

The item often took liberties with the *Ars Poetica*: the Sultan's

Favourite Emerging from her Bath was apt to replace the chaste Greek Venus Rising from the Sea. However at Dan's the Johnsons' repertoire was unimpeachable. Within a large picture-frame, in the glow of the lime and with the aid of flimsies and leafage, Mr & Mrs Mark and the boylike Mattie produced a live illusion of the biceps, bosoms, marble buttocks and angelic cheek of Bacchus and Ariadne, Venus with Mars and Cupid, and the icy Diana blinding the Hunter who had gazed upon her nude.

At The Grecian Theatre off City Road, London, under the management of Acrobat–Author George Conquest, there arrived sometime in the Sixties an intense young Irishman looking for work. He was big, blond and handsome, had served in the Royal Navy, possessed the physique of a prizefighter and a voice that had been rocked in the cradle of the deep. The melodious young giant became dogsbody to the Conquest Company, acting, clowning, stage-carpentering, writing and rehashing scripts of all sorts. Blossoming into a playwright, with dreams of being the second Shakespeare, he changed his name from Gilbert Hastings Farrell to the more regal style of G. H. Macdermott.

It was not his Bloodie Tragedies that brought him fame but a ditty called 'The Scamp' which he bought for half a guinea. The golden voice, the bullocking and buttery tone, the unconscious truth of the characterisation, caused a sensation:

If ever there was a damned scamp
I flatter myself I am he,
From William the Norman to Brigham the Mormon
They can't hold a candle to me.

They couldn't. Engaged at The Pavilion to fill a gap in holiday time, 'The Scamp' took, and the engagement at £10 a week went on it seemed forever. Many lyricists (including Leybourne's Hunt) caught the thunder-and-soup Macdermott tone and supplied him with a large battery of hall-stormers, but for years 'The Scamp' remained his song and his symbol.

Then one morning in 1878 G. W. Hunt, reading his newspaper at breakfast, found that the Russian was threatening the Turk, while the Imperial Government of Great Britain and Ireland was trying to warm up to the idea of warning off the Russian Bear. Hunt was seized with excitement and dashed off a song on the subject. Not quite Leybourne's style, he decided he would give it to the thundering Macdermott. He hurried round to the Irishman's lodgings, woke him, and there by the bedside tried out words and tune. That night at The Pavilion Macdermott sailed into it, the great voice found resonance in every corner of the Hall, and with all the Actor's art behind it the bull quality in song and man provoked a crowd-storm of hysteria:

The Great Jingo in Action, drawn from *The Halls*, 1900

We don't want to fight
But – by Jingo! – if we do
We've got the ships, we've got the men,
We've got the money too!
We've fought the Bear before
And while Britons still are true
THE RUSSIANS SHALL NOT HAVE CONSTANTINOPLE!

It was the biggest musico-journalistic scoop of all time. It was the swear-word 'Jingo' that set the nation to hum. Papers took it into their editorials, it flamed through every Pantomime, cartoonists had endless fun with the English Jingo terrorising the shaggy Bear, and the song entered every language that had the rudiments of a printing-press. Modest little men became war-minded, costers bawled it, ladies trilled it in drawing-rooms, the Jingo Spirit and the word for it stalked the land. Hunt, a little man with a big moustache, was Jingo Hunt for the rest of his days, and the ex-dogsbody of the Conquest Company was thereafter the Statesman of the Halls. He was advanced to the status of Lion Comique, putting Arthur Lloyd's nose out of joint in his own Theatre. In the event, the Russian refrained from attacking the Turk. Macdermott, giving Hunt a guinea, took the credit to himself, and there was some talk of a Knighthood being conferred on him in the Birthday Honours List.

Macdermott entered Dan's on Monday 9 October for a fortnight. The fit of war fever had cooled. Yet 'House Full' signs were up; the entrances were jammed, dockers and tramway men and barefoot youths crowded in Dame Street to catch a glimpse of the fur coat and silken whiskers of the big Lion Comique who had interfered in history. Inside at 9.30 p.m. the Band struck up the Jingo tune, Bars and Smokingroom emptied, there was a rush to the Auditorium and the whole House gave a prolonged ovation to the Cosmic Figure on the Stage.

These scenes of enthusiasm continued night after night. After by-Jingoing the Russians back where they came from to the delight of the labouring-man, escaped a moment out of his candlelit cave, the Lion would roar out some reverberating sentiment overflowing with love for all Mankind:

We're dear Old Pals, jolly Old Pals,
Clinging together in all sorts of weather,
Dear Old Pals, jolly Old Pals,
Give me the friendship of – Dear – Old – Paaals!

And all felt good and strong and powerful lifting their voices in the leonine roar.

Macdermott had cost Dan £50, and very probably had carried off another £50 from his Benefit. But the success of the Tavern Theatre in Crampton Court was now assured.

Old Dan Lowrey's wife, Charlotte, died this Autumn, and was buried in Mount Jerome close to the grave of Artois. The Old Comedian was alone now; he still came to The Star from time to time, travelling on the horse-tram or by cab to play his Comic Characters, and his convivial drollery enlivened the company in the Bars, adding to the Family quality of the Music Hall in Crampton Court. But the Tavern Theatre he had created was now for the most part out of his hands. He seems to have taken to gambling as a pastime, and it became common to say of a heavy gambler: 'Oh, he's another Dan Lowrey!'

The Star was forging ahead. The wealthy Findlater Family, with an eye to the future, began to invest in property in Crampton Court; the leading papers, the *Irish Times* and the *Freeman's Journal*, began to give space and cautious approval to this new kind of Nightlife which, it appeared, had the approval of the Prince of Wales, and George West, who had had Findlater financial backing for his Grafton, was finding he could not compete with the Lowrey imagination, grit and vigour.

Christmas was at hand. Again Dan Lowrey had a scenario designed that would give a dramatic unity to a whole night's Show, using all his current Artistes and their individual acts along with a shoal of local talent in the presentation of the Tale. Opening on St Stephen's Day he produced *The Magic Shamrock, or The Little Boy's Visit to Donnybrook Fair.* Represented by Sixty Performers. Scenes: House of the Leprechauns. Abode of the Fairies. College Green. Lakes of Killarney. The whole produced under the Direction of Mr & Mrs Pat Kinsella.

The Royal Patentee looked helplessly on. For the Law, *The Magic Shamrock* was a Music Hall show; for the Audience it was a Christmas Pantomime. Dan's Story-Show was the talk of the Town; the genial Pat and his thistledown wife were the heroes of the hour. 'The production of *The Magic Shamrock* will long be remembered as one of the most success-full enterprises in this City' – *Irish Times.*

CHAPTER SEVEN

1883 The Missing Link

In his Office, surrounded by his correspondence files, ledgers, engagement books, accounts with caterers, brewers, distillers, signed photos and pictures of Artistes, Clowns, Elephants, Serios, Troupes of Chicks, proofs of his advertisements, newspaper cuttings, copies of *Era*, *The Stage*, *Lady's Realm*, *Entr'acte*, his programmes and drafts of his posters fresh from the press of Powderley & Co., Colour & General Printers, Dan Lowrey was the dynamic centre around which all these fragmented lives and songs and lacy somersaults revolved. He had hardly any personal life: he was no longer Dan Lowrey but 'Dan Lowrey's'.

Already the Tavern Show was beginning to acquire an annual routine geared to the seasonal life of the City: the Christmas Show running over into the New Year; St Patrick's Day; the Easter Holidays; Whitsuntide; the long bright evenings of the Summer slack; Horse Show Week in August; darkening November days with the lights of the Theatre twinkling in the early dusk; then the Midwinter Festival at hand again with the sun barely lifting above the snowbound Dublin Hills.

He was now giving Grand Illuminated Saturday Matinées, especially when he had a big attraction to offer. These began at 2 p.m. and were designed for the ladies, children and family parties who might enjoy The Star atmosphere in the afternoon without indulging in the more adult delights of the Night Show.

His advertising campaign was incessant – two-inch column space in *Pat* and in its successor the *Irish Diamond*, three-inch column in the *Times* and the *Freeman's Journal*. His bright posters thirty inches long and ten inches wide were everywhere – in bars, sweetshops, tobacconists, bunshops, on brick walls and billboards. He himself phrased all the publicity, showman style, making everything larger than life – Engagement at Enormous Expense of, Resounding Success of, The Entire American Press is Unanimous that, Easter Monday Monster Attractions, Every Night The Star Shines Bright . . .

28 May – the return of the Great London Lion Comique, George Leybourne. And there he was, rings on the delicate fingers, cigar poised. The Masher charm had now a vintage quality and the great Roué of the Halls was ageing ere his time. But the magic was still there, in the mellifluous voice and in the bewitching personality which was his very own, for Leybourne off-stage as well as on was the most good-natured of men. Lowreyites loved the flexibility of his style, a rollicking repeatability in his 'Rams', a Dickensian whimsey in his 'Mousetrap Man' and 'The Little Eelpie Shop', a touch of the blue-rag in such tit-bits as 'They All Do It'. That week the Leybourne fever spread all over Town; in the coster taverns off the Daisy Market and in exclusive rooms behind the prim façade of Trinity the chorus was raised:

After the Opera's over
And tending the ladies is done
We gems of the very first water
Commence with our frolic and fun.

Early Ads in *Pat*

DAN LOWREY'S
"STAR" MUSIC HALL
DAME STREET.
Monday, November 13th, and during the Week,
MISS MARIE LOFTUS,
FOUR ARABS, MR. CHARLES BELL,
THE MURPHY'S
PADDY AND ELLA.
THE GREAT AMERICAN TEAM, Chester, Cullen, Lewis and Downey, Herr Adalbert FRIKELL, The Sisters WALLACE,
Monday Next—T.C.Everard. Ada Lundberg Dillon & Brady

Time and Prices as usual.

HARP MUSIC HALL.
ADAM COURT, GRAFTON STREET.

PROPRIETOR .. .. MR. P. LANGAN.

This Establishment open every evening with a grand variety entertainment.

Prices of Admission 1s., 6d., 3d.

The later Leybourne, from Hibbert, *Fifty Years of a Londoner's Life*, 1916

Leybourne took his last bow at Dan's amid scenes of enthusiasm. He had created a new myth: the Bohemian, the hail-fellow-well-met in opera cloak and topper, improvident and generous to the last degree, a living embodiment of the dreamworld of the man in the street. But he was worn out. He died the following year, aged forty-two.

'The announcement that Arthur Roberts the London Comic was to appear was sufficient to assure Mr Lowrey a crowded attendance' – *Times*.

Roberts with his hooked nose and high shoulders was a mercurial man. He used to deliver with gusto such pathetics as 'Tidings of Comfort and Joy', break into offbeat patter in an airy staccato, improvise characterisations seemingly ad lib, shut up of a sudden and silently mime the style of well-known figures on the Stage and in public life. The crowds came. In the presence of Arthur they were living it up in the slickest London Stageland style.

As with Leybourne and Macdermott, his style and rise to fame were as eagerly discussed in the drawing-rooms south of the River as in the sawdust drinking-dens of the Liberties. He was a Londoner, born in 1852, who had got a fair share of schooling before beginning work with a firm of solicitors. At the age of twenty he threw over the security of the Law and embarked on a Stage career. Nattier than most with his black moustache and pointed beard – the imperial – he eventually reached the rank of half a guinea a night.

Roberts was perhaps a bit too clever for the peculiar mood which was Music Hall. He lacked the Leybourne gift of being at one with the Audience, and was an intellectual wit rather than a Male Comic. A few weeks after his appearance at Dan's he left the Music Hall Stage and went into fashionable Burlesque, Musical Comedy and Pantomime. In these lavish settings (at The Gaiety under Edwardes) he found his true métier and for twenty years was 'the funniest man in London'. He lived in upper middle-class style – large house in Maida Vale, European vacations with his family, yachting, hunters and racehorses – at the very peak of the theatrical milieu in which the greater Artiste, Leybourne, had died in poverty.

Arthur Roberts by Augustus John, from Roberts's *Fifty Years of Spoof*, 1927

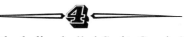

After the Male Comics the ladies (called Serio-Comics) were late starters. Star taste in lady singers was still for a mixture of music and feminine charm; while the dishcloth realism of Ada Lundberg was politely clapped, Dublin surrendered more readily to such sweet musicians as Jenny Lynn.

Of the Serio-Comics this year, Lottie Collins, tall and strong-boned with the Serio's face and the plastique of the Female Clown, was principally a dancer. Bonnie Kate Harvey was more on the Serio-Sexy side. She was billed as The Simple Country Maid, which she was not; in fact she was one of London's leading Girls in the Gaslight. In an interview widely publicised she agreed she was 'one of the Finest Figures on the Stage. Proportion, perfection, and natural golden hair – not a wig – which so many of the Serios have copied!' Her humour was tart, and the 'serio' element in her act lay mainly in the supple use of her ample attractions.

But neither Lottie nor Bonnie Kate broke the Victorian taboo as cheekily as did the Celebrated Characteristic Vocalist Bessie Bonehill. Bessie's gift was to exhibit her figure and personality in the guise of a man. She was English to the knucklebone, born at West Bromwich where as a small girl she had won local fame as a clogdancer. Her sharp sense of realism soon learned to see through the boys; she began to mimic the males, their cocky self-assurance, their raffish way with a maid; and in the Seventies these sharp-edged male personations attracted London attention and earned Bessie engagements at The Metropolitan, The Royal, The Oxford. Clement Scott wrote her a song, 'Here Stands a Post', a patriot piece which went through many versions until it finally became the sinewy 'Waiting for the Signal' which the fetching figure in the male attire sang with the angel cheek of a stiff little soldier boy.

On the high cars jingling through the streets Dan's posters announced: 'Tremendous Success of Bessie Bonehill!' Underlying the serio-satiric comedy there was a deep psycho-attraction in her act. The audience felt it as 'naughty', but it was never vulgar for it was presented with all the finesse of a breezy and soignée style.

But the Male Comics and the Serios were by no means the whole of the picture. All the teeming life of the Circus, the wandering one-night Acrobats and Animals of the Sawdust Ring, the Enchantments and Necromancers, the Puppets and Peepshows that had enlivened the streets – all now joined the caravanserai passing across the Stage at Dan's.

Among the Puppets, Codman's Punch & Judy and Jennion's Marionettes were outstanding. Like Punch & Judy (Pontius Pilate & the Jews), and indeed like most things in Theatre, the Marionettes had come down from the colourful religion of the Middle Ages. They had begun as little figurines of the Virgin, called 'marions' (marys) or 'marionettes', which were worked on strings to enact the Christian Mysteries for an unlettered people. At Dan's, with the Starlights dimmed and the limelight focused on the perky little puppets, their mimicry of life was curiously more convincing than actual life itself.

The Diorama presenting views of the United Kingdom was an early attempt to provide moving pictures. The comic paper *Zoz* describes it: 'A long picture wound on sticks and indicating (at the pleasure of the proprietor) Jerusalem, Madagascar or Connemara. An Artist travels with the outfit and paints in, as occasion may require, a cedar tree, a black man, or an outside car.'

Among the Novelties, the Clown Raffin with Performing Pig and Monkey

Through the streets in February and again in November came the cavalcade of Delhi & Poonah the Musical Elephants. People stood to watch them pass on their way to Dan's: the plod of the feet and the trained curl of the patient trunks brought a whiff of the glamorous Victorian Empire of India. The Elephants were sick on their second night and unable to appear 'in consequence of having experienced a sea-passage of twenty-four hours in the storm'. But thereafter they were put through their paces nightly by Captain Harrington; they rolled on globes, walked on a tightrope, stood on their heads, danced, played drums, trumpets and clarinets. As well as being a wonder in themselves, they brought respectability to Dan's, for it was known that the Queen Empress had commanded a performance of Delhi & Poonah for the entertainment of herself and the Royal Children. The Captain also presented the Wonderful Dog 'Royal' who had followed the Fourth Royal Irish Dragoons through the late War in Egypt to Cairo. After which the Elephants sat down to tea and were served by a Barbary Ape.

But even the high-grade publicity attending Delhi & Poonah paled before the presentation of the monkey-girl.

Farini the London Freak-Merchant was a phenomenon. In his youth he had been a brilliant acrobat who, Blondin-like, had crossed Niagara on a tightrope. Later he dressed his son as a girl and for years had him shot from a spring pedestal, thereby raising the eyebrows of the Purity League and attracting the masses, with the result that Farini was appointed as Technical Advisor to The Royal Aquarium, opened by a Prince of the Realm in the presence of the Nobility and Clergy in June 1876 as a centre of Highclass Music, Entertainment and Education in the Natural Sciences. It had been a dismal failure until Farini took over. He shot Zazel, a beautiful female, from a cannon. There was an outcry. Home Secretary Cross wrote to the Manager warning that he would be held responsible if the Lady were hurt. Farini placarded London with the Home Secretary's letter, inviting Mr Cross to come and be shot-up at his convenience. Zazel became the London Thing and Farini's reputation as a Freak-Merchant was firmly established. Giants, Midgets, Calves born with Two Heads, Siamese Twins, Aztecs, Earthmen and Ladies with Beards . . . he signed them all up at his Westminster Office, displayed them at his Aquarium, then sent them on the Stageland round. They satisfied the age-old appetite for gazing at wonders, and were of special interest in the storm of argument unloosed by Darwin's *Descent of Man*.

Darwin was led to assume that Man and the Higher Apes were descended from the same stock, a rude Prototype long buried in the mud of the past. But there was a link missing in the evidence: there was an unbridgeable gap between the lowest form of Mankind and the highest of the Apes. The kind of creature that would fill the gap – half-way between Man and Monkey – came to be called the Missing Link. This struck the popular and the scientific fancy and an enthusiastic search for

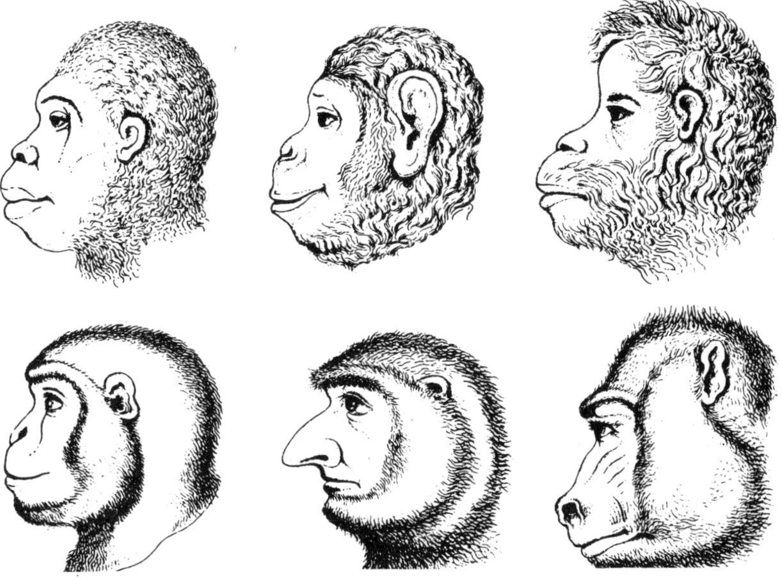

Haeckel's notion of Man's relation to the Apes, printed in 1868

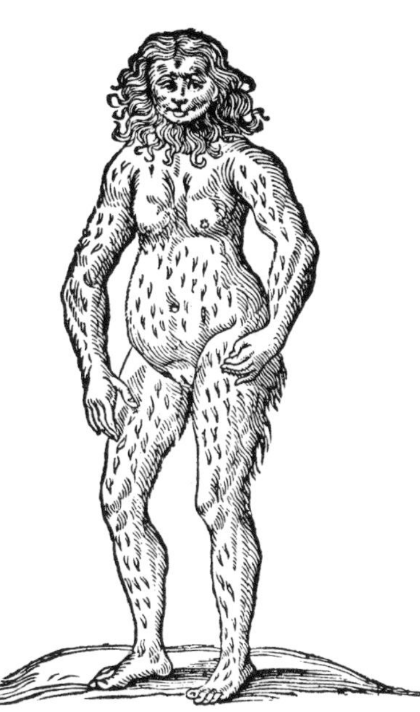

'The Missing Link'. A Dutch doctor's idea of the Female Ape, printed two hundred years before Darwin

the Link was instituted, both among living creatures and the bones of the past. The bones disclosed Neanderthal Man, Java Man, Heidelberg Man, but all attempts failed to light upon an appropriate living creature.

Farini was fully alive to the situation: if the Link were to turn up he would be Top of the Bill. In many corners of the world his agents were warned to be on the lookout and to sign up the Link if it appeared.

Claims were put in, but to no avail. Upon expert examination they were found to be either all-man or all-monkey: none was the long-sought half-and-half. Then early in the Eighties the exciting news reached London. The Link was found in Laos. And there was one unexpected feature of the find which caused Farini's heart to miss a beat. The Box-office would be high. For the Missing Link was Female.

A German traveller in Siam, Karl Bock, had observed a peculiar family of creatures in the private collection of the King. The creatures were remarkably hairy, they seemed in fact to grin out of a cloud of hair, and had been captured in the jungles of Laos for his Majesty's amusement. The Siamese called them 'krao', their word for monkey. By some means, not quite clear, Bock got hold of one of them, a young female; one authority states that he acquired her from an explorer who had actually penetrated into the steaming forests of Laos. And Bock, accompanied by the shivering little creature, arrived in London in October 1882 to announce the Discovery.

She was thereupon taken in hand by an Anthropological Authority, one Behrend, a Medical Doctor from Baltimore, who thenceforth became guide, philosopher, friend, and Business Manager to the little specimen. Doctor Behrend, it would appear, had himself penetrated into the impassable jungles of Laos and had seen there with his own eyes some twenty or thirty of the Krao Sub-Species chattering semi-intelligibly in the trees. A nurse, a comfortable woman, was found for the Krao, and all three – the Nurse, the Medical Manager and the Female Link – were added to Farini's payroll.

Dublin at that time had not quite begun to suffer from the paralysis of the intellect which later affected Joyce so much, and in matters of Science and the Modernist outlook it was little, if anything, behind London or Liverpool. Trinity College, the Royal Dublin Society, the *Freeman's Journal* and the *Irish Times* were not entirely averse to philosophical considerations, and polite society was already beginning to derive some benefit from Newman's Lectures on Liberal Education delivered some thirty years before. It was with some interest therefore that the City awaited the arrival of the Missing Link.

The Freak-Merchant, as soon as scientific curiosity was somewhat assuaged, sent Krao and her Entourage on tour. Dan Lowrey acquired the Dublin rights for September, booked The Rotunda Concert Rooms for a fortnight to have more scope for her Exhibition, and from Wednesday the 26th showed her at The Star each night at 9.30 p.m.

Following a flourish of primitive music Krao came on. The expectant crowd sat back, disappointed; apparently the long-lost Missing Link was only a small girl in a short blue frock, with red stockings and shoes and long black hair hanging down over her shoulders. The general feeling was that if this Thing was a Female Monkey then she was not so very different from the thousand-and-one little female monkeys, offspring of the great unwashed, who ran barefoot daily in the lanes of the City. What could be seen of her arms and legs in a sideview as she edged slowly on appeared to be copper in colour, and was presumed to be skin, which caused no very great consternation. Then the Krao turned round and faced the Audience full. Dan Lowrey chewing nervously on his cigar in the wings heard the House gasp. The extraordinary effect of being faced suddenly by the Missing Link is described by a pressman present:

> It is a revelation. Krao has a round, chubby, lanuginous face. Thick protruding lips, paunchy cheeks, and large soft dark eyes whose merits are wholly sacrificed since they have to shine over a nose that is as broad and as flat as any negroid's. The forehead, short and narrow, is densely covered with thick coalblack hair which must be cut once a month to prevent its overhanging the face. The hair also grows down the cheeks past the ears and supplies Krao with a pair of whiskers of a growth which is unusual in a six-year-old female. Ethnologists will perhaps agree that Krao is the mean – the hairy if not the golden mean – between the most degenerate of human Ladies and an advanced Chimpanzee.

Dr Behrend lectured on the History of the Sub-Hominoids and put Krao through her paces. She showed how she could press the thumb of her little pink hand backward as far as her wrist, and how, crossing her arms, she could make her fingers meet easily at the back of her neck. The Human Audience were invited to try it and failed. She then proceeded to empty her 'pouches' or cheeks of some fruit which, it was explained, she always carried there till she felt hungry. But these were small items on the Stage of a big Hall, and Dan with his keen sense of Audience realised that what had gripped the House was the fetching quality of the hairy little Thing's personality as it confronted Dublin across the footlights. The arresting thing about the Girl-monkey was not that, like all humans, she was subhuman, but that, like all Artistes, she enjoyed it.

Anxious to get the widest publicity for the act, and to bring the scientific merits of Music Hall forcibly to the notice of the educated classes, Dan invited a Select Audience of Trinity Professors, Savants of the Royal Society, Members of the Medical Profession, the City Analyst, some Veterinary Surgeons and the Gentlemen of the Press, to a special showing so that they might make a psycho-physiological examination of the Missing Link. Her Medical Manager addressed this Conference upon the habitat and biological background of the Sub-Species Krao, and informed them that this present specimen was constantly eating fruit which agreed with her mightily. The Savants were to take note that of fish also she was very fond and would eat it at any hour of the day.

Sir Charles Cameron, City Analyst, a member of the Committee who examined Krao. Cartoon from the *Irish Figaro*

Behrend then conducted the Girl-monkey through the ranks of the Select Audience that they might make a physiological examination, conducted with decorum. It was ascertained that she had a double row of teeth in the upper jaw, that there was an interesting absence of the upper cartilege of the ear and a lack of certain muscle in the arm which is peculiar to the Genus Homo. Krao's six-year-old eyes twinkled through her cloud of hair as the Savants prodded and hummed, and all agreed that she was an unresisting and pliable object. The body and limbs were then bared for their inspection, and it was ascertained that all was covered with black hair, wonderfully soft, and four centimetres long.

While Nurse was putting on her dress again Behrend outlined the steps being taken to provide the Monkey-child with a Human Education. Nurse had already taught her a few words of the English language, and when she was older she would be sent to school. Then Krao came forward and shaking each gentleman gently by the hand pronounced the words, 'How d'you do, Sir? Good-bye', and all were amazed how prettily she spoke. At the end she bowed them out, saying distinctly, 'Hope ge'men you come again.'

Cameron the City Analyst wrote saying that she was 'an anatomical curiosity worth paying a visit to see'. Dan Lowrey at once appended this letter in full to his Music Hall advertisement in the *Times*.

But indeed no one could resist little Krao and the success of her act was assured. Back in London, this hairy little offshoot of our species was soon earning the stiff figure of £100 a week. She grew more attractive every year. 'I don't remember her myself,' says Norah Lowrey, 'but my Father often talked about the Monkey-girl. They had her educated at a school, and she played beautifully on the piano.'

Time came when she could retire in easy circumstances. Back to the jungle? Not likely. As far as the Descent of Man was concerned Krao was on the up and up. She emigrated to New York, settled into an apartment, retired from the Monkey-business, had her hair done in contemporary style, and eventually contributed her piquant if hairy little genes to the evolution of American Man.

CHAPTER EIGHT

1884 The Star Shines Bright

Dan Lowrey's New Year Message to the People of Dublin:

> Speed the Past. Welcome the Future. Dan Lowrey entering on his fifth year of Management desires to return his sincere thanks to the Nobility, Gentry and the Public generally, who have bestowed on him such splendid patronage, especially during the past two years, being the most successful in the Annals of Music Hall Management in Ireland.
>
> The names of Macdermott, Ashcroft, Arthur Lloyd, Leybourne, Arthur Roberts and others, are proof that he has studied the wishes of his patrons. The success of the Performing Elephants and other Novelties was also gratifying.
>
> Encouraged by the liberal patronage bestowed Mr Lowrey is determined to, if possible, eclipse his best efforts. Engagements have been effected with Artistes of the highest repute, Novelties will be introduced hitherto unheard of on any Music Hall Stage in Ireland, and every attention will be paid to the comfort and convenience of the Audience.
>
> Wishing you all a bright and happy New Year. I am your obedient servant. Dan Lowrey.

Monday 3 March. Staggering Engagement. First Appearance in Ireland of Colonel E. D. Boone's Performing Lions. Assisted by Miss Carlotta.

Wednesday 5 March. Colonel Boone's Lions will parade the City this day from twelve o'clock to one. Mr Lowrey has undergone expensive preparation for the hoisting of these Royal Beasts from Sycamore Street through a large doorway onto the Stage. They will be put through their paces by the Colonel, and by Miss Carlotta, who will enter the Cage.

Monday 10 March. The Lions! House packed at 8 o'clock each night. Hundreds turned away! The enormous success attending this Engagement is unparalleled in the Annals of Public Entertainment.

Wednesday 12 March. The Lions! Select Fashionable Morning Performance for the special convenience of Families living in the Suburbs. At the termination of the Performance the Animals Five in Number will be fed in the presence of the Audience.

Monday 17 March. St Patrick's Day. Last six nights of the Five Performing Lions. At the Wednesday Matinée by kind permission the Boys of Artane Industrial School will attend. There is no need for apprehension, these savage Kings of the Jungle are thoroughly under control of the Trainer.

Friday 21 March. Benefit Night for Colonel Boone and his Wife (Mlle Carlotta). Mr Dan Lowrey Senior presented Mrs Boone with a handsome bracelet, and the Colonel with a medal. Then the great Cages were wheeled off the Stage amid scenes of enthusiasm.

The Star façade in Sycamore Street as it is today. The large entrance was first constructed to admit Boone's Lions

Monday 24 March. Return of Paganini Redivivus who has just concluded a brilliant series of Recitals in London. The *Irish Diamond* reports:

I have had the pleasure of hearing Paganini Redivivus for the first time last week. If he described himself as a trick violinist, or a fiddling acrobat, he wouldn't be far wrong. His great merit consists more in some remarkable feats on the instrument than in any surprising musical display.

Against that, the *Court Journal* had written of the Ghost's Concerts at the Piccadilly Hall:

He is master of everything that can be done on the violin and his range is very great. He can make the instrument sing in the most tender and pathetic accents, which is its great and chief merit. As a composer he has potent claims, and we cannot help an expression of profound surprise at the extra-memory he possesses enabling him to play for two hours of the most exacting character without a note before him. We believe Paganini Redivivus will leave us without making himself known, but not without making himself celebrated.

Harry Randall, celebrated in Drury Lane Panto, featured by Dan in this Year's drive

Now in a neck-or-nothing attempt to obliterate all rivals and to put Music Hall on the Dublin map, Lowrey presented the best available in Male Comics and Serios at his '*Maison du tout Plaisir*':

The Great Vance, Champagne Charlie Leybourne's Rival in the Wine-War. Hear him sing 'Sparkling Moselle'.

Nellie Power, Sailor Elf of the Covent Garden Pantomime *Robinson Crusoe*, and best serio-comic on the Music Hall Stage.

Florrie Leybourne, daughter of the late King George.

Bonnie Kate Harvey of the Perfect Figure.

Vesta Tilley, finest Male Impersonator of them all.

Ashcroft. Mr Lowrey quotes Shakespeare: 'We shall not look upon his like again.' 'A host in himself' – *Freeman's Journal*. 'Glad he has some new songs; we were all getting a bit sick of the Solid Muldoon' – *Diamond*.

Nelly Farrell the Glittering Star of Erin.

J. H. Milburn, the man of Many Faces.

Charles Coburn, taking the palm as the cleverest exponent of Character Comedy in the profession . . .

Vance 'Doing the Academy'

17 VANCE: "DOING THE ACADEMY IS QUITE THE THING YOU KNOW"

5

Monday 6 October. Premier Théâtre des Variétés. Mr Lowrey has pleasure in announcing the Return of the One & Only Chirgwin the White-Eyed Musical Kaffir. Chirgwin was now touching thirty and had had a long haul up out of obscurity. Of Cornish extraction and Cockney rearing, he had toured with the Chirgwin Family as a child; at thirteen he played a solo black act on the beach at Margate; at twenty-two he strummed with his brothers as Negro Minstrels on seafronts. Once during this act a bit of dust got into his right eye; he rubbed it, forgetting the burnt cork, and left a white patch round his eye to the mocking delight of the holiday-makers. He seized on the gimmick – anything at all to distinguish him from the swarm of burnt-cork minstrels who wailed and banjoed for coppers on the summer sands. Making up, he always left a diamond of

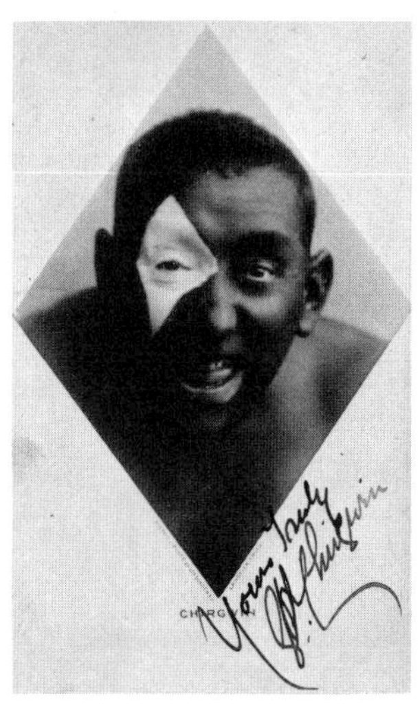

The White-Eyed Kaffir

white skin round his right eye and billed himself as The White-Eyed Kaffir. The Eye had an oddly hypnotic effect in the footlights and, combined with his native grit and weird vocal technique, brought him at last to the front.

At The Star he wrung Dublin hearts in a way no Cockney voice had done before. The Eye looking out of the African Mask had an uncanny sense of character: Scots, Yorkshire, Geordie, Midland, Eastender. Through all his range of song-moods and studies, 'My Fiddle is My Sweetheart', 'Jee-ho-sophat', 'I've Gotta New Girl Now', 'Up Go the Taxes' (to the air of 'Pop Goes the Weasel') he never ceased to be 'Chirgwin', a primitive *persona* that played a whole gamut of emotions upon a packed House. Sizzling with punster patter and word-antics, 'Ladies and Gympnums', topical sidecracks, 'chy-iking' with the Audience, engaging with quickfire backchat with the Boys on the Shelf – the Kaffir's act alone was enough to sell out the House.

In the direction of Drama, Lowrey insisted on his right to enliven the Night with 'Sketches'. These were mainly farcical pieces by two or three persons, lasting up to thirty minutes. But in the fluid pattern of Music Hall practically any act could be dramatised: a team of Rollerskaters produced a 'Skatorial Sketch', *Snowed Up*; and Jennion's Marionettes performed a Pantomime with Christy Minstrels, Acrobats, Jugglers, Skeletons, Fairies and Dancing Girls, all in miniature.

Patentee or no Patentee, nothing in the Theatre was going to be excluded from The Star of Erin. A Chirgwin, a slapstick Pair or a Dude Clown would be followed by an Operatic Sketch, a Harmony Quartette, Charles Clifford on the Harp, Welsh Vocalists, a Hungarian Soprano. And he advertised the selections from quality music that were being offered: airs, overtures and interludes from *La Mascotte*, *The Bronze Horse*, *La Somnambula*, *The Grand Duchess*, *H.M.S. Pinafore*, *Masaniello* . . .

The Kaffir offstage

Monday 10 November. Notice: The encouragement which has attended Mr Lowrey's efforts to bring to Dublin the best Attractions that money can procure has induced him to venture this week upon the Startling and Extraordinary Engagement of the World-famed Opera Bouffe Artiste – MISS EMILY SOLDENE.

Miss Soldene, patronised by H.R.H. the Prince of Wales, was the original Drogan the Pastrycook in *Geneviève de Brabant* (music adapted from Offenbach; first production at The Islington Philharmonic, 1871; at The Gaiety Theatre, Dublin, 1872). She will be accompanied by the distinguished Operatic Vocalist Rose Lee from The Alhambra Palace, London, and will render selections in costume from Offenbach's Charming Opera.

Tuesday 11 November. The Reception afforded Miss Soldene & Miss Lee last evening was one of the most brilliant on record.

Monday 17 November. Miss Emily Soldene, in grand costume selec-

Emily Soldene

tions from the Operas *Madame Argot* and *Chilperic* (in which, riding a Horse, she had played the lead at The Lyceum, London, and at The Gaiety, Dublin). Three nights each. 'Crowds thronged the Hall. A capital entertainment' – *Times*.

The Grafton had been closed since June. Rumour was that it would not open again.

And through it all danced the Chicks: the Orsinos, the Kate Paradise Troupe, the Clari Combination in Divertissements *à la Zingara*, the Rivière French Ballet of Ten, and the Three Sisters Grosvenor – the Daisycutters – ('Such a nice lot of beauties you are so you are! Oh I say!') – the blonde, the redgold and the brunette, kicking up dimities and muslins sprigged with rosebuds, displaying their skyblue paduasoys and bunty velveteens in cherry and plum.

Monday 1 December. Dan's posters in blue and red cried from the hoardings: See the Conquering Hero Comes! Return of the Profession's King, the rage of London's Variety Halls. G. H. MACDERMOTT. Copied by thousands, equalled by none. 9.45 each evening.

A latecomer hadn't an earthly chance of getting in. The Great Jingo Clown, the long beard, golden and curling and split at the chin, the colossal impudence in the torso of a toreador, the voice that had served before the mast and the astringent enunciation that smacked consonants like a nutcracker – in 'Old Familiar Faces', 'The Beautiful Sea', 'Down Went the Captain', 'Up Went the Price of Meat' and 'The Russians Shall Not Have Constantinople' – held the Stage for upwards of forty minutes at a time.

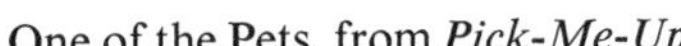

One of the Pets, from *Pick-Me-Up*

All had heard the rumour that the Jingo Broadside had been inspired by Prime Minister Disraeli and his Tory Cabinet, and the tones of the blond Giant bellowing in the gaslight were tinged in the ears of Dublin slumdom with echoes of powerful and distant Westminster. All thought of a social revolution was far from the minds of Dubliners; the little Labour Movement at Beresford Place (Liberty Hall) was a voice in the wilderness. The Dublin man living at subsistence level could, like his London counterpart, listen with delight to the Lion singing –

If ever there was a damned Scamp
I flatter myself I am he,
From Roger to Odger that Artful Old Dodger
They can't hold a candle to me!

'Roger' was the presumed Sir Roger, Claimant to the Tichborne fortune, and fair game perhaps. But 'Odger' was George Odger, a man who had spent his life and his energy in the working-class movement and whose great sin in the eyes of the upper class was that he had had the cheek to stand for Parliament. One night at the London Music Hall George Odger's son hissed the Great Macdermott as he sang this slanderous stanza. He was arrested by the Police and charged at Bow Street with disturbing the public peace, but the Magistrate held him justified and dismissed the case.

No hiss came from the Gallery at Dan's, and the posters cried for a fortnight: See the Great London Pet Tonight!

Macdermott touring as 'King Koko', from the *Entr'acte Annual*

10

Friday 26 December. St Stephen's Day. Grand Production of the entirely new Spectacular Entertainment, founded on Tom Moore's Magnificent Poem entitled *Lalla Rookh.* Written and Produced by Frank Hall. Brilliant Scenery, Music and Costumes.

After Emily Soldene, this was Lowrey's biggest challenge to the Gaiety Big Gunn. It might have been called a Musical Opera Bouffe; charged with the cultural prestige of Moore's long verse-romance, chock-ful of the glamour of the East, Sultans, Sultanas, magic moonlight and veiled maidens, it had gone like a fever through the English-speaking world.

Frank Hall had been Musical Director at The Royal, Westminster, and later Manager of The London Alhambra. He had all the musical and scenic know-how for creating the Lowrey Show. The story gave scope for lavish costume, pert peachiness, spectacular tableaux and limelit chiaroscuro, and found place for Contraltos, Sopranos, Operatic Profundos, Soubrettes, Comics, Dogs, Monkeys, Mimics, Blacked-up Knockabouts, Mystagogues, Jugglers, Acrobats, Actors, Hibernians, Dame, Princess, Turks, and the Orsino Chicks in silk sultanesque trousers suitably slit.

Christmas Eve. Mr George West announced that after spending £400 on alterations and decorations at The Grafton Theatre of Varieties he was unable to come to terms with his Creditors. The Grafton passed from the scene.

Monday 29 December. LALLA ROOKH. Tremendous & Unprecedented Hit!

CHAPTER NINE

1885 The Idols

In the *mélange* of Circus acts and wonders, Enchantments, miniature Drama, Opera airs, Wild Beasts, Midgets and Mystagogues, the Male Comic and the female Serio came more and more to be recognised as the intrinsic Idols of the Music Hall. In a predominantly male Audience, romantically minded, the true Serios were slow to catch on. Ada Lundberg this year made her fourth visit to Dan's. Billed: the most Artistic Low Comedienne before the Public. Each Character a Study. 'She is one of the best Artistes seen at the Hall for some time' – *Evening Telegraph*. But this critic was rather alone in his opinion. Ada was still ploughing the difficult furrow of the low-life female Clown, not yet taking the fancy of Victoria's Dublin to the extent that it was tickled by such sweet singers and fluent figures as Katie Lawrence and Bonnie Kate Harvey.

Nellie Farrell had little of the Lundberg bite. Billed as the Glittering Star of Erin, she was idolised as a singer of patriot songs such as 'Her Lad in the Scotch Brigade' which became the 'Tipperary' of the First Sudan Campaign; or that song with the fetching chorus:

We are still staunch and true to the red, white and blue,
Our loyalty is firm as a rock.
The sorrows of today will tomorrow pass away
For one black sheep will never make a flock.

Daisy Hughes was a Low-cut Lady. 'Her first song was attractive, and its rendering should not have been marred, as it was, by the *décolletée* she exhibited' – *Telegraph*. The split-bodice trick was a favourite one with Grand Opera singers in eliciting applause. Emily Soldene wittily describes the method: Prima Donna bows to the Audience – faint applause. She bows lower – applause warms up. She bows still lower till the gap yawns down the break of the bodice disclosing the 'lily boleros' – thunderous applause from the Music Lovers.

Poor Daisy (her real name was Alice Victoria Villiers) was subject to fits of depression. Desperate for success, she lived in a shadowland of dim faces, terrifying silences and handclaps of applause. One Friday in the August of 1893 she made her last low-cut bow at The Brighton Empire; late that night she threw herself from the balcony of the Grand Hotel and fell eighty feet to her death.

The West Bromwich girl, Bessie Bonehill, made her last appearance at Dan's this year in her trim and tailored act of male impersonation. She had brought the act to the perfection of an art-form and paved the way for the Boy–Girl Idol of the age, Vesta Tilley.

The Idol was born at Worcester in 1864, the daughter of Henry Ball, Comedian and Chairman of a local Tavern Theatre. As a tiny mite, watching from the wings, she was absorbed in the facial antics of her Father. The sensitive little mind became shaped to the male image. At four, dressed as a mannikin, she ventured out on the Stage. There was a Peter Pan quality – a fairy-like ambiguity of sex – in the little waif which had an odd fascination for the Audience. Father, glimpsing the boy–girl possibilities, wrote her some male-character songs, dressed her in little-man

The young Vesta, from *Recollections of Vesta Tilley* by Lady de Frece, 1934

costume and worked the Midland Halls and Free-and-Easies, billing her as Tilley Ball the Pocket Sims Reeves, and later The Great Little Tilley.

At fourteen she made her London début at The Royal, Holborn, in debonair man-studies written mostly by Father – 'The Pet of Rotten Row', 'Strolling Along with Nancy', 'Squeeze her Gently'. She was billed 'Vesta Tilley'. The name suggested the intriguing vestal or virginal quality in the boy–girl voice and figure. In her prime hit, 'The Gaiety Boys' –

I belong to a set of true-hearted boys
Out on the Ran-di-dan –

the he–she quality of the pert little masher excited the mass-imagination; Tilley Ball as 'Vesta' became the centre of a crowd hysteria, an Idol. At eighteen she was picked to play Sinbad the Sailor at Drury Lane under Harris and made the greatest impact ever seen in a London Theatre since the boy playing Rosalind in Shakespeare's *As You Like It* three hundred years before.

She was definitely as Dublin liked it. Strolling with consummate ease on the boards and playing such song-personations as 'The Masher', 'The Street Arab', 'The Prima Donna', 'Poor Jo', she electrified the Town. Critics searched for superlatives to describe the sensation. 'Impeccable artiste'. 'Unique powers'. 'Beautiful sympathetic pathos'. 'Perfection exemplified, down to the last detail of male attire'.

In the greenish light one saw a straight nose, wide mouth in a flattish face under a close-cut crop of curly hair, eyes frank, inquiring, wide apart. Figure slim and boyish, breasts and curves streamlined under hidden whalebone corsetting, the same twi-sex character being communicated in the infectious rhythms of voice and limb.

The Lowreyites were witnessing an art-form from Elizabethan and Restoration times which was only slowly coming to light again. Vesta achieved that nice balance between illusion and reality which induces the trance of Theatre and lets loose the dreaming desires. She was the Pretty Boy to the males in the Audience and the Masculine Girl to the feminine hearts, and thus her act was exquisitely arch and titillating.

Offstage she was quite normal, even innocent, in her sex life. In Dublin she had her first love affair with a young American whom she met in the street. She fell for him 'because I realised he loved his Mother, just as I loved my dear Father'.

Above a score of Male Comics were featured in this year's Programmes. Among them Sam Redfern came nearer than most to the true Music Hall style of wry and comic criticism of daily life. He was more of a patter-merchant than a singer; his topics were up to the minute and his 'stump speeches' were delivered in a droll manner enlived with snatches of song. A favourite ritual of his was 'Any Excuse for a Booze', in which he sang and acted the scenes in the celebrated Cruikshank drawing, 'The Drunkard's Fate'.

Another Sam, Sam Torr, now made his last appearance. Torr was an old Clown of the Theatre, red-nosed and down-at-heel, in battered hat and seedy frock-coat, flopping bow cravat.

The fox and the hare, the badger and the bear,

J. W. Rowley

The birds in the greenwood tree
And the pretty little rabbits so engaging in their habits –
They've all got a mate but me.
Oh Lor'!

J. W. ('Over') Rowley the Lancashire Lad who came to The Star in June of this year was a Comic in a bright and breezy style. He had the finest tenor voice in the whole of Tavern Theatre, and a bewildering repertoire of song-studies – Irish pathetics, English working-man, coster comics and starlit carols of the Dockside in which East End lad meets ladybird. His Irish morsels went down well in Dublin for Rowley had none of that whack-o'-me-blackthorn mania which Irishmen will take only from Irishmen.

His typical vein ran rather to the creation of the humble man without pretension to toff language or the lush life:

Down in a coalmine underneath the ground
Where no ray of sunshine is ever to be found
Digging dusty di'monds all the year round
Down in a coalmine underneath the ground.

In these ditties, as in those of Arthur Lloyd at his most typical, there is a rooted and racy Englishness. The words are in close relation to everyday speech – in contrast to the verbal extravagance of the Operatic Aria. This quality was novel and slow to take, in Dublin especially, where an escapist fantasy and a romantic inflation of speech survives in song and poetry to the present day.

Another hit of his was Fred Albert's little song-drama which used a whole series of topics and characters, each character created in dramatic style and each episode ending, 'It was only the way it was done on the Stage!' Topical events could be introduced ad lib, and Rowley would insert new topics nightly as events occurred. It was a sort of a Singing Newspaper.

To crown his act he would dive into handsprings of great agility, drawing from the Audience the concerted roar, 'Over, Rowley!'

Monday 26 October. Return of the Lion Comique! The Great Macdermott in Songs & Flashes of Merriment! This time his big Flash was his lampoon on Sir Charles Dilke.

Dilke was that rare bird, an English Liberal Republican. He had small love for the Crown, criticised the pensions granted to the Royal Children, took active interest in the Women's Trade Union League and campaigned for the raising of wages and the betterment of living conditions. He had joined the Gladstone Ministry upon the Liberal victory in 1880 and was on his way to becoming the greatest anti-Conservative power in the land. This year, 1885, he was President of the Board of Trade and in the throes of a war to improve housing when the blow fell. A Scots M.P. had occasion to take divorce proceedings against his wife, and he cited Sir Charles as the naughty co-respondent. The scandal was immense, the Diehards jubilant, and Sir Charles ruined for political life.

The Great Macdermott was quick on the ball with 'Charlie Dilke Upset the Milk'.

At Dan's the Dubliners cared nothing for Dilke's liberal policies – if they knew of them at all. To them he was just another of the Upper Crust caught meddling with another man's petticoats. 'The Great Macdermott was rapturously received' – *Telegraph.* Audience adored the ditty, sang and drummed their feet to it:

He let the cat – the naughty cat –
Slip out of the Gladstone bag –

and:

Won't it be a dainty dish
To set before the Queen!

The great square jaw wagging its curls of dandelion beard hammered the chorus down their open throats:

Charlie Dilke upset the milk
Taking it home to Chelsea . . .

and no one hissed the ex-sailorman turned Jingo Bard.

When Jem Mace, ex-Champion Bareknuckle Fighter of the World, stepped onto the Stage of The Star in 1885, it was clear from the long roar of acclamation that here was one of the great Idols of the day.

The Bareknuckle Ring or 'Fancy', was a revival of a Graeco-Roman sport. Christianity had stamped it out and Pugilism had consequently disappeared from every country of Europe except England where it lingered as a country sport, associated with old pagan festivals and patron-saints' days. The ritual was taken up as a fad among the young bloods of the aristocracy in the eighteenth century. Bouts were arranged between professional Bruisers for 50 or 100 guineas a side. It was a blood sport of the most primitive and enthralling kind; the Bruisers toughened their fists by pickling them in vinegar, rules were few, eyes were not seldom gouged from their sockets, each round went on until one or other of the combatants was knocked to the ground and the fight ended only when one of them was unable to 'come up to scratch', that is, a mark scratched across the centre of the earthen Ring.

Laws against Prizefighting were strictly enforced but at the same time it was sought to control the primitive urge by civilising it and the Amateur Boxing Board was founded by the Marquis of Queensberry who left his name to the famous Rules. Yet Prizefighting went on in secret. Matches for large stakes were held before small and select circles in out-of-the-way places, elaborate precautions were taken to dodge the Police, and the public avidly read the details.

The pattern repeated itself in America. State after State passed laws against 'The Fancy', serving only to drive it underground and add to the fascination. Fights were held in the out-back in the presence of the social celebrities of the day; they were ponderous, slogging affairs and the slow-motion murder might go on all day until dark or a downpour put an end to it.

These bloody barefist epics were first-class news and were reported with gusto in the Press on both sides of the Atlantic, so that the names of the most famous Idols of the Ring – Tom Allen, Jem Mace, Jem Smith, Jake Kilrain, John L. Sullivan – were as well known in London, Edinburgh, Cardiff and Dublin as they were in San Francisco. And the pick of the Pugilists, between battles, went on tour with exhibition bouts (legal, since there was no prize-money at stake), bringing the secrets of this latest Cult before the populace.

Mace was then in the sunset of his career. On a Stage decorated with the prize trophies of the United Kingdom, America and Australia, the Champion entered, stripped to the waist and wearing the great Belt of the World. A thousand throats roared inadequately what they felt.

The Hero's skull was entirely bald except for a patch of black hair at the back of the head and a big dark triangle of moustache under the nose; the waist had disappeared under middle-age spread, but there was no mistaking the extraordinary power of the shoulders and the rippling biceps. The House was charmed with his manner, simple and unassuming, and with the homely tones of his Midland voice. He was accompanied by an Expert in Ringcraft who drew out and exhibited the Champion's repertoire of parry, feint, lunge, blow and 'cowboy whiplash', and a Renowned Traveller & Lecturer gave a glowing description of the Hero's career, with graphic word-pictures of his most famous fights.

Jem said he was born in Beeston, a village of Norfolk. 'I began as a boy. You see, the men both on my father's and mother's side were either wrestlers or boxers. Scarcely a Sunday passed without me having a fight.' 'Oh no, sir, I was not intended for the Ring. I was apprenticed to a cabinet-maker, and happened to take up the violin for amusement. It was as a violin player that my appetite for fighting increased. You see, I used to play at a house frequented by soldiers and sailors, a mixed, rough lot, and I often had work with my fists.'

At fifteen he travelled with a boxing booth to fairs and race meetings, fighting local worthies for £10, £5, or often enough for coppers. 'It was sharp work. Match made at night and fight next morning. We always fought for what they'd give us.' He played the violin to eke out his earnings. Music, he found, was a great help in fighting: his style was indeed marked by a marvellous rhythm and precision, his swinging into action and his bewildering knuckle-obligatos appeared to be set to some hidden tune, and his whole approach was so concerted and confusing to the Bruisers of the day that he has been called the Father of the Scientific Approach.

In 1861, he challenged World Champion Sam Hurst. Mace weighing no more than eleven stone five pounds stepped into the Ring to face the bulk of the Champion standing six feet three inches and weighing over seventeen stone. It was the classic affair, brawn and slog on the one side, controlled strength and natural genius on the other. Mace looked as if he was losing badly in the earlier rounds, but as he settled down to the rhythm the spectators gasped at a display of feline fury and agility the like of which had not been seen before in a Prize Ring. In the eighth round Mace neatly slipped aside from a swinging bonecrusher, caught the huge man off his balance and crashed a fist into the great maxilla, taking the man-mountain off his feet, and the Title.

For eleven years he reigned supreme, the Pride of the Fancy, meeting the foremost Pugilists of America and Australia, battling in secluded fields, in stables, on rafts in the river, eluding the Vigilantes and the Police. The fascination of his style, 'like a controlled tornado', his modest

W. H. Lowrey, Leader of the Orchestra

demeanour and his complete dedication to Bareknuckle Fighting as a way of passing one's life made him a favourite everywhere. When the years slowed the tiger in him he retired from the Ring, unbeaten, and on his return to England joined Ginnett's travelling Circus. Coming to Ireland, he formed a Circus of his own, pitching on the fair-greens of country towns where among Clowns, Equestrians and Acrobats he fought all his battles over again and displayed the spoils of three Continents. At Dan's he had brought the Myth of Man the Fighter, sagas of the New York wharves and the sheep-pens of New South Wales, home to the Dublinman.

The old age of the Hero was mellow. To the rare visitor who came upon him, in Brighton, seated half asleep by the fire in his little home, he would smilingly show his old discoloured knuckles. 'Yes sir. They been knocked about a bit.' He died at Newcastle in 1910 and was laid in his last earth at Liverpool. Leaving a memory – the Artiste as Bareknuckleman.

Lowrey's victory over The Grafton had been complete. George West had been forced into the Bankruptcy Court with the result that his creditors had received only a shilling in the pound. The Star's only competitors now were the tiny Harp in Adam Court and the sporadic Mechanics.

The Grafton building in Anne Street abutted upon a property owned by Michael Gunn. Gunn, anxious to expand, had his eye on the empty building. Privately he was thinking that at some time in the future he might have to open a Music Hall of his own as the only way of dealing with The Star. Lowrey saw the danger, moved quickly and bought The Grafton for himself. 'It was a lovely little place,' Norah remembers. 'It had a Balcony, Stalls, and about four Boxes up above the back of the Balcony.' Its Bars and cuisine were among the best in Town. Dan had it overhauled and redecorated and opened it on Easter Monday as The Bijou.

The Bijou did not have regular evening shows except on Saturdays. It was used to take the overflow of customers from The Star at festive times and during the run of a big attraction. The Artistes doubled at the two Houses – as each item finished at Crampton Court cabs were waiting to take the performers trotting across the cobbled streets to The Bijou, and Dubliners stood to catch a glimpse of the Idols as they passed in the night.

The Autumn season of 1885 was barely underway when, in October, William Henry Lowrey was taken ill of a fever and died in a day or two. Coming so soon after the Artois tragedy, and striking into the heart of his family, this death of his son at the age of twenty-six was a shock from which the Guv'nor was slow to recover. It was also a great loss to the Theatre, for the brilliance of the Orchestra under its gifted Conductor had been a prime factor in the success of The Star. Business was abandoned for a week. On Friday the funeral took place and the following Monday The Star reopened with Deputy Leader James Munroe promoted to Conductor of the Band.

CHAPTER TEN

1886 Returned from the Dead

Roger Charles Doughty Tichborne was a dandy young subaltern in the Sixth Dragoon Guards, eldest son of Sir Edward and Lady Tichborne of Tichborne in Hampshire, the Family seat for 800 years. He was born in Paris, French-speaking until the age of sixteen, educated at Stonyhurst, commissioned in the dashing Sixth, in love with his cousin Katherine Doughty, and heir to the ancient Baronetcy and the immense Estate.

In 1853, finding the world too small for him, he sailed to Valparaiso. Thence he took ship, the *Bella*, Jamaica-bound. The ship was never heard of again.

The Family were informed that the *Bella* must be presumed lost with all hands. Lady Tichborne would not credit it. The second son died soon after and there was a wild scramble among the Family for the vast fortune. The Mother prayed that the lost Roger would reappear. She put advertisements in the papers in England and in the Antipodes. One of these was read far off in Wagga Wagga, New South Wales. And on Christmas Day 1866 a figure huge and sunburnt turned up at Tichborne House and said he was Roger the Missing Heir.

Lady Tichborne recognised him at once and received him with rapture. Many of the old servants greeted him with tears of joy, remarked on the family resemblance in his face and reminded him of many incidents of his childhood which he seemed to have forgotten. Not so the Family who regarded him as an impostor. Miss Katherine Doughty looked down her aristocratic nose at this huge bulk of a man who claimed to have been her sweetheart in time gone by. He spoke with a vulgar accent and weighed twenty-five stone.

In May 1871 the Civil Case began in Chancery, lasted 102 days, cost £200,000, and set all England talking. Sir Roger or not Sir Roger? – the argument swept through all classes in the land. The Claimant stated on affidavit that, the *Bella* gone, he found himself adrift in an open boat, was picked up by a passing ship and carried to Australia, his memory lost. There he had taken the name of Tom Castro and worked as cow-hand until one day in Wagga Wagga his attention was drawn to Lady Tichborne's appeal and it all came back.

Cross-examined for sixteen days, he became entangled in a mesh of blundering ineptitudes. He could certainly recall incidents of his childhood, but his attempts to speak French, or even upper-class English, were pathetic. Asked to pronounce 'fellow', he said 'feller'. Asked the French for 'Mister', he said 'Mongsewer'. Asked whether the Jesuits had taught him poetry at Stonyhurst, he said 'Humpty Dumpty sat on a wall . . .'. It was Music Hall *in excelsis.*

A young woman was produced who claimed to have been his sweetheart and swore he was Arthur Orton, a butcher of Wapping. The Jury stopped the case, the Claimant was committed for trial in the Criminal Court for perjury, and the fun began in earnest. A Fund was opened for the Defence; loans were obtained by the sale of Tichborne Bonds, puppets of all the principal figures in the Drama and sticks of Tichborne candy were sold in the streets.

The Criminal Trial at Westminster Hall lasted 188 days, one of the longest and most sensational trials in English history. The Claimant, not allowed to speak in his own defence, sat fuming at a table which had to have a curve cut out of it to accommodate his large stomach. Outside the

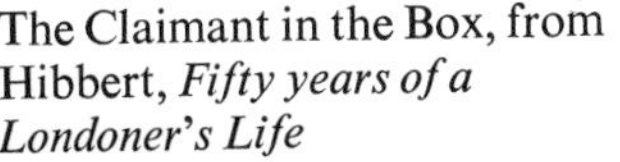

The Claimant in the Box, from Hibbert, *Fifty years of a Londoner's Life*

crowds were jam-packed in the streets to watch the shoals of witnesses coming from Wapping, from South America, from New South Wales. The Judge took a month in summing up and condemned the Claimant to fourteen years penal servitude.

Sir Roger, or Tom Castro, or Arthur Orton, whichever, went to Millbank Prison, then to Dartmoor. He served ten years. Released on ticket of leave, he was booked at once for the Music Halls.

11 January 1886. 'In order to give the Public an opportunity of beholding the most Remarkable Man on Earth, Mr Lowrey has engaged Sir Roger Tichborne, the Claimant, who will nightly give a startling history of his Past Life, Trial, Conviction & Imprisonment.'

The Claimant, appearing in elephantine evening dress, had lost nothing of his girth in Dartmoor. He was tall, rotund, of dark complexion, and as solemn as an undertaker. He was greeted with cries from the Gallery: 'Cheers for Sir Roger!' Roars and groans rocked the House. As soon as quiet was obtained he began his Address, referring to the generous manner in which his appeal to the Irish people had been met. Voice: 'Yer a fine man, Sir Roger!' He bowed as gracefully as his *embonpoint* would permit, continued: 'I am now asking you to come to my aid in obtaining a Royal Commission of Inquiry.' Voice: 'Wagga Wagga!'

When the laughter had subsided he calmly continued the sentence, 'a Commission to investigate –' Voice: 'Life is too short for that!' Cries: 'Put that man out!' Scuffle. Voice: 'Go on, Jumbo!' The Jury, he was heard to say, had been handpicked. Voice: 'How d'yeh know?' That information, he said, had been obtained by a miracle. Uproar.

The Claimant cartooned as a Police Chief in *Punch*

The Tichborne Claimant

When order had been more or less restored the Claimant was telling how the detectives, Clarke and Meiklejohn, had been instructed to find jurymen who were prejudiced against him. Here a boisterous youth guffawed. Claimant looked up, pained, contracted bushy eyebrows, put hands in pockets and observed, 'If you wish, sir, to come up here and address the Audience I am willing to give way.' Cheers.

'I am not asking you to aid me out of your hard earnings.' Voice: 'Ah sure you'll always be welcome!' 'All I want is that the Law may be meted out to me as it is to any of you here present.' Voice: 'Bedad, you'd better ask more than that, avick!' Prolonged applause. 'And when I have obtained a Royal Commission of Inquiry I shall stand before you in a different light.' Voice: 'May yer shadda never grow less!' This remark delighted the House, and even the Claimant smiled, continuing, 'To return to my subject –'

A bell rang in the wings. Time up. He thanked them for their kind attention and hoped to see them back next evening when he would 'resume the thread of his discourse'.

This extempore comedy went on for a week. Never before had there been such Audience-participation in a show. Everyone had a chance to raise his voice and shoot his wit.

Thereafter the Claimant went his way telling his puzzling Tale in the Circuses and Nightlife Halls of many lands. He died on April Fools' Day 1898, penniless; a Paddington undertaker buried him without charge. The Family allowed the inscription: 'Sir Roger Charles Doughty Tichborne' on the coffin, but would allow no monument upon the grave. Of all the Mystagogues who appeared at Dan's he was the most mysterious.

Johnny Patterson, the Hibernian Clown from Clare, was also popular this year. He spent his life travelling on the wagons, and now and then having a Circus season in the Halls and Rinks of Cities at home and abroad, often in company with his fellow-Clown, Johnny Quinn. He composed some of the best songs of the Century – 'The Stone Outside Dan Murphy's Door', 'Goodbye Johnny Dear' and the evergreen –

Now her parents they consented
and we're blessed with children three,
Two girls just like their mother
and a boy the image of me.
We'll train them up in decency
the way they ought to go –
But I'll never forget the garden
where the praties grow!

All his songs have a touch, at once humorous and wistful, and the words give a glimpse of common life in the real Ireland which seldom gets into song or story. One day when the Big Top was pitched at Castle-pollard, an enchanting lake region in the Midlands, he went into the local inn for a drink and met Miss Bridget Donohue. The Clown's eyes twinkled, the lady's twinkled back, and his little song of the romance circled the world:

Then Bridget Donohue
I'll tell you what I'll do,
Just take the name of Patterson
And I'll take Donohue.

Well, he took her, and she travelled with him on the wagons till the end.

American Circus-lovers were charmed with Johnny Patterson's songs and antics when he toured with Ringling Brothers. Back in Ireland, he had a season with Ginnett's at the Earlsfort Terrace Skating Rink and then came for a week to Dan's, billed as Clown & Bagpiper. The critics would seem to have overlooked him.

He went his way with comic lines of worry painted on his face, Clown's trousers flapping round his heels, falling into the laps of maiden ladies at the Ringside and delighting the children of whom he was one. He never bothered to take out copyright or publish his work, and his songs were appropriated left and right by Big Names in the business. During the Parnellite Split and the storm of partisan passion it roused, he composed a song calling for unity among Irishmen. On the night of 19 May 1890 he sang it under the Big Top pitched at Castleisland in Kerry. There was an uproar, benches broken, heads split. The old Clown died in hospital during the night from injuries received. His bundle of manuscripts passed to his son, and we have Johnny Quinn's word for it that these little masterpieces, claimed by many, were indeed the work of his old friend of the Sawdust Ring.

Unlike Sir Roger, Viscount Walter Munroe, who appeared at The Star in May 1886, made no claim to Aristocracy. This was a stage-name, adopted no doubt in the style of Lord George Sanger. He was an Irish Character Comic & Stepdancer, and had been an old Grafton favourite in such ballads as 'The Agricultural Irish Girl':

She's a Fine – Big – Woman
and she knows that same
And early in the morning
she'll possess my name.
But I feel so dreadful nervous
I don't know what I'll do
When I think that I must tackle
Oh – Twelve Stone Two!

The Viscount struck different people in different ways. English Chance Newton (who knew him well): 'Breezy, genial, generous, his comic singing was a sheer joy.' Irish *Pat* (at The Grafton): 'Of all the caricatures of Irishmen that crowd the Music Hall Stage, Viscount Munroe is about the worst.' No doubt his style was a shade too full of tin-pan-alley sound and factitious fury for ears trained on Ashcroft and the controlled uproar of Pat Kinsella. Still, his 'O'Hara' had some of the frenzy of the true Absurd:

First we wiped the floor with him,
Dragged him up and down the stairs,
Then we lugged him round the room

Under tables, over chairs.
Then we jumped upon his face
Before he'd time to say his prayers –
Rags and bones were all we left
Of the Man who Struck O'Hara.

Earlier this year The Star had featured another of Farini's Freak Attractions. He had acquired a whole Village of Primordial Man. His first experiments had been with Zulus but, finding that these objected to 'being sold from one white man to another like cows', he acquired African Pygmy replacements and constructed his 'Village of Earthmen', designed to display Man in his primitive condition. These Little People comprised males and females, shown in their huts of leaves and twigs, hunting with their poison darts, making their mud pots, eating their meals of elephant steak and tapioca pudding and dancing their savage rites of war and wedding round a fire of coloured paper and blazing lime. Having perfected the experiment at the Westminster Aquarium, he sent the Sub-Culture on tour.

Dan Lowrey, being to Dublin what Farini was to London, and giving the City a window on the world, had William Summerfield and Jack White to design the lights and sets. The Earthmen were introduced. N'Kon N'Koi, a kind of Captain or Chief, a Giant in his own country, forty-two years, height four feet nine inches. The Chief's Favourite Dancer. Wife of the Chief's Favourite Dancer. N'Ko, a fine shot and a good Hunter not afraid to tackle a Lion singlehanded, nineteen years, four feet three inches. A very affectionate little Earthgirl, N'Toi, twelve years, whose parents had deserted her in the Desert. Nightly shows were not enough, the Village was set up every day, on view from 2 to 4 p.m., admission 6*d.* Dons from the dim recesses of Trinity and dwellers in the decay of their tomb-like Georgian rooms came to gaze at the denizens of the Dark.

N'Kon N'Koi and his hutful went on to spend Christmas at the Crystal Palace. Farini, advanced in age and anthropoid wisdom, retired with a nice fortune, devoted himself to his garden and became an authority upon the cultivation of the Begonia.

A pair of coloured banjoists, from a song-front of the Ethiopian Serenaders

That Autumn, the coloured posters in the City Streets announced the Bohee Bros. Joyce pictures them in the Nightown episode of *Ulysses*:

> Coloured coons in white duck suits, upstarched sambo chokers, and large scarlet asters in their buttonholes, leap out. Each has his banjo slung. Their paler smaller negroid hands jingle the twing-twang wires. Flashing white eyes and tusks they rattle through a breakdown in clumsy clogs, twinging, singing, back to back, toe, heel, heel, toe, with smackful clacking nigger lips.

Darkest of all Dan's dark Idols, George & James Bohee were born in the Fifties at St John's, New Brunswick. George went strumming on the New York Stage as a child, but while there was a vogue for blacked-up acts there was not much scope for a pure-bred coloured boy. Later, however, he teamed up with his brother and toured on this side of the Atlantic with Haverley's Minstrels.

The pair took London in a big way. Their season in the Halls was dazzling; they were wined and dined by Society hostesses, patronised by Earls and seduced by Countesses; and they were engaged to teach the Royal Infants – including the prodigal Prince of Wales – to tickle the banjo-strings *à l'américaine*. Dressed in smart white linen suits, lithe muscles rippling under the material, their voices blending with each other and with the banjo's bickering 'A Man's Best Friend is his Mother' they directed The Gardenia, an elegant night haunt in Leicester Square. It was an exotic bloom, a new religion, and the handsome fellows grew so accustomed to high life that they eventually lost all they had.

Their Society fame and Royal refinement had preceded them to Dublin and a full house at The Star heard the rich timbre of their voices harmonised in tune with the plangent strings – 'a-ha-bout a-ha mi-hile fro-hom tahn' –

In an ivy-cover'd lil cot
about a mile from town
Dwells a maiden that I dearly love
and I'll meet her when the sun goes down.

Dance. Heel-and-toe shuffle in offbeat two-pulse, then the Bohees banjo to banjo go string-plucketting into the Nightown refrain:

And it's O-o-oh
How I lo-o-ove
Pretty lil Mai-ai-rihy

The Two Macs, from *Pat*

She's the keeper of a dai-ai-rihy
O-o-o-oh!
How I lo-o-ove
And I'll meet her when the sun goes dah-ah-ahn.

According to a son of Jack White, the Stage Carpenter, the harmony of these men was so moving that they actually cried and the Audience wept with them. And all over Dublin boys were playing imaginary banjos with their fingernails and shuffling in the offbeat two-pulse.

Winter came with mists, foghorns moaning in the Rivermouth, and laughter rocking Crampton Court. 'Are you coming out in a minute?' 'No, I'm coming out in a rash.' Biff. Whack on the head. Thinfellow slumps. Fatfellow throws a somersault. Thinfellow trips him up. Thud! Fatfellow ends up looking pained standing perfectly still upon his head. Here are The Two Macs, progenitors of all the pairs of Comic Colleagues down to Laurel & Hardy times.

Back in the dimlit Sixties John McNally was a curlyhaired Dublin boy, clever if not too well fed, with a gift of verse-making in his own brand of English and a desire to get out of the ghetto of back-street life. He managed to get a spot on the Bill of the Rotunda Skating Rink singing his comic poems of the scenes he knew: 'Dublin Monuments', 'Bills that are Posted on the Wall'. Round the same time an English Comedian, Mike MacCabe, was appearing at The Widow Connell's. At MacCabe's Benefit the young Dublin jackeen McNally was invited to do his own particular act. MacCabe's experienced eye noted the inspired streak of Dublin absurdity in it and they paired up as Hilton & Curly, Blackface Comics, filling bills at The Widow's and The Grafton.

A fresh wind blew in the business with the arrival from America of Ferguson & Mack. These Artistes were pioneers. Having cast off the traditional corduroys and cutaway coats, they had created a new type of comic Irishman, burlesques with bald heads and shaggy whiskers. Hilton & Curly took the hint, unblacked their faces and designed a new masque for themselves: a Pair of Opposites, the one padded out stout and hefty, the other thin, the one stupid, the other quick, both lunatic, both skulls bald on top and padded to take resounding wallops, limbs galvanic, wit and action high-speed and unexpected, living in a world of quickfire cross-talk and lithe leg-action. This was the Huroo class of Comics with a difference.

They toured America gagging and wheezing, biffing each other on false foreheads with thuds that echoed through the House, breaking into delicate footwork, gazing at each other in sad wisdom and knocking each other down. In the cosmopolitan atmosphere their act went like wildfire.

They were billed as MacCabe & McNally until their London agent gave them a neat title. The Two Macs.

Back in Dublin where the imagination was more alive to the Irish Handy Andy than to the Human Absurd, the full flavour of their comic creation was for a long time missed. The Macs were more than Irish Whack-o'-me-blackthorns. They burlesqued the very fact of life itself. In

THE WILD MAN OF BORNEO
HAS JUST COME TO TOWN
THE WILD MAN OF BORNEO.
THE WIFE OF THE WILD MAN OF BORNEO.
THE CHILD OF THE WIFE OF THE WIFE OF THE W. M of B.
THE DOG OF THE NURSE OF THE ETC. ETC.
THE TAIL OF THE DOG OF THE NURSE OF THE ETC; ETC; ETC.
THE HAIR OF THE TAIL OF THE TAIL OF THE DOG OF THE ETC, ETC, ETC, ETC,
THE FLEA IN THE HAIR OF THE TAIL OF THE DOG OF THE ETC, ETC, ETC, ETC. ETC.
THE WHISKERS ON THE FLEA IN THE HAIR OF THE ETC. ETC. ETC. ETC. ETC.
THE WIND THAT BLEW THROUGH THE WHISKERS OF THE FLEA IN THE HAIR OF THE TAIL OF THE DOG OF THE ETC. ETC. ETC. ETC. ETC. ETC. ETC. ETC.
KEATING'S
H.G. BANKS LITH
THE GREATEST SUCCESS OF THE SILLY SEASON
SUNG BY
THE TWO MACS

particular, they latched onto the scientific obsession of the Victorians and reduced them to the ridiculous:

The Wild Man of Borneo
has just come to Town!
(*Zulu Shuffle. Biff. Falls. Up.*)
The Wife of the Wild Man of Borneo
has just come to Town!
(*Bellywobble dance with palm-leaf. Whack. Down. Up.*)
The Child of the Wife of the Wild Man of Borneo . . .

and so on down the larrupping litany.

Just before Christmas 1886 Dan was interviewed by a journalist from *Sport*:

– Do you find it difficult, Mr Lowrey, to keep up a constant change?
– You bet. Considering that I have to engage some Artistes as long as fifteen months in advance, and even then I am sometimes short.
– Now, really, Mr Lowrey, do these Artistes receive such large salaries as they are reported to? Salaries such as £30 and £40 per week appear extravagant for twenty minutes work per night.
– So it may appear. But I can assure you I have often paid as much as £50 per week to an individual star. A very low salary with me is £9 a week.
– What performers take best in Dublin?
– Ticklish question. Haphazard, I think that Ashcroft, Vesta Tilley and The Two Macs have been my best draws.
– How many people and how much money does the Hall hold?
– Roughly, 1,100 people, or about £50, represent a good House. People are always going in or out. Last Saturday was an overpowering night. It took me all my time, with the assistance of my men, to turn the people away. By the by . . . I think you could not get in yourself!
– Finally, what are you going to do for Christmas?
– These special Christmas Shows are too troublesome, although those already produced, especially *Lalla Rookh*, have been highly successful. Artistes, to undertake the study and preparation of these pieces, will not be satisfied with less than a month's engagement, and before this time is up my Metropolitan patrons are tired and long for something new.

In fact it was becoming clear to Dan that the typical Music Hall Bill, well planned and well balanced, with constant variety and with the Orchestra to thread all the items together, had a dramatic unity of its own, suited to the temper of the new times and the new Audience.

LEFT The Two Macs in 'The Wild Man of Borneo'

CHAPTER ELEVEN

1887 Here We Are Again

John L. Sullivan, Champion Knuckleman of the World, was a god to Irishmen everywhere. He had been floored but once. Handsome Charlie Mitchell, pure-bred English, had earned world headlines when at Madison Square Garden in 1883 he knocked down John L. in the first round. Rising from the ground Sullivan went berserk and the Police had to intervene to save the Englishman from being murdered.

Early this year Dan booked Mitchell to fight an exhibition with Jem Smith, Heavyweight Champion of England, who was seeking a match with the great John L.

Every move of the approaching Pair was publicised as if they were visiting Royalty. They travelled on the mail boat with their Touring Manager Mr John Fleming, landed at Kingstown and took the train to Westland Row where a clamorous crowd was gathered. The Welcoming Committee included representatives of The Star Theatre, officials of the Amateur Boxing Clubs of Dublin and County, journalists, the Editor of *Sport*. That night it seemed all Dublin was afoot to see the man who was about to face John L. and the man who had knocked him down. Small boys jostled among the legs of the crowd to catch a glimpse of the 'puckers'. *Sport* relates:

> The applause was so thunderous that Mr Fleming found it utterly impossible to introduce the pair. But identification was unnecessary – there was no mistaking the rollicking good-humoured Hibernian guile of Smith in contradistinction to the subdued steadfastness of Mitchell.

The inimitable Arthur Lloyd

Smith's physique and rock-like slugging earned mass admiration; a gasp came from the House as each thud went home. The Englishman, taller, a dark Adonis, showed the jauntier and more elusive style and drew scathing remarks from 'the fourpenny sages upstairs'. On their final night the Editor of *Sport* went on the Stage and presented Jem and Charlie with gold lockets set in rubies and diamonds, subscribed for by their admirers, and everyone was happy.

Except Michael Gunn. His gilt-edged Gaiety was not designed for such gladiatorial displays. But being a practical man he knew he must cater for the needs of the times. On the site of the Old Theatre Royal in Hawkins Street he had built The Leinster Hall, and had opened it the previous November as a venue for Concerts, Oratorios and visiting Circuses. This year, going one better than Lowrey, he engaged the Great John L. Sullivan himself.

Cordons of Police had to be called out to control the crowds. The City, enthralled, heard the Brooklyn–Irish brogue, gazed on the flaming moustache, the bulging thighs and thews of the Hero and the Ladies were invited to 'shake de hand dat shuk de wurrulld'. As a finale to his fisticuffs he thanked Dublin for the tremendous welcome he had received and in his deep, soft, tragical tone tendered his sympathy, and the sympathy of the Irish in America, with the Cause of Ireland's struggle for Home Rule. The Hall cheered and wept.

Michael Gunn shook the huge hand at parting. He had won that round.

A Christy Minstrel, from *Pick-Me-Up*

2

Once again the peculiar velvety voice of Arthur Lloyd was heard at Dan's and The Star clientele felt the warm outflowing personality which was the gift of the Lion Comique. He was fond of Dublin and Dublin was fond of him; his song sheets were in all the music shops and sold by the hundred: 'Not for Joseph!', 'The German Band', 'The Organ-Man', 'It's Wonderful how we Do it but we Do', 'Aurelia was always Fond of Soldiers', 'The Brewer's Daughter', 'Promenade Elastique', 'Song of the Dutch Clock-Man', 'Immensikoff' (a Cockney study), etc. etc. He was the first song-writer fully to realise the money value of his work.

He had created a whole hymnal of nonsense rhymes, like:

Pollywollyamo nogo soki
Pollywo-a-lumpo shoes two tees
Slopey in the eye ah flatnose beauty
Pollywollywollyo jolly Japanese!

which were chirrupped all over Town, especially at alcoholic outings when tongues became tangled in the syllables. Ever since 'Not for Joseph!' the common touch was a distinctive mark of his song-making, and he had a knack of precise detail –

Just by the Angel at Islington
Close by the clock that is always wrong –

which reminds one of the precision of T. S. Eliot in *The Waste Land*, bringing poetry down to the street:

To where Saint Mary Woolnoth kept the hours
With one dead sound on the final stroke of nine.

In Lloyd's work there was always what F. R. Leavis has called 'an irresistible rightness' in word and phrase, and it was set to an infectious beat, as in his 'Yokel Yodel':

I fancy I can see her now
Down at Farmer Flynn's
Picking up the newlaid eggs from the cow
And milking the cocks and hens.

'Pure' music at Dan's hardly existed. It had to be linked to the visible, the breath-taking, the comic, the ravishing, the pathetic, the cleverality. Such music was provided by American Christy Minstrels. A large Troupe of Twenty-five arrived in the Spring with a non-stop fund of song, dance and instrumentation. Quick pop-up gags, crass crosstalk, elastic legantics punctuated the incessant twanka-panka-panks of the banjo which the Bohees had made all the rage.

In a somewhat different vein were the Jung Frau Kapelle, four ladies and eight gentlemen from the Swiss Mountains, directed by the Family Seebold, presenting forty different instruments with Chorus and Yodel. In colourful Swiss costume they filled The Star with the soulful strains of liberty, the cowbells and the mating calls, in a dreamwhite Wonderland among the snowdeep Alps.

But the daddy of them all when it came to putting classical music into Tavern Theatre was Paganini Redivivus.

It was dawning on Dublin that those who said the Ghost was the grandson of the Giant O'Shaughnessy, and those who said he was a son of R. M. Levey, might both be right. The solution of the puzzle seems to be that R. M. Levey's real name was O'Shaughnessy. He was himself a son of the bagpipe-playing Giant, but had changed his name to Levey on the grounds that it was more musical. He was twice married and had many children. One of his sons, Richard Michael, tall and eccentric as his grandfather, went playing the violin through Europe, was picked to play the part of Paganini's Ghost in a London Show in which he was got up to represent the Maestro, became possessed of the part and lived it all his life. He introduced the Galleries to some of the purest violin music of the day.

'Serio' remained a vague term for a female singer who was not quite a female soprano nor a stage sex-kitten nor a comedienne, but who had a touch of all three in her make-up. 1887 brought, among others, Alice Leamar, one of the most sophisticated Girls in the Gaslight and a devastating danseuse. She and her sister Kate had tripped it right to the top in the new vogue for 'Sisters'. Most of these 'Sisters' were real sisters, and the relationship gave an enticing air of innocence to the performance.

When the staff of the *Sunday Times* set up a raffish little restaurant, Café Vaudeville, the Leamar Sisters helped to manage and to perk it up, and the place became known from one of their toney titbits as 'Paradise in the Strand'. They were both fashionably buxom beauties who assumed a demimondial air, attenuating their vowels to the exclusive Night Club tone in their ditties:

Two Girls of Good Society
We dance, we sing,
We're models of propriety –
Too wise to wear the Ring.

Alice Leamar, from *Pick-Me-Up*

As for the 'good Society', Alice and Kate were daughters of Cokey Lewis, nicknamed from the trade he followed in the New Cut. Cokey became a devoted attendant upon his prosperous girls.

The whiff of Café Vaudeville was relished at Dan's. Youths whose parents had not yet quite mastered English were muting their vowels to mouth the Leamar refrain:

Romano's! Italiano's!
It's Paradise in the Strand.
At Romano's – as Papa knows –
The wine and the women are grand!

December. 'Slap-Bang!' 'Here we are again!' Enter the Great Vance, Pondrous as a pachyderm. Clobbered in startling colours, puce, lemon and bottle-green. Cream curlybrim topper, eyeglass, goldknob cane, diamond studs as big as little saucers. He leaps from the wings on large canarybright spawgs, and the floors of Dan Lowrey's echo with the thunder of a thousand boots:

Slap-Bang! Here we are again!
Here we are again! Here we are again!
Slap-Bang! Here we are again!
Such Jolly Dogs are we!

Orchestra, *sforzando*, heard for a moment above the din. Then:

To balls or hops of course they go
And each man does his weed,
They stick by one another
As they've previously agreed,
And they always seem so jolly, Oh!
So jolly, Oh! so jolly, Oh! –
Slap-Bang! Here we are again!
Here we are again! Here we are again!
Slap-Bang! Here we are again . . .

No need for him to sing, they sing it for him.

This hulking Dandy who set everybody wild and music-lovers mad was nearing fifty. Born Alfred Peck Stevens, he had tried life as a lawyer's clerk in Lincoln's Inn Fields, wandered off in his teens with a band of strolling Players, and by dint of hard work and a readiness to tackle anything on the planks made the grade in a distinguished Liverpool greasepaint Company, which included Robson and Barry Sullivan. This acting experience, in all kinds of parts and conditions, shaped his style when he took to the Tavern Halls.

About 1860 he made his first break from Regular Rep and toured with a one-man Show of his own devising, 'Touches of the Times'. In this he danced and sang his way from one end of England to the other making odd forays to tread the plank-and-barrel scene in obscure communities across the borders of Scotland and Wales, quick-changing through twenty separate parts per performance. This method evolved into the typical Vance brand of One-Man Comedy.

For four years he dragged his trunks, paraphernalia and the largest feet ever seen in the business, through the wilderness of the Theatre, until J. J. Poole (inventor of the 'Lions Comiques') brought him to London and gave him a chance to display the full spectrum of his talent at The White Lion, Edgware Road. His act included Toff types – 'The Galloping Snob of Rotten Row' – and low-life drolls – 'Peter Potts the Peeler' (expert in courting cookies).

In 1886 he was engaged by The Oxford, where they wanted a Heavy Swell to offset the impact made by Leybourne at The Royal, Holborn. Then began the long rivalry, Dude versus Dude, Vance versus Leybourne – which was to be the toffier of the two? Nightly they outbid each other in the Wine War. Leybourne made the Town drunk on 'Champagne Charlie', Vance replied with 'Cliquot, Cliquot, that's the Wine for Me', and they sang their way down the vintage list, 'Moet et Chandon', 'Cool Burgundy Ben', 'Sparkling Moselle', until in the end the heavier Vance came down to earth with 'Beer – it's the same for a Clerk as a Peer'.

Light swell against heavy swell, they never ceased to vie. Against

Vance's trained actor's technique, his meticulous care in costume and make-up, his voice raw as a gapped razor to cut the most beer-happy Gallery down to size, Leybourne had nothing to offer but the expansive warmth of his personality, his light tenor, his natural flair. Serious musicians and Concert Hall singers thought both men mad and the Public even more lunatic to listen to them, yet their vogue spread through the United Kingdom and fixed the Lion Comique as the main dynamic of Music Hall.

Vance had arrived in Dublin in 1874, and appeared at The Round Room of The Rotunda with his own Company, 'Vance's Varieties'. Patronised by H.R.H. the Prince of Wales, and the Aristocracy & Clergy of Great Britain & Ireland, the large-footed Lion regaled the City with 'Beautiful Girls', 'Eaton Square', 'Arthur Fitzflat', 'Pal o' Mine' and the biggest hit of all, 'The Shah of Persia', a noted Dandy among the international set.

He then took his Troupe on tour through the south of Ireland – Munster Hall, Cork (a week); Theatre Royal, Limerick (three nights); Town Hall, Waterford (three nights); Athenaeum, Kilkenny (two nights). And the Munster mots and the mashers thumped and cried:

Shlap-Bang! Here we are agin!
Here we are agin! Here we are agin!

His mission to Ireland accomplished, he returned to London to carry on the study of the Stilton Set. But in this kind of act Vance was no spellbinder. His ungainly size and low-comedy mug made it impossible for him to compete with Leybourne, but he was saved by his versatility. He took up Cockney types – 'Costermonger Joe', 'Going to the Derby' and 'The Chickaleary Cove', the ditty of a flash crook of the New Cut:

I'm a Chickaleary bloke, with my one-two-three
Vitechapel was the village I was born in;
To catch me on the hop,
Or on my tibby drop,
You must wake-up very early in the mornin'
I've got a rorty gal, also a knowing pal,
And merrily together we jog on.
And it doesn't care a flatch,
So long as I've a tach
Some pannum in my chest – and a tog on!

For some roles his writers supplied him with a rich mixture of Slanguage – backslang and rhyming slang, flash phrases and the dialect of the race-course, the oyster-restaurant, the fruit-market – a forerunner of the argot ditties of Albert Chevalier.

On his large feet he lollopped along, even more loved, loathed, pictured and caricatured than the Great Comedians of the Century – Disraeli, Parnell, John L. Sullivan and Sir Roger Tichborne.

The death of Leybourne left the Dandy field to Vance. But the Slap-Bang singer, tireless worker though he was, was ageing. Still, his song-sheets, carrying coloured prints of the Lion Comique in character togs, continued to spill by the score onto the counters of all the music-shops of Dublin, Cork, Limerick, Galway, Belfast, and lay piled on the pianos of every lady's drawing-room – 'The Roaring Boys', 'Anastasia', 'Howling

RIGHT Vance 'Walking in the Zoo'

GUNN

Vance as 'Miss Wobbinson'

Swell', 'Poor Married Man', 'Jolly Dogs', 'She Lodges at a Sugar Shop', 'You Walk to Covent Garden in the Morning', 'Doin' the Academy is Quite the Thing y'know', and the ineluctable 'Miss Wobbinson'.

The Great Dude's last appearance in Dan's was in December 1887. The following year, on St Stephen's Night, while he was appearing wigged as a barrister at The Sun in Knightsbridge singing in solemn tones 'Are You Guilty?', he fell unconscious on the Stage; a troupe of dancers tripped on, hiding the great recumbent body – on with the Show – discreet dropscene – worn-out body carried off. He was forty-nine. There was a tremendous Burial Service, streams of carriages, thousands on foot, Wire-walkers, Tumblers, Clowns in funereal garb, Chicks, Serios, Character Comics, miscellaneous Knockabouts . . . pit, stalls and galleries. His last mass-Audience role.

Tuesday 10 November. Death strikes again. Annie Lowrey, aged forty-nine, the beloved wife of Daniel Lowrey Junior, died this night in The Bijou (late Grafton) Theatre.

Four sudden deaths since his take-over – Artois, Old Dan's Charlotte, William Henry, and now Annie, daughter of the portrait-painter, who had been his wife and comrade at The Malakoff and at Crampton Court.

The Funeral went to the Roman Catholic Cemetery at Glasnevin on Saturday. On Monday The Star reopened with 'Professor Dewynne the Man with the Mysterious Fingers, See his Remarkable Shadowgraphs'.

CHAPTER TWELVE

1888 In the Drame of Dan's

Joyce coined the word 'Drame' to express the connection between the Dream and the Drama. On the dreaming screen of the mind all kinds of grotesque and ideal and primitive images are thrown up from the dark depths of the Human Memory – The Girl, the Girl–Boy, the Adonis, the Skeleton, the Wonderman, the Bird, the Beauty, the Old Wise Wizard, the Wolf, the Pair of Opposites, the Witch, the Eternal Clown. . . . In the dream of Theatre, in the trance of the lights, the colour, the dance, the music, these images out of Man's dark experience, the archetypes, in an endless variety of shape and shadow, appear before the footlights within the proscenium frame and vitalise the latent energies in the mass audience, hypnotised, revealing Man to himself.

With Mlle Senide in January 1888, the fairytale of Beauty & the Beast entered the Drame. She was Viennese, very pretty, leading a troupe of Lions, Tigers, Panthers and Bears. Dublin flocked to watch the lovely Viennese tease and pummel her Beasts, make them fawn, crouch, beg, put her head in the Lion's mouth, make the Bear fire a revolver, play tig with sleek and snarling Panthers, interrupted time and time again by breathless cries from the House: Enough! Enough!

She had been in love with animals from her girlhood:

> At the age of sixteen I prevailed upon my mother to purchase for me two young panthers and four young hyenas which I had seen in a show at Hamburg, and to my delight I was allowed to bring them home to Vienna where I kept them for four months. But as they grew up the expense of their keeping increased and my parents insisted on getting rid of them. I had to yield, but I decided that on the very first opportunity I should renew acquaintance with my pets. Having heard they were sent to Berlin, I followed them there and soon became their owner for a second time, adding to my collection a lion, a bear and eight wolves, with which I started on tour through Germany, much to the sorrow of my parents.

On her Benefit Night, admirers presented her with a gold medal. She had held back mealtime for the Animals and fed them on Stage, drawing

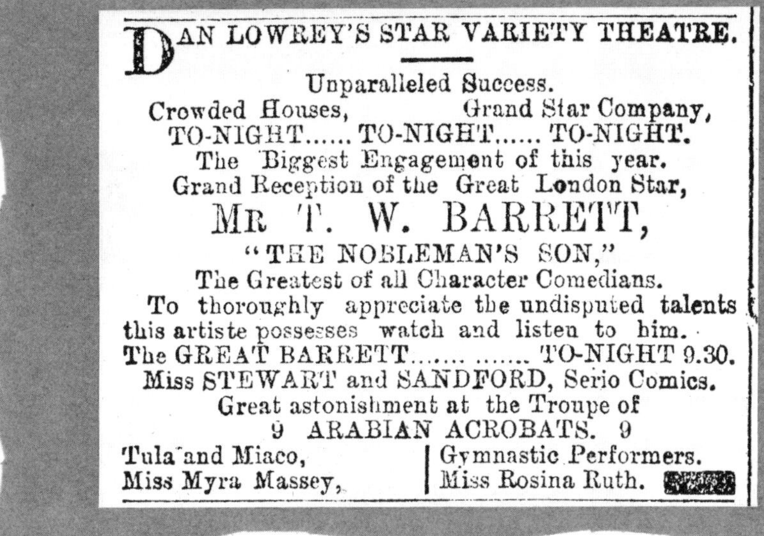

DAN LOWREY'S STAR VARIETY THEATRE.

Unparalleled Success.
Crowded Houses, Grand Star Company,
TO-NIGHT...... TO-NIGHT...... TO-NIGHT.
The Biggest Engagement of this year.
Grand Reception of the Great London Star,
MR T. W. BARRETT,
"THE NOBLEMAN'S SON,"
The Greatest of all Character Comedians.
To thoroughly appreciate the undisputed talents this artiste possesses watch and listen to him.
The GREAT BARRETT....... .... TO-NIGHT 9.30.
Miss STEWART and SANDFORD, Serio Comics.
Great astonishment at the Troupe of
9 ARABIAN ACROBATS. 9
Tula and Miaco, | Gymnastic Performers.
Miss Myra Massey, | Miss Rosina Ruth.

The *Irish Times*, 19 April 1888

grunts from the brutes and gasps from the House as she snatched meat back from slavering jaws. At about eleven o'clock, when the Hall had emptied, a photographer from Robinson's of Grafton Street arrived. Mlle Senide took a Cage of Lions on Stage and while he set up his dark-box and focused the lens she inserted her head in the Lion's mouth. The Beast was sleepy, the Girl tired, the cameraman fiddled with his apparatus. 'Make haste!' she hissed in the dusk. Suddenly the magnesium-flash flared, the Beast, startled, gnashed his teeth gripping her by the face, she pulled it partly free, he lashed out at her with a claw, Carl Beckmann, her Manager, rushed into the Cage, drove the Beast off, carried her out in a dead faint, clanged the door. A doctor put five stitches in her cheek and dressed the wounds on her breast.

Next evening she wanted to return to the Stage, but the doctor would not allow it. In a few days the Beauty left for England and went on to The Concert House, Stockholm, to display her beloved Beasts.

The Irish element was particularly strong this year. As a comic writer 'Ballyhooly' Bob Martin of Ross was now at the peak of his London fame. The London Gaiety Pantomime (1887), *Miss Esmeralda*, had been sprinkled with his lyrical essays in the Absurd and E. W. Coleman, from The

Bob Martin's 'Killaloe'

Gaiety, introduced them to Dan's. 'Killaloe' is a prize specimen. It enacts the fate of a teacher of French who came to the village school:

When a boy straight up from Clare heard his mother called a mère
He gave Mossoo his fist between the eyes.
Says Mossoo with much alarm, Go and call for Johnny Darm,
There's no such name, said I, about the place.
Comment, *he made reply. Come on yerself, says I,*
And I scattered all the features of his face.

Oh boys, there was the fun, you should see him when 'twas done,
His eyeballs one by one did disappear
And a doctor from the south took some days to find his mouth
Which had somehow got concealed behind his ear.
Then he swore an awful oath he'd have the law agin us both
And he'd lave both Limerick and Clare,
For he found it wouldn't do to teach French in Killaloe
Unless he had a face or two to spare.

Now I'm glad to find 'tis true ye are plased with Killaloe
And our conduct to the Teacher they did send;
But I've tould you all that passed, so this verse must be the last
That's the reason I have left it to the end.
We're all Irish tenants here and we're all prepared to swear
That to the Irish language we'll be true,
But we all wid one consent, when they ax us for the rent,
Sure we answer them in Frinch in Killaloe.

Pat Feeney was, after Ashcroft, the most finished Irish Song-Comic of all. He often appeared in the costume of Robert Emmet, a romantic figure hanged for organising a rebellion and attack on Dublin Castle in 1803 – a ghost which has forever haunted the Dublin mind. Offstage, he emptied his pockets to help the Land War and collected some thousands of pounds to alleviate distress in his native West. Yet his comic *persona* was never of the raw and rabid kind but delightfully soft and stealing, cocking a humorous eye at what becomes of the peasant when he gets into power:

Ten years ago I stepped aboard
A ship for England bound,
My heart and pockets both were light
Though I'd not got a pound.
I was but a young greesheen then
Without deceit or sham
But times and things have altered with
Meself, and now I am –
Misther Michael Murphy, a man of great ability
Known and respected by all the gentility
Patronised by all the nobs amongst the great nobility
For Misther Michael Murphy is a Well-Known Man!

Pat composed this song to words by a fellow Irishman, Tom Browne. Among his other compositions were 'How Paddy stole the Rope', 'Maguire's Backyard', 'Goodbye Pat and Goodbye Mick', and:

George Lashwood and his Daughter

Musha bad luck to the gamblin'
For I'm in a funny fix,
Out of four pounds nine and sixpence
I've only three-and-six.

The ghost of Robert Emmet never appeared again in the Drame of Dan's. He fell ill the following April, broke to the wide. Lowrey gave a Benefit in his aid, but Pat died in May, aged thirty-eight. He was soon forgotten. Years later, Sidney Page of the Middlesex County Council discovered his neglected grave, and had it renovated as a tribute to one of the fine Comic Spirits of the Age.

George Lashwood, who arrived in Dan's on Easter Monday 1888 for a week, was a young man on the way up to the Comique pinnacle. He had a little of the Leybourne style about him, transposed into the cheeky insouciance and faultless attire of the New Mode and he became the glass of fashion in which every starveling clerk in every counting-house saw himself.

The year after this appearance at Dan's he got his first London engagements, serving three Halls simultaneously and rapidly became the new Beau Ideal, enrapturing boys and girls alike, humorously fluting through 'My Poll', 'Riding on the Top of a Car', providing the masculine day-dream 'Three Women to Every Man', and luxuriating 'In the Twi-twi-light'. On the sentimental side he struck unerringly the mood of the Young Britons, the new Romans fighting on the farthest marches of Empire to preserve the White Civilisation – 'The Death or Glory Boys', 'The Gallant Twentyfirst', 'Where are the Lads of the Village Tonight?', 'Motherland', 'The Last Bullet, or a Tale of Lucknow'. Harold Scott notes that, as far as social psychology goes, often as much may be learnt in a flash from one of his songs than from three whole books.

George Lashwood was one of those upon whom assurance sits 'like a silk hat upon a Bradford millionaire'. He was as hard as nails, carefully counted the shekels, unlike Leybourne 'who had lived hard and died hard-up'. In 1916 he made a big splash in the Courts. He was sued by William Chappell, Manager of Fritz's Agency, for slander, libel, assault and wrongful imprisonment. Fritz's was typical of the new streamlining that had entered into People's Theatre as it became Big Business. It secured engagements for the Artiste, dividing the takings: 40 per cent to the Hall, 25 per cent to Fritz's, 35 per cent to George. One pay-day at The Hippodrome, Gloucester, out of the takings of £244. 12*s* the Manager handed £92. 12*s* to George as his share. George in his dressing-room sat down and did the sum for himself, came to the conclusion he was three pounds short, sent for the Manager, gripped him by the lapels, shook him, called him a thief, threatened to throw him through the window which was on the second floor, and sent for the Police. Chappell sued for damages, Theatreland flocked to the Court of King's Bench, the Jury found for the Plaintiff and the Beau Ideal lost £150. Lashwood died in 1942, leaving £131,323.

Millie Hylton, one of a family of five sisters all of whom went on the stage, was born in Birmingham. She made her début, at the age of fifteen, in the Panto *Queen of Hearts* in her native City, percolated through the Halls and arrived at Dan's in May of this year at the age of twenty. As Male Impersonator she dulcetted 'Oh! the Rhino!', 'Life's High Road' and 'Something Sweet'. A week after leaving Dublin she got her chance on the London Halls and took it to such good effect that the developing Syndicate took her up and groomed her to be the People's Idol, competing with Vesta Tilley, the London Idol. Her sprightly insouciance sustained the role. She surpassed all her sisters (except perhaps Letty Lind, who won fame as a skirtdancer) and began to figure largely in the Song-Sheet Sales. Years later (October 1896) she came again to Dan's, impeccable twisex humoresque, singing 'Mary's a Fairy':

A cheap tourist ticket and a cheap ditto suit
With two or three quidlets to spend
Completed my outfit and fitted me out
For pleasure and joy without end!
Away in the mountains and close by a lake
There stands a farm house all alone
And Mary the daughter of Farmer McGrath
Is conquered and made all my own!

Mary's a fairy, a fairy is Mary,
And like a canary she warbles and sings.
Never contrairy is sweet little Mary
For Mary's a fairy – but minus the wings!

Vesta as a Soldier Boy

In 1897, in tights and spangles she played the title role in the Gaiety Musical *The Circus Girl*, and came with the show to Gunn's Gaiety the following February. By 1902 she had topped the Bill at The Empire (formerly Dan Lowrey's). She was among the first of the He-Girls of Brummagem Britain, singing through the blood-and-thunder of the first German War, and seeing the end of Music Hall and of much else too before her death in 1920 at the age of fifty-two.

Millie sparkled, but Vesta Tilley shone. Quite in a class of her own. When she came on 10 September 1888 for a fortnight, Dan, still suffering from the shock of his wife's death, billed her as the First Ray of Sunshine of the Year.

On Christmas Eve Nelly Farrell, the Irish Brilliant, appeared at The Star with her new song 'My Boy's Birthday'. 'As an Irish comedienne she received a cordial welcome' – *Freeman's Journal*. It was her fifth and last visit. In January of the following year she appeared at The Belfast Alhambra, was taken ill with typhoid and died in February. Aged thirty.

Among the Serios, the rosyposies, the arch-eye soubrettes, the lesbics and the bursting bodices of the Hebe handfuls, came Ada Lundberg, nearly a hundred years before her time, a fish out of water.

Ada found herself immersed in the older period of Tavern Theatre become Music Hall. She first saw the light in Bristol in 1850 in a dull grey respectable milieu. She ran away from home, aged eleven, to join a travelling Circus. Stranded, she sang and danced in taverns, played farce and melodrama under one-night canvas roofs, exhibited her tight little charms in Poses Plastiques by the light of the flickering lime, learned what life is like at the grass-roots after midnight on the Village Green, and made an early hit with 'My First Young Man'. She sang this in the character of a teenage devil-may-care tinged with the ironic wisdom gained in the sawdust and in the smell of horsedung behind the Circus vans.

Katie Seymour, from the *Sketch*

A later song-study, 'Bessie Barlow', brought her London engagements at The Marylebone, The Middlesex, and at length in 1875 to The Pavilion, the Centre of the World. Her style was slow to catch on for it was dynamic, new, created out of her own sharp experience of the Hidden England, the reality kept well out of sight behind the establishment façade. She shocked many by her harum-scarum outspokenness; she lacked the ladylike quality of the Mrs Caulfields and the Mrs Brians whose approach to the Halls was by way of melody rather than by character creation, and who for humoresque were content to trot out ladies' versions of the Male Comic songs, yet on the other hand she lacked the houri-hebe juice injected into their Stage *mélange* by Gaslight Girls of the Marie Loftus vintage. 'When that lady ceases to mistake double entendre for wit she will please better' – *Pat*, April 1880.

Now, on 30 July for a fortnight, Ada Lundberg made her last appearance at Dan's, aged thirty-eight, sharing the stage with the Beloved Pair, Arthur Lloyd & his Katty. Taste had shifted ever so little. 'The success which attended Miss Lundberg's performance was increased by her production of some new songs' – *Telegraph.*

Ada's flavour was tart, raspberry rather than strawberries and cream. She was a pioneer of sorts, seriously comic in a way the Serio-Comics seldom were, caustically revealing the People to themselves. Her most disturbing feminine study, sung in the character of a drunken woman, was 'I'm All Right up to Now', a forecast of the horde of feminine misfits boozing their way through the boredom of the New Century. Other incisive delineations were 'Such a Nice Girl Too', 'All through Sticking to a Soldier', 'That's a bit of Comfort for a Poor Old Maid', 'Tooraladdie'. Hibbert, who himself took a wry view of human nature, notes: 'Ada Lundberg, a delightful exponent of Cockney humour who must have sung "Tooraladdie", while she polished a boot and her nose alternately, thousands of times at the London Pavilion'. Yet it is the rarest thing to find her figuring in the Song-Sheets. She died in September 1899 and was quickly forgotten.

As far as dancing was concerned, the English Openair-Girl style which had displaced the puffball pirouette of the Italian Ballet was now itself being transformed by French style and the Can-Can. Leg-action had become more electric and the accent was on lingerie, svelte limbs flashing in a shadowgraph of rainbow silk and lace petals. Foremost in the new mode came attractive little Katie Seymour, aged nineteen, billed as Serio. This was the only time she came to Dan's in a solo turn. Born in Nottingham, she had gone into Panto there as a child and had appeared in George West's Grafton at the age of thirteen. Later, in 1890, she found the true medium for her skirtotechnics and nimble footwork in Musical Comedy at The London Gaiety under George Edwards, electrifying the Town with her pickanniny dance in *A Runaway Girl*, the demure doll duet in *The Chorus Girl*, and a titillating Japanese *pas de deux* in *The Shop Girl.*

At the turn of the century she went to America with *The Circus Girl*, and returned heralded by a fanfare to a new Ballet in The London Alhambra which was to be 'utterly modern'.

Katie illustrates how the old Italianate Ballet, having gone through the

Leg Action, from *Pick-Me-Up*

Music Hall and become dynamic in the process, returned and gave a refreshing shock to the Fashion Theatre. She danced the hectic Nineties Era to its end and died in September 1903, just two months after the curtain fell for the last time in the Old London Gaiety. Aged thirty-three.

On Tuesday 21 August 1888 at half-past nine, as the Daisycutters popped on Stage to musical chords, the form of a man fell thirty-five feet from the Gallery – and landed on the head of George Kennedy, a Cornet-player who was seated on the left of the orchestral box. For a moment it was thought to be some gag, a dummy figure, and the Audience sat expectant. Then Mr Lowrey and the ticket-checker rushed forward to the two figures lying in a heap and began to carry them out. At Mercer's Hospital the injured Bandsman was found to have his head badly lacerated and many of his teeth broken by the cornet which he was playing at the moment of impact. The Stranger from on High had scalp wounds for he had come down head-first.

He was a young man named Kenny of 19 Michael's Lane off High Street, engaged as a Coffinmaker by Messrs Nichols, Undertakers. It was said he had been sitting quietly with his wife in the Gallery, slightly drunk, saw the Girlies bounce onto the Stage beneath and remembered nothing after that. He was taken to College Street Station and charged with attempted suicide. There can be no doubt that the man jumped deliberately because there was a grating in front of the Gallery which would have made it impossible for anyone to fall over.

The Cornet-player took over six weeks to recover. Of the Coffinmaker nothing more is known.

CHAPTER THIRTEEN

1889 End of an Age

The bells of Christchurch rang the New Year in; a bedlam of organ-grinders massed in Chancery Place and the crowds linked and sang 'Two Lovely Black Eyes' and 'The Wearing of the Green'. An unrest swept through the Town. 1889 . . . Eve of the Nineties, End of an Age. The weight of the long reign of the Widow Victoria was felt as a burden; old faiths, old dogmatic attitudes began to be shaken loose, rich and poor glimpsed the dawn of the New Century at hand and felt as Dryden had sung:

'Tis well an Old Age is out
And time to begin a New.

Hope for Home Rule was at fever pitch. The word was become a fetish that would bring all kinds of everything for everybody. Parnell hit world headlines. The long Inquiry into the 'Parnell Letters' published by the London *Times*, implicating him in the Phoenix Park Murders, finally came to an end and found the 'Letters' to be forgeries. Pigott the Forger fled to France and blew his brains out. Crowds hugged, kissed and danced in the streets, Ireland was Ireland. And there to prove it was Charles Stewart Parnell. And John L. Sullivan.

On New Year's Day Dan, shaking off his own unhappy past, expressed the feelings of all. 'Another Year is Cancelled from the Calendar of Time – one which I trust may carry away with it the sorrows and afflictions which many have had to bear. Throughout the world Ireland's vicissitudes are proverbial and it is my earnest desire to join in the common hope that her darkest days have passed and that 1889 may bring to her the realisation of those noble aspirations of all great nations – Peace, Happiness & Prosperity. To the Public:

Wealth abundant with healthful cheer,
A very, very Happy New Year.' – Daniel Lowrey.

Tuesday 22 April. At the Mageough Church at Palmerston Park, Daniel Lowrey of 1 Sycamore Street married Annie, daughter of Thomas Tierney, an Officer on the Mail Boat. Dan held his chin up. 'Speed the Past, Bring on the Future.' The Bride was twenty-four.

In April this year Ashcroft topped the Bill. 'W. J. Ashcroft is Mr Lowrey's chief artiste and is a greater favourite than ever. His peculiar style is different from all others, and it goes without saying that he is perhaps one of the finest exponents of humorous Irish character on the Stage' – *Irish Times*.

Ashcroft at forty-three had an immense repertoire of personations and singing-tales – 'I haven't been Home this Morning', 'Norah Kearney', 'We had Half a Day', 'A Quarter to Two', 'McGinty the Swell of the Sea', 'Wreck of the Ragamuffin', 'The Swimming Match', 'Just Pay our Respects to McGuinness'.

There was a soft side to his humour, depending upon charm of melody and gentle whimsy, an old-world quality which could still seduce Dublin. But it was becoming more and more removed from the dominant mood of the New People; it evoked no primitive passions, let loose no such exuberance as did Munroe's 'The Man that Struck O'Hara', or Bob Martin's 'Killaloe'. This very superiority in quiet and classic style was one of the reasons why Ashcroft was bypassed in the Halls by comics of lesser range and feelings less refined.

In 'The Brick Came Down' (lyric by Tom Browne, composed by Michael Nolan), a doggerel-ballad of three labourers – Gannon, Burke and me – his soothing voice and light touch tempered the lunacy of the material:

But Burke came round this morning and he woke us up at five,
To get us on the job by six he somehow did contrive.
We made a start, but just at noon we both chucked up the work
And just to get him on the spree we played a trick on Burke.

At this point the Ulster voice tinged with accents of North America broke into patter:

Burke, you know, is our Gaffer. One of those men you never hear swearing. But he is a gambler to his heart. Well, when I said to Burke, we're not going to work any longer, he said we were doing wrong, but when I said to him, Burke, we'll toss whether we work or not, says he, I'll be wid ye, and he was. How is it to be, says he, the best of two out of three? Divil a fear of it says I, going over and picking up a brick, Do you see this? I do, says he. Well then says I, I'll toss this brick into the air and if it stops up we'll go back to work, and if it comes down we won't! Well, what do you think happened? –
The brick came down! We had half a day.
We've been boozing up and down
Challenging to fight the Town,
Burke's locked up and Gannon's hid away
And I expect the sack tomorrow morning.

Twinkling feet danced through the intricacies of a drunken jig, and the whole House, Orchestra, Bars, Smoking-rooms, gave tongue to the Refrain: 'The Brick Came Down . . .'

John J. Stamford, Manager of Ashcroft's Belfast Alhambra, wrote him a number designed to display both his vocal gifts and his versatility on many instruments; the music was by Shamus O'Connor:

My name is Macnamara, I'm the Leader of a Band,
And though we're small in number we're the best in all the land.
Of course I am Conductor and we often have to play
With all the fine musicians that you hear about today.
Chorus:
When the drums bang – the cymbals clang,
The horns will blaze away,
McCarthy puffs the ould bassoon
While Doyle the pipes will play,
Hennessy tootle-i-toots the flute,
The music is simply grand –
A credit to ould Ireland, boys,
Is Macnamara's Band!

Ye should hear us play The Last Rose of Summer *in nine flats, and the man, woman or child that wouldn't lift their fut when we strike up* Garryowen *must be either deaf or a cripple. Talk about your Grannydears and your Cold Crame Guards – they're not in it with us –*

When the drums bang, etc.

Here 'Macnamara' breaks into a dancing quick-march up and down the Stage, his nimble fingers snatching up one instrument after another, blowing the bassoon, tootling the flute, beating the drum with the knob of his baton – A One-Man Band.

Whenever an election's on we play on either side,
The way we play our fine ould airs fills Irish hearts with pride;
If poor Tom Moore was living now he'd make yez understand
That none could do him justice like ould Macnamara's Band!

Sure we're not consated, but there's nobody like us. I must go now, as the boys are waiting at the Corner, but if at any time ye're in want of a Band to play at a Wedding, a Christening or a Dog Fight, we shall be pleased to come on the shortest notice and the most reasonable terms. Cash in advance, and –

When the drums bang – the cymbals clang . . .

The gusto and break-neck beat of this song have left it ringing in all ears. Yet the character that clung most to Ashcroft was 'The Solid Muldoon'. He played it in frock-coat, muttonchops and tall hat – the self-made man of the Successful Generation, bluff, honest, generous, and proud of it – and it made such an impression both in Europe and in America that he was always referred to as the Solid Man.

He lived that part before the footlights but offstage there was no solidity; his life became more and more of a shifting phantasmagoria as the years went on. To add to his troubles, Stamford, who as Manager had made the fortunes of The Alhambra where others had failed, resigned this year to take over The Shakespeare Inn. Ashcroft's marriage with Kitty Brooks was breaking up. Things were moving to a tragic crisis.

In May 1889 Jake Kilrain & Handsome Charlie Mitchell returned for another Sensational Sparring Match. The House was packed to suffocation and the feeling in the air was ominous, for since his last appearance here Handsome Charlie had done an unforgivable thing. He had stood impudently up to the Hero, the great John L. himself.

All Dublin had the details. It had happened late in 1888. Unknown to the world the Ring was set up and the fighters stripped at the Baron Rothschild's Estate near Chantilly.

It had been raining for thirty-six hours. The Fight began with the two Pugillists slithering in the mud. Icy rain fell from a winter sky, gusts of sleet were blown on the wind. Sullivan went like a tiger for the Englishman, exploding into the pile-driving attack which no man had ever stood up to. But Mitchell could take it; he was at the peak of his form, had his tactics prepared and fought to a plan. Sidling, retreating, clowning, jeering at the big man's inability to land a telling punch, he kept the Champ facing into the punishing wind and sleet. When he felt the want of a breather he took a fall to end a round.

'For Godsake, man, stand up and fight!' John L. roared in fury. 'Don't run away!' Mitchell only gritted his teeth and grinned. He ducked, weaved, slid aside in the mud. Half-blind with anger and pelting sleet the Champ sledgehammered ever more wildly at the empty air. Under the darkening sky and the downpour, after thirty-six rounds spanning three hours and ten minutes, the backers, dripping like drowned black rats, agreed to call a halt and declare the Fight a draw. Sullivan was fit to be tied. Ever after he referred to Mitchell as 'that bombastic sprinter!' The news that the Hero had been fought to a draw ran quickly round the world. Every street-urchin in Dublin knew the ins and outs of it – it was some slippery English smart-alec business to belittle the Irish Giant!

There was a big contingent of dockers in the Gallery. The Ring was set up, the cicerone came before the footlights to introduce 'your friend and favourite', the Englishman stepped into the Ring. The beginning of a clap was suddenly drowned by a fierce and prolonged hiss. The cicerone appealed for a hearing. The crowd began to murmur like an angry hive. A big man rose and called cheers for John L. Sullivan 'whose parents came from Ireland!' There was an uproar, hats and sticks flew, half the House were on their feet. On Stage the cicerone gesticulated, raised his voice and made several ineffectual attempts to get a hearing in face of the mounting passion of the mob.

Mitchell shouted to him to call time and start the bout. This evoked a storm of jeers: 'Walk-around Charlie!' 'Lie-down Charlie!' 'Charlie the Sprinter!', and eventually 'Mitchell the Coward!'

With raised chin Mitchell walked firmly down to the footlights and asked to be allowed to say a few words. His very stance exuded a quiet power. One by one the heckling voices died away. He spoke modestly, incisively. 'Someone in this House has just called me a coward. Well, I'm not hiding anywhere, I'll be here for a week, and let you just trot that man out!'

Shamefaced laughter and some applause followed this neat hit and the bout began. The exhibition was tame. Both men were off form in the prevailing hysteria, and the conclusion brought a very mixed reception from the crowd, with more whistling and catcalls from the Gallery. This time it was Kilrain who advanced to the footlights; he protested against all the talk there was of Sullivan, as if there was no other boxer in the world. Raising his voice he declared, 'I never said I would beat any man, but I am ready to fight any man'. Police cordons were drawn up at the entrances as the House emptied into the street.

It may be said in passing that John L. successfully defended his World Title against Kilrain in one of the last Bareknuckle sagas of the Century; after seventy-five rounds, the Challenger's seconds (Mitchell was one of them) threw in the sponge to save the stunned and stupefied Kilrain from what might well have been a death-blow.

The Mitchell riot at The Star reminds one of the later *Playboy* riots at The Abbey Theatre, during which Yeats advanced to the footlights, faced, the storm of protest and firmly declared: 'I have never learned to bend the knee!' Both Dan Lowrey's Star and Yeats' Abbey were essentially People's Theatres, thriving on the emotions of a passionate race. In Dublin perhaps more than in any other modern city, the story of the Theatre is closely bound up with the history of the times.

RIGHT Sketches from *Pat* with 'Lowrey' misspelt. The dancers are Pat Kinsella and his Wife

LOWRY WEATHER.
CHANGES TO THUNDERS OF APPLAUSE.

Old Dan in his last years

Pat Kinsella bubbled through the Drame. He was by now an institution; eyes crinkling in a rubicund face, melodious Clown of the Liffeyside Halls, known to every child at the Christmas Shows, friend to all the world, advertising himself as 'always to be found at the One Lamp in Grafton Street'.

He had acquired the little Harp in Adam Court when Lowrey had acquired The Grafton, and ran it on free-and-easy lines, saying it was the one place left in Dublin where a man could bring his pint into the auditorium and enjoy the show. Under Kinsella's genial management, The Harp held its own for many years. Its style was rough and ready. As soon as the doors opened there was a wild rush to get to the Gallery. In the stampede up the stairs the weak were tripped up or hand-pushed out of the way. The object was to get to the front row, take off your jacket, hang it on the protective rail, lean over and hurl abuse at the more moneyed latecomers down below. A fat man was always asked: 'Who ate the dog's dinner?'

Pat saw the comic side of serious things and tumbled into burlesque. When the Shah of Persia paid a State Visit to England in July, 'His Ever-Serene & Sublime Highness the Shah of Dublin, King Patroshki Kinsella' arrived in Dan's, where he 'kept the Audience on the best of terms with themselves' – *Telegraph*. In Horse Show Week came the 'Eminent Jockey & Animal Surgeon Mr Patrick Kinsella'. With war threatening, 'Admiral Pat Kinsella' enacted the Defence of Dublin – 'has to be seen to be believed' – the *Jarvey*. When Tom Costello came singing his robust 'Died like a True Irish Soldier', he was followed by 'General Kinsella' singing 'Died like a True Irish Tailor'. Percy French, editor of the *Jarvey*, said of him: 'He is the bright particular luminary of all Stage-gazers.'

'Wednesday 3 July. At his residence, Wentworth Cottage, Terenure, Mr Daniel Lowrey. Aged sixty-six. Funeral will leave above address for internment in Glasnevin Cemetery on tomorrow, Friday morning at 10 o'clock.' – *Freeman's Journal*.

The Funeral of the Old Comedian passed as unnoticed through the Dublin streets as he had passed through these same streets as a child clutching his mother's hand, more than fifty years before.

Of latter years he had come less and less to The Star of Erin which he had dreamed of and brought into being. 'I have no recollection of him on the Stage,' writes Norah, 'but I have heard him on one or two occasions when he had to make a presentation to an Artiste, talking to the Audience and they did not want him to go off, he was very witty. I believe that on one occasion when he was talking to the Audience my eldest sister Jeannie who happened to be at the side of the Stage made signs to him to come off. She evidently thought he had talked long enough, but he just said to the Audience, "Ladies & Gentlemen, my grand-daughter is telling me to finish, do you wish me to do so?" There was loud applause and cries of, 'No! we would like some more stories!'

The Press appears to have ignored his passing. His name, style and Stage career dropped out of the Dublin Myth, eclipsed by the name and *persona* of his son. An oilpainting of him which hung in The Star today lies unnoticed in the Civic Museum. He was one of the creative spirits of his time. By turning his back upon the ruins of the past and calling The Star of Erin into being he opened the floodgates to the new ultra-national age, yet no scholar traces his footsteps in a thesis, and there is no Dan Lowrey Industry in the Book Market. A People's Theatre, it seems, is no subject for Masters of Arts. 'I believe he was born in Roscrea,' writes Norah. 'The principal thing I remember about him is that he was never pleased with the way my hair was done.'

Music remained as much part of the atmosphere of a Night in Dan's as did the Beer, Wines & Spirits. For a couple of weeks in November 1889 the Stage was dominated by 'Les Militaires'. This was an Orchestra of twelve ladies, all skilled instrumentalists, conducted by Mrs Hunt. They were much talked of, and came fresh from the Yorkshire Festival and from a dazzling success at Michael Gunn's Leinster Hall.

Dressed in dashing Hussar uniforms with tricorne hats, they played selections from Opera and Opera Bouffe, as well as international marches, waltzes, quadrilles, Irish and Scottish airs. Insistent calls from the Gallery brought 'The Harp that Once thro' Tara's Halls' which, rendered with full orchestral score, provoked mass emotion. All shades of politics disappeared in a sort of race-feeling; they ended up with 'God Save Ireland'.

Mrs Hunt's Ladies' Orchestra, from the *Strand Musical Magazine*

Thronged Houses and scenes of enthusiasm lasted a fortnight. All felt that a friendly settlement of the English–Irish problem was just round the corner.

An Age was indeed passing from the Stage. This year saw the last appearance in Dan's of the Great Macdermott. The luxuriant daffodil wig and curlycue whiskers trembled to the resonance of the deeper voice, and in between stanzas he was up and down the Stage playing three or four characters at once, gruff, wheedling, droll, falsetto, placing his gags with the precision learned long ago when he was dogsbody to the Conquest Company. 'His appearance was the signal for an enthusiastic reception. The old Jingo is in voice and style even better than ever' – *Times*.

He had jingoed at The Star for the last time. But back in London, the unofficial Jester of the Tory Reign had one final part to play. In December a certain Captain O'Shea filed a petition for divorce against his wife, Kitty, for adultery. The whole Music Hall world was thrown into disarray, for as the adulterer the Captain cited no less a man than Charles Stewart Parnell. Parnell, the Uncrowned King, become a god since his triumph over the London *Times*, was found to have had a scandalous secret life. One night, when the Captain came home unexpectantly, the Chief was obliged to step out the bedroom window and run down the fire-escape. Liberals of all shades were appalled. Ireland was paralysed. The Great Macdermott grasped at the theme of a lifetime:

Charlie Parnell, Charlie Parnell,
Oh you notty boy!
Why did you ever interfere
With another's joy?

Political uproar drowned the stentorian voice and the Lion went on in dumb show, taking a breath to roar out the telling lines above the din:

You want Home Rule for Ireland
And you can't Home Rule yourself!

Poor Charlie Dilke's spilt milk was thin stuff compared to this foaming brew. Macdermott lambasted the fallen Irish Idol and whipped Houses up to orgies of sadism with all the intoxicating comic power at his command. No English voice had the nerve to protest: the Chief who had made a laughing-stock of staid Westminster was fair game. That fine Artiste Charles Collette had been prohibited by Authority from singing a Home Rule song at the Trocadero in April, but Macdermott's impudence suited the Party Line. The Old Lion was at his most ebullient; Audiences were hoarse with cheering and sick with laughter when Mac pattered the Bedroom Scene in his best Melodrama manner and finicking uppercrust accent:

Heavens! Wot a situation! Hardly time to draw on one's gloves!
No chance of avoiding detection, no way to save the lady's
reputation – no way, no way – Oh yes, fthank Goodness there is
one! Ah happy, happy, fthrice happy fthought! –
The Fire-Escape! The Fire-Escape!
It was indeed a merry jape

When Charlie Parnell's notty shape
Went scorching down the Fire-Escape!

The Stage seemed afloat in a sea of howling faces bearing the Great Macdermott in triumph along forever. Until October 1891. Parnell died suddenly from nervous exhaustion. *Comedia finita est.*

The Old Lion Macdermott gradually faded out, gone grey in the face and solemn, living prudently on the Theatre properties in which he had invested the profits of his Tory thunderbolts, rather peeved to the end that no title came his way from an ungrateful Government. He became a churchwarden and a pillar of the Church. He had always been something of a religious man. The first few bars of his Jingo song were exactly the same as the Kyrie in Mozart's *Twelfth Mass.* He died in 1901.

Four months of wedded life was all Dan and his new wife Annie had, for she died of pneumonia on 31 August of this year. Yet Dan's motto remained: 'Speed the Past, bring on the Future!' and with the help of his son Daniel, now a competent assistant-Manager, he pressed on. The Theatre remained open on Monday, eve of the funeral, starring Vesta Tilley the London Idol. 'One of the best performances Mr Lowrey has ever presented to his patrons' – *Freeman's Journal.*

CHAPTER FOURTEEN

1890 Infinite Variety

In his New Year Address to the Public Dan Lowrey, having reviewed his management over the past ten years and seeing himself and his Night Rite as a public institution, continues:

> An outside public can never comprehend the difficulties which a Manager has to surmount in order to attain that perfection in production which he so wishes for the enjoyment of the Masses, and situated here in Ireland his must be a gold-baited offer to coax the Big Stars across the water from London, Paris and elsewhere. Yet glancing over last Year's engagements, I think I may humbly say my endeavours will bear favourable comparison with any other Manager in the Kingdom . . .
>
> In the future as in the past it will be my constant study to merit the confidence of a generous community, and I shall strive with incessant energy to eclipse if possible all former efforts. A special Agency has

Programme Cover from 1890. Figures down and across: Macdermott, Nelly L'Estrange, Horace Wheatley, Charles Clifford the Harpist, Harry Melville, Dan Lowrey, Old Dan, Dan the Third, Vance

> been opened up in New York in order to secure everything worth securing even in America, and already several big Transatlantic engagements have been effected. In addition to these I have numerous startling Novelties to present, and almost every Star of repute in London and the Continent has been booked for 1890.

The Bill for the Year hardly bears out that assurance. As far as Male Comics and top-rank Serios are concerned, this first year of the Nineties is perhaps the leanest of all at Dan's. It seems as if he was running into financial difficulties in trying to compete for top-class London talent; that through his New York Agency he was attempting to keep up a show of 'modernity' with cheaper and less high-grade material from American Vaudeville.

Surviving from the past Age, Ashcroft and Pat Kinsella out-topped everything in the Song–Comic line, while Paganini Redivivus returned and dominated the scene in a class of his own. He had a big success the previous year at the *Folies Bergère* in Paris, and had been presented by the Directors with a replica of the costume worn by the Maestro when he played at the Paris Grand Opera sixty years before. The Lowreyites were delighted with this distinction. The 'devilish' quality which had come down from the days of The Shades and the Caves of Harmony was resonant in the Ghost's playing of his own composition, 'The Demon Violinist'.

Apart from these vintage items, the spate of English and American 'novelties' made the Town conscious of the new concept of Theatre which was beginning to affect Music Hall: the idea of 'Variety'. The *Jarvey* notes:

> The Star is crowded nightly, as it deserves to be. Mr Lowrey has never presented to his patrons such a succession of marvels in the vocal, acrobatic or dancing acts as can be seen now in Crampton Court week after week. The public are certain to see for themselves what kind of talent pleases in the big hall of the big city.
>
> America is represented very largely, and certainly the Artistes sustain the great reputation for A-Oneness which the 'grandest country in the world, sir', has always claimed. . . . If you want a place to spend the evening where, like Sam Slick, you can smoke, put your feet up and 'spit and feel to hum', the Star is that particular location.

Yet America was not to everybody's taste. A letter to the *Jarvey* derides the transatlantic pseudo-Irish Comic, his verbal diarrhoea of Ochs and Begorras, his old frock-coat that doesn't fit, tall hat that was in fashion in the time of Noah, and whiskers flapping loosely from the hair. . . . Cause for complaint also is the coloured Comic in a ragged suit and a hat that is little more than a brim . . .

Although Dan had come to realise that the full-length type of Christmas Show he had attempted was not properly attuned to Music Hall, he nevertheless saw there was room for a 'Variety' type of short Panto as part of a Night's Bill. American groups especially were providing such fare. Michael Gunn held that Lowrey's Music Hall licence did not cover such coordinated items: that they were 'dramatic' within the meaning of the Act. The question remained simmering; legal opinion would not risk a prosecution unless it could be proved that the 'dramatic' item in question had actually been performed upon a Legitimate Stage. It was felt that a House of Commons Inquiry should be set up to consider the problem. Meanwhile Lowrey was determined to go as far as the obscurities of the Law allowed.

In January, to celebrate the new Decade, he arranged a Spectacular Extravaganza, *China*, in which a hundred Artistes took part. The script was by Jacques McCarthy of *Sport*, a lively writer who had scripted several Pantomimes for The Queen's Theatre. The nucleus of the Show was supplied by the visiting Harry Barnes Company of sixteen, supported by a Corps de Ballet and augmented Orchestra. There were five scenes, affording scope for scintillating costumes, choreography and sets, comics, chorus and topical songs, the accent being on spectacle and femininity. Dan advertised: 'Wanted at once, thirty Young Ladies, aged seventeen to twenty, to take part in this Production. Apply personally today at The Star.' There was a rush.

It seems likely that Lowrey brought the idea of this very early form of 'revue' back from his visits to Paris. It made an immediate impact. 'Last night there was a crowded house to witness the first production of *China*. The scenery and panoramic effects were very satisfactory and a ballet of nearly 100 dancers was on the stage. The other items on the programme are also attractive and altogether Mr Lowrey has provided an entertainment which cannot fail to be acceptable to the patrons of his music hall' – *Freeman's Journal*.

Among this Year's Novelties, Cliquot the Swallower, from *Pick-Me-Up*

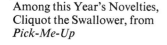

All through the Year he piled on 'dramatic' items which were barely, if at all, within the letter of the obsolete Law. Bruce's London Combination played a two-act Absurdity, *A K-Night in Armour*, with scenes in a London street and in a Baronial Hall, showing comic adventures with armour and butler and housemaids performing a Candle Chorus. The Four American Maxwells played the Blood-Curdling Comic Tragedy Burlesque, *Faust Reversed*. Folloy & Harvey's Boys produced *A Night in McGinty's Kitchen*, a species of Irish–American Cabaret in which the libretto gave scope for ballads, heart-scalders, wrestling, football and fisticuffs.

Hardly a week went by without some such 'dramatics'. The celebrated McCarthy Family of Six, who had more than fifty Sketches in their repertoire, could produce a new one every night if required. The Bradys sang Operatic Sketches, and Pat Kinsella swung on the flying trapeze in a Historical Sketch, *The Indian Mutiny*.

Variety could not exist without a continuous flow of 'novelties'. The Stage of The Star was become a Magazine of 'sensational pictures in action'. Joseph Darby jumps eight feet from a given mark onto the face of a man lying on the ground. Patsy Walshe nightly walks half a mile round the Stage in three-and-a-half minutes, Audience timing. The Aerial Demons dive from the roof through a Magic Balloon. Grant the Ventriloquist articulates six figurines in his 'International Congress'. Howard's Diorama unrolls the 'World We Live In', the painted pictures being set off by limelit scenery and mechanical effects, interspersed with narration, pianoforte solos and sparkling duets. Mlle Merveille displays her Canine Equestrian Troupe of Siberian Boarhounds and her flock of Performing Cockatoos. Kitty Lindsey brings her Mexican Troupe of Educated Donkeys from the Big American Hippodromes. Laughing Donkeys, Singing Donkeys, Dancing Donkeys, Spelling Donkeys. See the Great Donkey School. Marvellous Comprehension.

Professor Baughman & Miss Aldine are the World's Crack Rifle & Pistol Shots – 'Buffalo Bill can take a back seat!' – the *Jarvey*. The Baldwin Cat climbs a rope fifty feet high and, in precise imitation of Professor Baldwin the Renowned Parachutist, makes a parachute descent 'amidst the uproarious applause of the house' – *Freeman's Journal.*

This year saw the first appearance of Professor James Finney, Champion Swimmer of the World, in conjunction with his sister Marie. They performed in a glass tank on Stage, eating, drinking, singing, waltzing, somersaulting, gathering eggs, picking up coins in their teeth and sleeping – all under water.

'I remember the Finneys well,' says Norah. 'They suggested an advertisement stunt to my Father. James Finney was to be in a small boat on the Liffey close to O'Connell Bridge, being rowed by one of our men. Marie was to walk over the bridge with a friend, when she was to see her brother fall out of the boat, mount on the balustrade and plunge to his rescue.'

Dan agreed, arranged for boat and boatman. All went well. When Finney below saw the approach of his sister and friend he 'fell' overboard into the water. Marie coolly let a few minutes pass until a crowd had gathered, then crying: 'Oh, my dear brother!' threw off her ulster and appeared slim in a swimsuit – she was just eighteen – and began to climb up on the balustrade helped by the frantic friend. As she stood poised for the dive before the gaping onlookers, the hands of a Sergeant of the Metropolitan Police gripped her firmly by wrist and ankle.

– Now what's all this, missus?

– My brother! My drowning brother!

But the Sergeant hoisted the lady down from the parapet. It was a case, he considered, of female suicide. Dan Lowrey who had been standing close by came forward to her rescue, tried to explain that it was an advertisement, no harm intended.

– With all due respect, Mr Lowrey, sir, I'll have to take this young woman into custody.

The case came before the Magistrate, Mr Keys. The Court was crowded with Artistes from all the Playhouses, the entire staff of The Star, a phalanx of the Press. Marie Finney appeared, charged with attempting to jump into the Liffey thereby endangering her own life and collecting a crowd.

Defending Counsel, charmed to be holding the Stage while the celebrities of the Theatre sat in the Audience, gathered his gown and played to the Gallery. 'Can you swim?' he thundered at the six-foot Sergeant.

Sergeant confessed himself a non-swimmer, having a natural dread of water. (Laughter.) Counsel, proceeding, proffered his solemn and sincere gratitude to the Sergeant for preventing his lovely client from going into the Liffey, and averred that the lady, if she knew as much about Anna Livia as he did – as, unfortunately, we all did – would be eternally grateful to the Officer who had prevented her personal contact with that not too salubrious stream. (Prolonged laughter.)

Upshot: Mr Keys agreed to mark the suicide charge 'no rule', and imposed a fine of £1 for collecting a crowd.

That evening at The Star the lady swimmer was presented on Stage with a bouquet and a diamond ring. 'Needless to say,' adds Norah, 'the House was packed that night and for the rest of the week. It was a much better advertisement than if Marie Finney had succeeded in diving from the bridge.'

Among the most primitive Jesters to appear at The Star was the American Frank McNish. Billed as Humorist, Dancer & Storyteller, his one-man show, 'Silence and Fun', was more than usually full-blooded in its comic suggestion, and belonged to that phase of American Vaudeville before managers tried to tone it down and make it fit for ladies. His playlet was set in the kitchen, his props simple – table, chair, a couple of barrels, a sweeping-brush. Riding his hairy broomstick the funman danced on twinkling feet from barrel to barrel, barrel to table, table to floor, floor to chair to table again, spun his broomstick in arabesques, did splits, rolls, cartwheels, piled the furniture up, somersaulted to the top of the lot, King Broom erect, music crescendoing, spun in the air like a goat in a

A Trio of Sisters, from *Pick-Me-Up*

witches' sabbath and landed on the brink of the Orchestra pit, providing the Audience with an excruciatingly comic experience – all without a word.

Yet McNish was never among the greats: the Audience was too predominantly male. Only with Fanny Leslie did a comparable act in the female line turn up.

One of the Sisters Jonghmanns, from *Pick-Me-Up*

Flocks of lace-leggy Chicks were now practically a thing of the past. Pairs, trios and even quartettes of 'Sisters' eclipsed the Ballet. A Fleet Street journalist remembers them thus:

> . . . the most deplorable feature in music halls. These terrible young (or middle-aged) persons who were announced as the Sisters So-and-So and who were inevitable on every Stage, always succeeded in putting a portion of the Audience into a bad temper. Their short coloured skirts, their fixed smirk, the mechanical steps of their dances, their metallic voices – these things have left an impression not pleasant to recall. They couldn't sing. They couldn't dance. And their make-up proved that they couldn't even paint.

Yet the Sisters, by and large, were curiously seductive and remained the rage of the Nineties. Young men of the privileged and wealthy class flocked from the Bars when the turn of the Little Pets came on. One of them, Cranstoun Metcalfe, distils the essence of the attraction:

> You made your way, if you were lucky, to the bar that separated the Promenade from the seats on the second floor. The number was changed, the Orchestra played something lost in the tumult of clapping hands, played it a second time, and you saw the only thing you and the rest had come to see – charm and freshness incarnate on the Stage: two girls dressed exactly alike – in blue, wasn't it? – with fair hair curling from under mob caps, or Dutch caps, or some kind of cap that was exactly right, with laughing eyes in piquant faces. . . . And their absurd little songs could not have been improved upon, for them, for they were exactly the kind of song they could sing. . . . Of course it is drivel, but it wasn't drivel coming from them. It was because they were freshness and sweetness incarnate, and because they had the gift to waft this freshness and sweetness over the footlights, and up into the hot and crowded Promenade.

Not all of the Sisterhoods comformed to this type. We have already met the sophisticate Leamars. The Sisters Richmond (Josie & Lulu) had come to Europe from America. They delivered their ditty, 'Pretty as a Butterfly', in dinky male jackets and kneebreeches, choker collars and shirtcuffs, the whole effect topped with short boyish wavy hair.

The Four Sisters Jonghmanns provided some very refined musical fare. They dressed in old comedy style with impeccable taste, their stage presence was a picture and their singing was excellent. Little wonder, for they were daughters of Ferdinand Jonghmanns, the buffo vocalist and Musical Director of The Oxford.

Dan billed The Three Sisters Levey as 'the finest specimens of womanhood ever seen'. They too had musical connections: they were granddaughters of the Giant O'Shaughnessey and half-sisters of the Ghost of Paganini.

Yet the Dutch-cap type of Sisters with their twittering little ditties were by far the most successful. Many youths of the upper classes were mesmerised into matrimony by the innocent insouciance of these sisterly Chicks. The Bilton sisters, Belle and Florence, cast such a spell. Belle married young Lord Dunlo and when he succeeded to the Earldom she reigned at Garbally Park in Galway as the dazzling Countess of Clancarthy.

CHAPTER FIFTEEN

1891 Ameringloirish

1

By the beginning of 1891 Lowrey was forced to admit that he was finding it difficult to secure 'Great Stars of the Theatre firmament'. A new element had entered the business – the chains of Music Halls, the Theatreland 'Empires' and the Syndicates, and he was finding that The Star as a Family business could not compete with these growing monopolies. Under such Syndicates the old-style Music Hall, which had emerged out of Tavern Theatre, with its personal and particular atmosphere, was losing much of its savour and becoming the large, impersonal, fashionable, jingo-jaunty Variety Theatre.

Dan, now fifty and full of life, was still ploughing his own furrow. For the most part he acted as his own Agent, travelling frequently to London, seeing the best artistes there were to be seen, and booking them if he could for The Star. He thought nothing of making the trip to Paris to see for himself what the French Cirque, The Hippodrome, the Night Clubs, had to offer in the way of colourful sensation and clownery; his daughter Jeannie accompanied him on these trips and transacted business in French with Managers and Performers. More than any of his children Jeannie was, in Cocteau's phrase, 'bitten with the Red and Gold Disease', and he came to rely on her as his amanuensis.

The opening of his Agency in New York in 1890 made it possible for him to 'import' American vaudeville, and thus to bypass the London Syndicates, at least to some extent. But the flood of streamlined American items, highly polished, yet rather superficial and lacking in personality by English and Irish standards, was influential in accelerating the change from local-colour Music Hall to the sparkling and insubstantial Variety Theatre in which wit was to become wisecrack, character was to evaporate, and spangled Spectacle 'a whinny on the tinny side' was to replace the old enchantment.

Yet Dan's publicity campaign was more energetic than ever. His Powderley Posters still coloured the Town; his advertisements in the Press were daily, his notes to the Public well-timed and reverberating. He had developed a 'colossal' prose of his own in describing The Star and its Items – Dan Lowrey's World-Famed Palace of Novelties. The Crystal Palace of Ireland. Terrific Cannonade of Entertainments. Dazzling Explosion of Attractions. The present enormous organisation is positively unparalleled in the history of Music Hall Entertainment in Dublin. Patronised by the Classes, popularised by the Masses. Truly as compared with others we are as a Whale amongst minnows.

He snatched at every opportunity to publicise The Star, its comfort, its quality. 19 February. This is the Night! The Greatest Weed Night of the Century. The World-Famed Tobacco Manufacturers Messrs J. & E. Kennedy's Grand Free Smoke Night. Everyone entering The Star Theatre tonight will be presented with a free package of Kennedy's New Combination Flake, the most delicious Puff yet invented.

Charitable Benefits were frequent. Dan was generous, but there can be no denying such a Benefit meant wide publicity. 18 and 19 June: Benefits in Aid of the Funds for the Families of the late Inspector Doherty and Brigade-man Burke, who lost their lives in a gallant effort to save life at the recent fire in Westmoreland Street. Carriages thronged Dame Street, the Boxes glowed with diamonds. The Star was bursting at the seams.

1891 provided an abundance of Serios – Eva Johnson, Louie Frampton, Virginia Frances, Rose Sullivan, Marie Le Blanc, Kitty Nolan, Clara Bell, Maud Mildew, Eunice Vance (daughter of the Great), Lizzie Villiers . . . At one time it took a girl of spirit, an Ada Lundberg or a Marie Loftus, to go it solo in the Taverns and Tents and, if she was good and tough and lucky, eventually to be successful in the Halls. But now with the Syndicates ensuring salaries and engagements, with the fashion magazines featuring Ladies of the Variety Stage, and with convention beginning to break up in the Nineties, more and more girls were slipping off the stays of respectability and having a go. Each had her own bit of fetchery, but most were mediocre – only one in a hundred had what it takes to become an Artiste.

Among the best of the Year's bunch was Lily Marney, billed 'the Female Feeney', beginning to make a mark with her rollicky-jollicky style. Joe Lawrence's daughter, Miss Victoria, was now billed for the first time as Vesta Victoria, but her name was in small type – she was still in the chrysalis stage. Katie Lawrence was extremely pretty, poignantly sweet, but her big moments were still some way off. Billie Barlow too was still on the way up, a baby-eyed *ingénue* making famous the phrase: 'What on earth can you do in a case like that?'

There was a similar plethora of Male Comics of whom more than fifty appeared. They included Tom Coyne the Celebrated Lump of Irish Fun; Pat Bergin the one-legged song-and-dance Artiste from Golden Lane; Pat Rafferty; Horace Wheatley; J. W. Rowley; Tom Costello still marking time with 'Died Like a True Irish Soldier'; Ashcroft; Tom Maglagan; Michael Nolan of 'Little Annie Rooney' fame; The Two Macs; and T. E. Dunville, one of the most disturbing Artistes ever seen in The Star.

It was Pat Rafferty's second and final visit. Pat appears to have been Birmingham Irish, emigrated to America and returned. He made his début in English Provincial Halls and came to the London Stage at Seebright's Music Hall in 1888. He had a long innings as Comedian of the second rank, giving attractive renditions of such light-weights as 'Dancing to the Organ in the Mile End Road'. Some of his items, like 'Norah my Village Queen', were very run-of-the-mill: her eyes were like diamonds, he clasps his blushing love, and I will be as true to thee as are the stars above. His own composition, 'McAnulty's Garden Party', is of the jigtime feed-for-all variety, but lacks the inspired lunacy of such grub-time classics as 'Miss Hooligan's Christmas Cake'. More poignant in its humour was his honey-toned 'Swinging on Riley's Gate'. Even the love-scene lacked the usual gush:

When my daily toil was over
I would haste to meet my Kate,
Eight o'clock each night you'd see us
Swinging on Riley's gate.

Then in the Nineties came his big hit, 'Katie Connor', a perfect mixture of realism and fantasy:

The Mask of T. E. Dunville, drawn from an old print

Lily Marney

On my honour Katie Connor
is the nicest girl you'd meet.
I dote on her, I'm a gonner,
she's just nice enough to eat.
Near the water I first caught her
in a little fishing town;
But just lately she's turned stately
and my brain's turned upside down.

He clowned gently in two voices through the last scene of all:

Then we parted and I started
for the mighty ocean's brink.
Kate looked squeamy, she could see me
take a brick to make me sink.
Near the water she bethought her
– Jack! she cried. Said I – Too late!
– Jack me jewel, don't be crewel,
come back, Jack, and marry Kate!

Thereafter Pat topped Bill after Bill for forty years in English Halls. He died in 1952, aged ninety-two. The song still lingers.

Two visitors of note appeared in the Audience in 1891. One of them (in January) was Michael Gunn. He bought a ticket at the door, entered and sat out the Show, paying particular attention to *The Burglar*. This was advertised as a 'Dramatic Gem' with scripted dialogue, stage effects and music. Gunn noted the dramatic details and added them to the evidence he was preparing for the House of Commons Inquiry which was to come. Dan boldly billed *The Burglar* in big type on his posters for the following week.

The other visitor (29 June) was an unobtrusive little man with a big puff of moustache. He too had a pencil and sat in the Stalls noting each item attentively. He took home the Programme to his rooms at 12 Northumberland Road, filed it in his collection, and sat writing notes of the items in a school exercise book. As a result, that night's entertainment may be reconstructed:

1 OVERTURE BY THE BAND, *Chevalier Breton* (Hermann)

2 LYDIA YEAMANS, *the Australian Nightingale*

3 CARRIE LAWRIE, *BURLESQUE BALLADIST & DANCER*

4 LITTLE BILLIE BURROUGHS, *Negro Comic*

5 BILLIE BARLOW, *CHARACTER COMEDIENNE*
(At 9 o'clock)

● INTERMISSION ●

6 OVERTURE BY THE BAND, *L'Enchantresse*

7 THE FOUR ENGLISH FLASHES, *Acrobat Dancers, in their specialty, 'HIGH LIFE'*

8 *America's Big Four in Screaming Sketch,* NIAGARA'S FALL

9 HORACE WHEATLEY, *featuring among other hits 'HUSH, HUSH, HUSH, HERE COMES THE BOOGIE MAN!' as sung by him in ALI BABA at the Dublin Gaiety last Christmas.*

The little man was Joseph Holloway, an architect, who knew every play, every actor, every item of Theatre that appeared in Dublin during his lifetime. His figure was as well known backstage at The Queen's or Dan Lowrey's as it was in the exclusive environs of The Gaiety. Wrapped in a long black coat, with bowler and umbrella, he threaded the Nightlife scenes, gathering material for his Diaries: they were bound into volumes at the end of every year, and piled up until they eventually overflowed from his rooms, spilled into the hall and blocked doors. Holloway's diaries constitute a unique record of contemporary Theatre.

7 September. A fanfare of advertisement heralded the return of W. J. Ashcroft. By now he was the Grand Old Man of Irish Character Humoresque, a voice and a style from a more dim-lit Theatretime. All the developments in comic singing had passed him by – the Leybourne toff, the Vance dude, the Chirgwin grotesque, the rainbow spectrum of Arthur Lloyd, the Macdermott journalese, the intellectual blue-rag of Arthur Roberts, the Lashwood slick – yet he was still amazingly impressive.

Critics felt the difference, but it was difficult to put a finger on it. Here was a solid Artiste, a personality that rang true. Some of the lilt, the mellow tone and lack of boisterousness, may still be heard in the words of 'The Crockery Ware' (*allegro moderato*):

McGoveran carried the crockery ware,
The cradle was handed to me,
Murphy sat on top o' the cart
Houldin' the clock on his knee.
The horse set off at a funeral trot,
He was staggerin' under the load –
He'd good stayin' powers, but it took us two hours
To travel a mile o' the road.

After many adventures, falls, bangs, breakages, arguments, blood-lettings and free-for-alls – sung and danced through by Ashcroft with musical chimes, trot, reverberations, flutings and curdling effects – the six Characters tangled in the relics of the clock and the crockery-ware reach journey's end. One might contrast this with the tale of a similar 'Flitting' as sung by Marie Lloyd (*see page* 149). Ashcroft's 'Crockery Ware' illustrates the art of the musical Actor: there is little of his own inner personality and problem distilled into it. Marie Lloyd's song on the other hand is resonant with the stress of her own personal predicament: it is 'Marie' in a way 'The Crockery Ware' was never Ashcroft. From this one may see why Ashcroft, though a constant success in Ireland, England and all over the New World, was never to be numbered among the Lions Comiques who, one and all, no matter what their material, were always enacting dynamic aspects of themselves.

Yet seen in retrospect Ashcroft is a major figure. He presented a rural people, not only to Dublin and to Belfast, but to London, the English Provinces and America. Through his controlled artistry he let the public feel that the Irish peasantry were not quite the savages which the 'atrocity' stories of the Establishment Press made them out to be. It was the time of the Land War: the sympathy of the British and American public was all-important, swayed the issue in the heel of the hunt and the great Land Acts were forced through at Westminster. It seems probable that Ashcroft (and with him Pat Feeney, Nellie Farrell, Pat Rafferty, Pat Kinsella, Robert Martin of Ross, Percy French, and the Clown, Johnny Patterson) all unwittingly influenced history more forcefully than did the Great Jingo Singer.

The one-week stay this Autumn was Ashcroft's thirteenth appearance in Dan Lowrey's, a record for a star-turn. It was also his last.

His temperament, always sensitive, strained by the feeling that somehow he had lost his way in life, assumed a bitterness that found no outlet on the Stage, and he grew morose. His marriage with Kitty Brookes broke up. His closest friend, Old Dan Lowrey, was dead. He drifted through the crowds alone. In October 1895 he tried in the shades of his Alhambra to cut his throat, failed and was taken to a Belfast Asylum. He recovered, grew a beard to hide the scar and returned to the Stage.

In September 1900, he was bankrupted to the sum of £2,450, and to meet the demand his little Theatre, The Belfast Alhambra, passed from his hands. His Dublin friends rallied round and presented him with a Benefit at The Lyric Theatre; it lasted five hours and featured more than thirty turns, among whom the Solid Man himself appeared, charming a packed House as he had done so many times before.

Further spells in the Asylum followed, but Ashcroft kept returning to the boards. He appeared at The Empire Palace (late Dan Lowrey's) May 1901, March 1905, October 1906, New Year's Eve 1907, in May and again at Christmas 1908. Actor Bramsby Williams says of the ageing Comedian: 'He had lost nothing. Whatever he might have been years earlier, he was still to me one of the greatest Artistes I have seen in fifty years and I have seen a few. . . . He was a genius.'

But there was no cure. On Wednesday 2 January 1918, he died in the Purdysburn Asylum. There was a large gathering at the funeral service, conducted by the Reverend Dr Murphy, Chaplain to the Actors' Union, at St George's Church, Belfast. 'An upright and a thoroughly religious man,' he said, 'which to some of the unco' guid may seem strange in a Comedian.'

Monday 14 December. Important Notice: Mr Lowrey has just received a telegram from America to state that Miss Mattie Lee Price the Magnetic Lady sails from New York to Dublin on the *Teutonic* on Wednesday next.

The *Teutonic* docked at Queenstown in Cork. To meet the Magnetic Lady Mr Lowrey and his Reception Party travelled by steam-train on the Great Southern Line; his party of invited guests included figures of Theatreland, Medicos, Gentlemen of the Press. At Queenstown, on the edge of the greylit Atlantic, they went out in the tender to meet the Magnetic Girl. The day was overcast but dry. The rails of the *Teutonic* were crowded: exiles returning for Christmas, hard-hatted businessmen, actresses *en route* for Europe, bewhiskered gentlemen in sealskin coats looking with misty eyes on the Island from which their parents had come. Flushed and smiling Miss Lee Price came aboard the tender and received a bouquet and a polite acclamation. At Mr Lowrey's request she there and then obliged with a demonstration. She made strong men helpless. The Press took enthusiastic notes.

'The Electric Kiss'. An early experiment in Animal Magnetism: the Lady is being charged while the Lover with hand on heart awaits the passionate spark. From a German woodcut.

Science was news and Electricity was just now the thing. It was to be the cause, the cure, the elucidation and the end of everything. And Miss Matilda Lee Price was full of it. She was from Georgia, slim, twenty-five, of medium height and extremely charming. But behind her frank American smile and trim little figure she possessed some very remarkable powers. She had only to lift a little finger to heave bulky gentlemen off their feet. A darker Age would have dropped her in the duckpond as a Witch; but in the enlightened Nineties such peculiar powers were referred to as Electrodynamics, and the unknown current in the fingers of Miss Mattie which could move mountains of flesh was put down to Animal Magnetism. She had caused many a shock back home, and had been touring North America for ten years displaying her attractions on the Stage.

On Christmas Eve 1891 the Georgia Magnet made her bow at The Star. Her Manager detailed her history, outlined the various psycho-electric theories put forward to account for the energy which shot from her person – 'a psychophysical fluid carried within the network of the human nerves – as in certain eels – origin of life – the Magnetic Poles – attraction, repulsion – Ying – Yang. Very likely the secret of the Universe.' The discovery of her gift, he said, dated back to childhood. Teachers and schoolmates were surprised at the odd things which happened to books, desks, and doors which she touched. She fingered nothing which she did not vitalise. She put a hand on a playmate's shoulder one day and the child was sent sprawling as if from the kick of a mule.

Gentlemen from the Stalls were invited to come on Stage and assist in the experiments. She made babes of them; even her lightest kiss was a knockout. Six men tugging were unable to move the Magnetic Lady. For finale she selected three of the heftiest, put them sitting on top of each other in a chair and to the great admiration of the House raised the entire load weighing over forty stone off the floor by the merest friction of her hands on the sides of the chair.

But Dan Lowrey's triumph was the Private Manifestation. Invitations were issued to a 'Committee of Inquiry' which consisted of the Lord Mayor and Members of the Corporation, Judges of the County Court, luminaries of the legal, medical and journalistic professions and the Savants of Trinity, to attend at a private examination of the Magnetic Lady. Superb publicity. Yet there was more to it than that as far as Dan was concerned; for apart from his personal interest in the latest Scientific Experiment there was the Great Showman's delight in his art and, more deep-seated than all, the pride of a grandson of poverty-stricken emigrants from Tipperary playing host to the Lord Mayor and the Bigwigs of the Town.

On St Stephen's Day, Michael Gunn's Pantomime at The Gaiety, *Ali Baba*, had a skit on the Female Magnet – 'a very good parody on the Magnetic Lady in which the composition of the Committee of Investigation is mercilessly ridiculed' – *Irish Independent.*

But no parody could picture the actual scene. The Manager 'speaking with grave decorum' introduced Miss Lee Price to the distinguished gathering and the experiments were proceeded with. An eyewitness records: 'Doctor Franks and Surgeon Thompson held an ordinary chair and pressed it down against the lady's palm. They were unable to move it and, in fact, Miss Price's countershove threw them off their balance.' There followed a curious experiment. She had three of the Committee of Inquiry go on their knees, raise their arms, grasping in their six hands a hickory stick along three-quarters of its length, leaving a quarter free. She placed a palm against the free end of the hickory and made it describe a large circle, while the rest of the stick remained immovable in the vicelike grip of the kneeling Experimenters. The part of the stick where the pivoting took place was found to be warped and twisted. Bearing in mind the nature of the hickory, they felt it was an incredible feat, 'except on the assumption that the girl by friction had charged the molecules of the timber with a magnetic force negatively opposed to the current which exuded from herself, hence the highly charged attraction'. The pretty Georgian's hands, scrutinised by Doctor Franks, bore no marks of pressure.

The Gay Nineties. Yet one cannot help thinking of those three earnest Fellows on their knees holding up the hickory stick for little Miss Price to finger it limp before the Lord Mayor and the Judges of the County Court.

CHAPTER SIXTEEN

1892 The War of the Halls

The War that had been smouldering between Lowrey and Michael Gunn now came to a climax. The House of Commons had appointed a Select Committee to inquire into the question of dramatic items in Music Halls, and sittings were fixed to begin in May. Lowrey opened the Year in a fighting mood.

In his New Year Address to the City he disclosed that plans for the reconstruction of The Star were already in the hands of a Dublin Architect. Not only would he produce Sketches and dramatic items, but he would also push his demand for the right to produce Opera Artistes and short Musicals from the Legitimate Stage.

It was going to be an all-out effort. To finance his extensions and to attract the kind of Stars he wanted, he enlisted the aid of Adam S. Findlater, one of the foremost among the Dublin masters of Commerce. The Findlater Company had been behind George West at The Grafton, and had long had an eye on The Star as a promising investment. Lowrey mortgaged the bulk of his property in Crampton Court to Findlater in order to finance his attack. It was done privately, but there are few secrets ever in Dublin. Gunn, fearful that Lowrey might break his monopoly and win the day, quietly planned to open a Music Hall of his own.

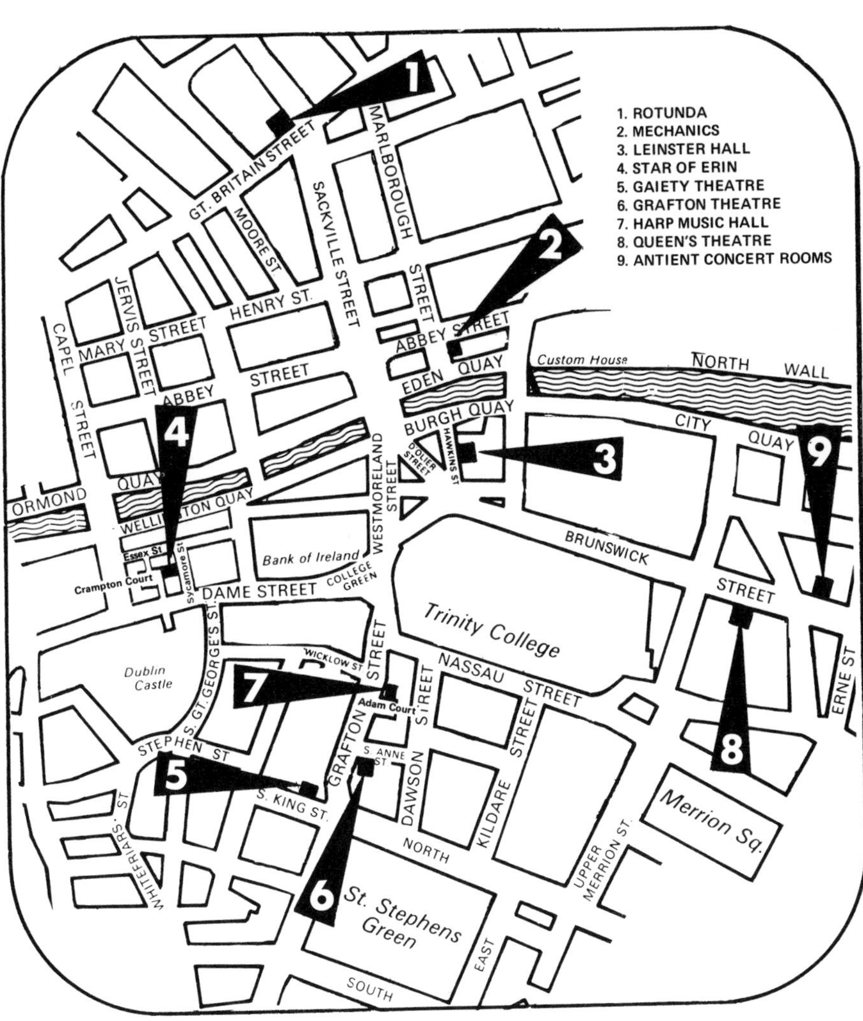

Sketch map of Dublin Theatreland during the War of the Halls

Among the Male Comics this Spring, Paul Pelham, from *Pick-Me-Up*

Now with money to spend, Lowrey secured and promoted the best in distinctive Music Hall items – those popular acts in a popular atmosphere which no large Fashion Theatre could achieve: the Male Comic and the Serio. He opened the Year with Lily Marney.

Lily was a true-blue Music Hall Serio, exploiting her own highly-flavoured individuality and bringing it through the successive stages of the Character she sang and acted. She made her own of Felix McGlennon's ballad, 'Hold Yer Head Up, Patsy McGann'. Opening, she is the Old Man advising his Young Hopeful:

Hold yer head up, Patsy McGann.
Hold yer head up like a man.
Sure if you let it down
There'll be trouble in the town. So –
Hold yer head up like a man, McGann!

Patsy-Lily passes through the lady-killing and dolling-up stage, and at last comes to grips with the problem of Woman:

He courted a girl called Bedelia O'Flarity,
Bedelia was shapely and tall,
She stood six feet something while poor little Patsy
He stood five feet nothing at all.
They got on alright till he wanted to kiss her,
He looked at her lips with a sigh:
Though he stood on his tiptoes he still couldn't reach her
She looked down and whispered him – Try. Ah –
Hold . . .

The Audience swayed and roared, 'Hold yer head up like a man, McGann!' Gunn's Gaiety could not compete with such an orgy of mass-participation.

The leading male Comic of these early months of 1892 was Tom Costello. Tom who had been throwing his voice and his weight around for years had now acquired the packet of songs which brought him right into the roar of the arena. Halls rang everywhere with his 'Comrades'. Audiences rocked in the rich waltzy sentiment – 'sharing each other's sor-rows, sharing each o-ther's joys' – dominated by Tom's great voice, his sturdy thirty-bob-a-week figure in shirtsleeves, braces hanging down.

Vance's primrose pantaloons, the smart frockcoat of Ashcroft – these were not for Tom. Claiming to have been born in Connemara, the son of a blacksmith and a laundry-girl, he projected himself as Birmingham Celtic and broadly down to earth. Tall, strong and handsome, he had made his début in Wolverhampton, sang in Dan's for the first time in 1887, then did America. Lacking the finesse of Ashcroft, the gentle charm of Pat Feeney, and using rather featureless material which projected nothing of his songful working-class self, he relied a shade too much on a gusto and a strength of voice which were easily parodied. Then came 'Comrades' and the shirt-sleeves. Thenceforth he was made.

Tom Browne, Felix McGlennon and other writers who had a finger on the public pulse supplied him with a sheaf of pathetics and humoresques that found their way into all the Albums – 'The Song that will Live Forever', 'At Trinity Church I Met my Doom', 'The One-Legged Family' – and a series of shirtsleeve studies – 'Father's Come Home with his Money Alright', 'He's in Regular Employment Now', 'Once More I Sent the Needful Eighteen Stamps' and 'His Funeral's Tomorrow':

My poor heart aches with sorrow.
I hit him once, that's all,
Then he heard the angels call –
And we're goin' to plant him tomorrow.

And as Tom Costello threw his weight about on Stage, Dan was bringing his to bear in the War of the Halls.

Gunn's plan was now made public. The Champion of Offenbach, Verdi, Goldsmith, Pinero and Shakespeare *à la mode* was now angling to black out Crampton Court by applying for a drink licence and building a Music Hall of his own alongside his Leinster Hall. This application would not be dealt with until the Autumn.

It was the intimate fusion of the Bars and Halls (the Tavern Theatre touch) which gave the Nightlife atmosphere to The Star, The Bijou, The Harp, an atmosphere which the 'fast' set was coming more and more to relish. If, in addition, Lowrey were allowed to gratify the taste for Opera and Drama, The Gaiety might well close down.

Lowrey needled Gunn all through April by advertising Operatic titbits by his Orchestra. This excellent group of musicians was now led by W. A. Millward who had a true theatrical flair, welcoming the Audience in with the Overture 'Poet and Peasant' and playing them out to the strains of 'Home Sweet Home'. This month he played selections from one of the most popular of Gaiety Operas, *La Bohème*.

On the eve of the Inquiry he engaged Arthur Lloyd with his son and their Touring Company to put on a series of Musical Sketches of the grand old Lion's own composition. Followed by the Trio of Glynn, Kelly & Bland in 'Fistic Burlesque' entitled *Police! or the Interrupted Prizefight*. The Lawmakers would have some fun trying to distinguish between a Drama and a Bareknuckle Burlesque.

Tom Costello in his Swank phase, from *Ariel*

5

Thursday 12 May. 'The Select Committee of the House of Commons appointed to take into consideration the Licensing & Control of Theatres and other places of Public Entertainment met yesterday under the Presidency of Rt Hon. D. Plunkett, First Commissioner of Works, when Mr Michael Gunn Proprietor & Manager of the Gaiety Theatre was examined.' – *Freeman's Journal.*

Mr Gunn's evidence was to the effect that under the Theatres Act of 1847 places of public entertainment had to have a special licence, under specific conditions, before they could stage a Play (Comedy, Tragedy, Farce, Opera, Burlesque, Burletta, Pantomime), and that the Music Halls (being still in essential a species of Tavern Theatre, closely connected with the consumption of alcohol, and with smoking allowed in the Auditorium) had not such a licence, and were not eligible for it. He stated that he had seen a Sketch called *The Burglar*, which had a cast of three and lasted about thirty minutes, performed at The Star. He added that in the National Theatre of Varieties, The Mechanics, the Manager had presented a sort of Pantomime and the Attorney-General had taken an action against him. This case, the Queen *v.* McNally, had been heard in December 1890. It was charged that McNally, lessee of The Mechanics, had staged *The Spirit of the Lake or Paddy Whack* on St Stephen's Day 1889; that it had run for thirty-eight nights, and that his House did not have a Patent under the Act to produce a Play, which this Pantomime was deemed to be. McNally was found guilty and, since the Act imposed a penalty of £300 for each such performance, he was ordered to pay penalties amounting to almost £11,000. The fine, it appears, was never paid. In fact, McNally replied a few days later with a military spectacle entitled *Rorke's Delight, or the Fight for the Colours!* Dublin might smile at the memory; but the colossal fine was a warning that the Royal Patent was no joke.

The Committee retired for some months to consider their verdict.

Dan's latest extension plans were passed by the Corporation. In June The Star was closed for rebuilding and business in the meantime was transferred to The Bijou in Anne Street, recently redecorated. It was a jewel indeed. All during June, July and well into August Dan Lowrey's hummed and sparkled there: lithe ladies walked on wire, Pedestallists pirouetted in mid-air, Acrobats catherined in wheels of colour, Birdie Brightling plucked the bickering banjo-strings, Rowley delivered his Cockney carollings, the Great Vento ventriloquised with a life-size figure of Lottie Collins scattering her limbs in 'Ta-ra-ra-boom-de-ay'. Sisters, Sisters and more Sisters stretched their legs to the gartermark in the Cachucha. Visitors sipping a Guinness or a bock in the Refreshment Bars might well think they had been transported to the Bar of the *Folies Bergère*. Horace Wheatley, launched on his long solo run, danced from the knees down, barely seeming to lift his feet from the ground. Sketch followed Prima Donna followed Tenor followed Feminine Panto-Acrobats in the quick-changing scene; American Specialties jostled Midland Clogdancers, Comics, Black Tit Bits; the House floated in waves of harmony, tobacco and alcohol, Serios sizzled, Jack Seebold and Lizzie Dent yodelled from Alpine peak to peak . . . Dan Lowrey's in Anne Street was the in-thing that Summertime.

The Supper Party Set, from *Pick-Me-Up*

In July Trinity College celebrated the Tercentenary of its foundation. The students staged a Play in The Gaiety interspersed with topical ballads of their own concoction. Among the famous names they introduced were Mahaffy, Traill, Palmer the mathematician, Carson the Tory lawyer, and – Dan Lowrey. These last two were picked for their dictatorial powers.

Dan's inclusion in such a constellation of Bigwigs shows how he had become a byword in Dublin, and in Trinity. He was on easy terms with many of the University lights, meeting them in the Clubs and in the Freemason Lodges (he was himself Grand Master of Lodge 101). Trinity dons were always invited to his Scientific Manifestations; and as for the students, they were among the most constant and most rumbustious of his customers. Even Divinity students were wont to disport themselves in the gods.

On the night following a Rugby match, especially if the College won, team and followers would descend upon The Star to celebrate and Dan, on the lookout for mischief-makers, often prowled through the House disguised in an old coat and tweed cap. The students' favourite sport was 'prigging' – swiping mirrors, jugs, tankards, juggler's balls, wigs, grease-paint, notice-boards, 'right under the nose of Dan' – trophies for their rooms. Norah relates: 'We had a very comfortable lounge in the Theatre, with nice armchairs, carpet, a fire in Winter and a coalbox. One night my Father noticed five students leaving with a hunchback amongst them. He said: "Just a moment, gentlemen!" and found the coalbox in the hump. This was going too far. He decided to send for the Police. They pleaded, he gave in, gave them a severe telling-off and let them go. Years later a clergyman appeared in his Office, smiling. "I was the hunchback," he said. "You were kind to me that night, Mr Lowrey, and saved my career!" '

The goodwill of Trinity was one of his greatest assets. As far as the University was concerned, the War of the Halls was won.

Hammer and saw went non-stop in the dust of demolition and reconstruction. Design: double the seating of the Auditorium without destroying the elegant style of the interior.

This time the Architect was James Joseph Farrall. Where O'Callaghan had been a Church Architect *par excellence*, Farrall was the top name in Commercial building. He was Consultant to all the leading Banks and business groups, and was employed in particular by Messrs Findlater in designing their many shops. He was a very wealthy man, possessed a fine tenor voice, and took a keen interest in Star investment possibilities – as did Adam Findlater.

To begin with Farrall removed all the partitions which separated the Bars from the Auditorium on each of the three floors, throwing the whole interior into one open area. Two tiers of Boxes were built, twelve in all, for the Supper-Party Set. Stalls, Pit and Galleries were extended. The seating capacity was now about 1,100, as against 600 in the old House. Orchestra Stalls held 280, the Pit Stalls, 174, the Boxes, 80, the First Gallery, 250, the Top Gallery, 280. Counting those standing in the Promenade, and those in the new Refreshment Rooms, the total capacity would now be 1,600.

The ground at the back of the Theatre towards the River, occupied by a large yard and stables, was purchased and a tall three-storey structure was erected on the site as an Annexe: this was to house the new Bars and Refreshment Rooms, two for the Ground Floor, one for each of the Galleries, all self-contained. In spite of rumours to the contrary, The Star was not going to revert to the status of a luxury Free-and-Easy; Dan made it clear to the papers that customers would not be allowed to carry drink into the Auditorium.

Kate Santley. The Divine Santley came to Dan's from Fashion Theatre and the Legitimate stage

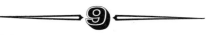

The stage area was enlarged by removing the dressing-rooms which had abutted onto it, and placing them above the Manager's Office towards Sycamore Street. Gaslight was retained in the starlights and gasaliers of Stage and Auditorium, but the new City Electricity was installed for footlights and corridors. This added fresh fascination.

The new-look Star was ready for the Dublin International Season, the Horse Show Week. The cost – £3,000.

Saturday 20 August. Grand Re-opening Night. Invited guests added tone to the occasion and all floors were sold out. The electric footlights added new depth and definition to the scene. The Hebes serving the drinks were in new high-necked gowns; doormen and attendants wore dark gold-braided uniforms with brass buttons. A special souvenir Programme was printed on pink silk, with Kate Santley Celebrated Burlesque Actress topping the Bill.

9

In presenting The Divina Kate Santley Dan was fairly flying the Dramatic and Operatic flag. Kate was a second Emily Soldene, an educated musician finding her feet in the circussy Opera of the early Fashion Theatre, and not averse to showing a leg in the Music Halls. She came to The Star trailing litanies of colourful acclaim, in Shakespeare, in Panto, Comic Opera and Opera Bouffe. The Orchestra Stalls and the new tiers of Boxes fluttered like dovecotes with the plaudits of white-gloved ladies, Gaiety clientele, lured to Dan's in the sacred name of Kate.

The Santley was no chick now. She seems to have been born in Germany about 1837 but her family emigrated to South Carolina where she was educated. During the Civil War, when she was in her early twenties, she came to England, earned her keep as a professional musician and educated herself for the Legitimate Stage. Her chance came with Charles Kean's Shakespeare Revival; she made her début in Edinburgh as Ophelia, then played Jessica to Kean's Shylock.

Soon she put a foot across the fence into Illegit at The Oxford Music Hall, creating a furore as a flustered kitchenmaid singing 'The Bell Goes A-Ringin' for Sair-ah!'. As Peri in the Drury Lane Panto *Beauty and the Beast* she stole the show, and thenceforth she was offered one part after another. Her next move was to undertake the management of The Old Royalty Theatre in Dean Street, Soho, and in seven years she had saved enough money to buy the lease. Here she produced an Indian Comic Opera, *Vetch*, with herself in the title-role, and it was a rage. In March 1886 Michael Gunn brought the fetching divinity and her *Vetch* to his Gaiety.

Now, in 1892, still game for an adventure at a reasonable fee, she accepted the invitation to Dan's. Eternally slim, provocative, dipped in the witchery of *Vetch*, King Carrot and Cunegunde, she was adorable. Her voice, never outstanding, was beautifully controlled – she was not of those who had more leg than larynx – and her arias, dramatesques, popular numbers and choice bits of Operatic buffoonery were rapturously received.

Dan, in full evening attire, watching, seeing all classes happy under his roof, had a vision of what he might achieve. Already he had phrased it: 'A National Theatre of Ireland. Companion piece to a National Parliament. And a National University.'

10

As well as exotics like the Santley, the new Audiences venturing to Crampton Court were treated now to the best in international Serios and Comics. Compared with the dearth of the previous Year, a single month now saw Bonnie Kate Harvey, Marie Loftus, and the rejuvenated Charles Coburn.

Belonging to a similar stratum of popular culture were the 'Enchantments'. Chief Enchantment of the Year was Monsieur Guibal the Thought-Reader. Guibal had been Professor of French in a girls' school in Dublin before taking to the Stage in his mystifying act of thought transmission. He had a hypnotic presence, and how much of his act was due to common conjuring and how much to psychic powers no one could ever tell. Como the Dublin Mystagogue was his pupil. One night at The Star, lost in concentration on the Frenchman's act, poor Como slumped in his seat and died of heart failure.

This kind of psychic spiritism was in vogue again. Earlier in the Century, in the wake of Darwin and the Scientists, it had been hooted off the Stage by the atheistic Moderns as antiquated mumbo-jumbo, and had been cheered by the Spiritists who still believed in an Unseen World. An act of this kind put on by the Brothers Davenport in Liverpool in 1865 led to a riot; the clamouring factions, Moderns versus Spiritists, practically wrecked the Theatre, and certainly wrecked the Davenports' English career.

The Nineties took a different view. Telepathy and suchlike extra-sensory phenomena must have a 'scientific' explanation. The cause of course was Electricity. Guibal at Dan's was careful to explain that the new 'energy' which he had discovered was 'an influence, an inflowing and out-flowing current, which the mind may become attuned to and learn to control'. He performed in conjunction with Miss Greville, whom he hypnotised, and the effect was weird. In a twilit House the lady all in a glimmer of white looked like the sleepwalking Lady Macbeth, moving among the Audience and chilling all to silence. In this trance both her mind and body seemed absolutely under Guibal's control, and she performed any action whispered to him by members of the Audience.

Such an attraction was pure Music Hall, intimate and Lowreyesque. The Gaiety had no answer to this kind of primitive magic actually taking place on the floor of the Hall.

On 19 August the House of Commons Committee published its Report. It recommended, in brief, that short Sketches which were not pieces taken from the Legitimate Stage might be allowed in Music Halls. But the War had gone far beyond the question of Sketches. In billing Kate Santley, Lowrey showed Gunn, the House of Commons, and whomsoever else it might concern, that he was determined to produce what he liked, from Drama, from Opera, and from the comic sensuals called 'Pantomime' and 'Musical Comedy' in Fashion Theatre. He had the bulk of the Press, the University, the Garrison, the growing Commercial interest and the horde of Lowreyites behind him. But Gunn had the Law and the Attorney-General on his side, and the Lawmakers had small love for democracy or for the dangerous notion of a People's Theatre.

Michael Gunn, Proprietor and Manager of The Gaiety Theatre

12

In October Michael Gunn's Application for a six-day Licence in respect of his proposed Music Hall in Hawkins Street came before the Court of the Recorder. Edward Carson, Q.C., appearing for Mr Gunn said the Hall would cost £15,000 and would be of the finest quality and well-conducted. He applied for a Licence to serve drink all over the House, including the Auditorium, where customers might rest their glasses on ledges affixed to the backs of the seats. This was out-Lowreying Lowrey.

The Application was opposed by the Police, by various Church bodies, by three Temperance Societies, by the Coffee Palace Association, by Mr Daniel Lowrey and Mr Patrick Kinsella.

Among precedents for such a Licence, Mr Carson instanced The Harp. 'The gold-mine!' muttered Mr Kinsella. (Laughter.)

Summing up after long argument the Recorder waxed eloquent. He asked if there was not a danger to the bloom of female modesty in such a proposed mixture of young men and maidens, smoke and intoxicants. No such licence, he said, had been granted in England in recent years; a large number of such had in fact been refused. Mr Lowrey had assured him that he found his Hall could pay on its merits alone, with the licence for Refreshment Bars outside the Auditorium. For this and for many other reasons, legal and moral, he must refuse Mr Gunn's Application.

Norah Lowrey's account is less eloquent: 'He told Michael Gunn to stick to his own business.'

13

Following this victory, in November, Dan booked Charles Godfrey. Godfrey was an Actor who had solved the problem of turning Legitimate Drama into Music Hall fare in a way which left the Law helpless to interfere. Born in Southwark about 1857, he got his first smell of greasepaint when he worked as a waiter in The Surrey. He served his time as Actor in obscure Halls, Saloon Theatres, and on tour with fit-ups, general utility man, giving potted versions of *Hamlet* and *Sweeney Todd the Demon Barber*. Quick to learn, he seized on this idea of 'potted Legit', a melodramatic narrative sung, acted and monologued as a one-man Play.

He tells how he made his first essay in Luby's Music Hall with a song-monologue, *Poor Old Benjamin the Workhouse Man*. He developed this into what he called a Song-Scena. A Tramp comes looking for a night's shelter at the Workhouse Casual Ward. The Janitor appears jangling his bumbledom keys:

> *Janitor* (*Godfrey*): *Be off, you tramp! You are not wanted here.*
> *Tramp* (*Godfrey*): *No. I am not wanted here. But at Balaclava, I was wanted there!*

The Hall exploded. The mass Audience, identifying with the ragged and wretched veteran of the Charge at Balaclava, erupted into a howl of applause. Authority intervened. Officers of the Household Brigade objected. Unwise to incite the masses. Bad for Recruiting. Managers were warned to cut the scene. Godfrey overnight found himself Number One Turk of the time.

His Song-Scenas became a must in the Halls. Some were of his own composing, many were contributed by Le Brunn, Harrington, Wal Pink. Most were of a military kind giving full scope to his commanding personality, and of a sort to smooth the ruffled whiskers of the Household Brigade – 'Nelson', 'Balaclava', 'The Last Shot', 'Inkermann' – all with staging and scenic effects, costume, make-up, lighting, props. Managers of Legit had to grin and bear it: a Song-Scena could hardly be prosecuted as Drama under the Act.

The Great Actor-Vocalist liked living it up. He grew careless, took to drink, arrived merry and late for engagements, band-parts missing, costume and props left behind at some tavern *en route*. The Artiste seemed to live in the lurid light of one of his own Song-Scenas. A highbrow Critic, asked about a Godfrey number, said he had never heard of it; next morning Godfrey hired forty-six street-organs to play the tune under his window.

Dan Lowrey to cap his triumphal Year billed Godfrey in his latest Scenas. Consternation. He arrived for rehearsal with one eye half-shut and one half-open, no music, no costumes, no scenery, all left behind in his trunks 'somewhere in Liverpool'. A hectic search through the music shops turned up some of his older pothouse poetics, and the Great Actor staggered on Stage that night giving an unimaginably realistic rendering of –

Hi-tiddly-hi-ti
I'm – orl – ri'!

Mr Lowrey's thoughts on the occasion are not recorded.

The long Year ending, Dan with Jeannie and Daniel the Third sat in the Office to draft the Christmas bombshell: Miss Cora Stuart, in the Fashionable One-Act Musical Comedy *The Fair Equestrienne*. Not only was Cora one of the most fetching figures of Fashion Theatre but she had played *The Fair Equestrienne* at Gunn's Gaiety only two years before.

Lowrey lost that round. The House was packed for the Matinée on St Stephen's Day. No Cora. Mr Lowrey appeared on Stage, very solemn, and read aloud the letter he had received on Christmas Day from Gunn's Solicitor:

> Dear Sir:
> Mr Gunn, patentee of The Gaiety Theatre, instructs me to draw your attention to the fact that your intended performance at your Theatre of Varieties being of the nature of a Stage Play, will be a clear infringement of patent rights, and also illegal. So that not only are the patentees entitled to interfere, but any member of the public can put the Attorney-General in motion . . . Mr Gunn trusts that you will not permit any performance which would necessitate the Law being put into motion.
> Yours faithfully, etc.

Mr Lowrey said that he had engaged Miss Stuart at £60 a week, that at that moment she was with her cast in his Office, and that he would take immediate steps to ensure that her admirers would not be disappointed. Meanwhile the Audience had to make do with the Boxing Kangaroo.

The *Evening Telegraph* carried the full story. Michael Gunn had the article reprinted and inserted into the Programme of his Gaiety Christmas Pantomime, headed, 'A "Star" Star Stopped!'

CHAPTER SEVENTEEN

1893 Pinnacle

Dan withdrew the piece, but he had no intention of withdrawing Cora Stuart. In a scurry of effort a new Musical entitled *A Dress Rehearsal* was rehearsed and substituted. Cora at thirty-seven was still a considerable Circe and bewitched an overflow House. Rarefied perfume from Box and Stall was wafted up to the Galleries while Mr Lowrey in swallowtail smiled on the scene.

The tale of Michael Gunn's Christmas Letter was given wide publicity. Mr Lowrey wrote to the *Times* to say he was sending out invitations to a Free Show, an afternoon performance of the disputed piece, *The Fair Equestrienne*, with the divine Cora in the lead as Lady Kitty Clare, full score and wardrobe. The carriages rolled up in the bleak winter daylight. Gunn fumed. He could not prevent Lowrey from having his friends to a Free Show. The Town thought it a great joke, and that was all that was needed. Dublin finance was convinced it was high time to move into Crampton Court.

With characteristic attack Dan now billed the nattiest of the Nineties Naughties, Miss Fanny Leslie, in a new Musical Sketch, *The Tyrant Love*. Fanny was a Cora Stuart with a difference. Wide of face and hip, in skimpy blouse and knickers, she was a very fetching, fashionable and feminine buffoon. English born, début in America, back home as a Serio, then into Musicals and Fashion Burlesque.

The new Star was too small to contain all her worshippers. *The Tyrant Love* was specially designed to display the essential Fanny in a whole cluster of comic incarnations, showing her beauteous bounce and bump, her footwork, her guitaristics, her splits. It wasn't exactly illegal, but many were glad it was dark as they hurried to The Star to see Fanny in *Love*.

More in the Music Hall tradition was Marie Kendall (May), then in the first bloom of her long career. A rage of the Nineties, Marie was a brilliant low comedienne with a flair for the sauciest hits and hats, song-talking to the People in their own tongue in true Tavern Theatre style – 'My Old Man is One of the Boys and I am One of the Girls'. Figure trim and flitsome as a dragonfly, small serious face with close-set eyes, voice radiating her own sharp self, she personified the Grand Old Days of cold water in the dressing-rooms and the camaraderie of the road. Her personality, undisguised and outgoing (secret of all the great Comics and Serios) still rings in her words: 'It was plain honest vulgarity, like Hampstead Heath on a Bank Holiday.' 'Warm, happy, intensely human atmosphere.' 'We would be booked for just one week, sort of on approval. The first Friday evening was always one for excitement; we girls had no separate dressing rooms, we all used the one big one, and as each turn came off we would all buzz round and ask: "Have you got your notice?" that is, have you been told you will not be wanted next week?' 'To visit every Town was just like going home. The Orchestra began to play your music, your number went up in the frame, the turn before yours coming off would say "Nice House tonight, Marie". And you went on and . . . there they were.' (From an interview with *T.V. Mirror* much later.)

That sense of belonging, that identification of the Artiste with Audience, was to reach its pinnacle with Leno and Marie Lloyd.

These new times brought new Chicks. John Tiller, a Manchester man with a seat on the Cotton Exchange, gave his spare time to organising concerts. Using the know-how acquired in Cotton he trained a bevy of girls to sing and dance in concord. The combination of strict training and the natural zest of the girls gave new life to the ancient art and soon the professional Halls were crying out for Tiller Girls. In 1890 the Cotton Man opened a school of dancing to keep up the supply. At Dan's their sparkling song-and-knicker act sent them, legs, laughs and lingerie, to the top of the Bill. It was another notch in the breakaway exhibitionism of the Nineties. Innocent maidens from the waist up, 'they display a considerable ability in revealing that portion of the feminine attire which goes in twos' – *Pick-Me-Up*.

As a final move in the game of putting Dan's on the theatrical map (before The Star Company shares were put on offer to the money-men), the *Irish Times* arranged for an interview with Mr Lowrey and published it in their *Weekly* on Saturday 3 June:

> The dingy days of the penny gaff, the shouting Lion Comique, the broken-stringed piano, the cracked-voice patter vocalist, the tawdry, low-bosomed highskirted cantatrice, the thundering gallery chorus, the gibing pit, the straggling lights, dense clouds of smoke, pounding of pewters, the brutal badinage, the roars, the rips, the ructions – all that has changed. The Music Hall is now a rival of the Playhouse of today.
>
> I passed down the Court, entered the Vestibule, inquired for the High

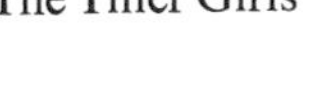

The Tiller Girls

Priest. Devotions were in full flow. Mr Lowrey led me to the Sanctum and sat me in a comfortable armchair.

– This House was not always called The Star? – Oh dear no. It used to be called The Monster Saloon. The proprietress was a Mrs Connell.

– Do you think the Music Hall has now reached the height of its perfection? – No-o, said Mr L. with an intonation which cold print cannot convey. – The Music Hall is only in its infancy. I contend that it will pass the Theatre by and by.

– Is the Hall coming more into vogue among respectable and intelligent people? – Undoubtedly. Concert-hall people are increasing every year. And take the fair sex, when would you see a lady in a Music Hall a few years ago? well, they come here now and are exceedingly delighted.

– When does your House close? – At a quarter to eleven.

– What have you to say of your Audience? – Everything that's kind. There is not and never was a better behaved Audience in the United Kingdom.

– On what line of amusement do you most depend? – All-round Variety to please all parties.

– A last matter, Mr Lowrey, is this concern going to be floated as a Limited Liability Company? – It is. The Prospectus will be out at the end of next week.

The genial proprietor then showed me round from floor to floor,

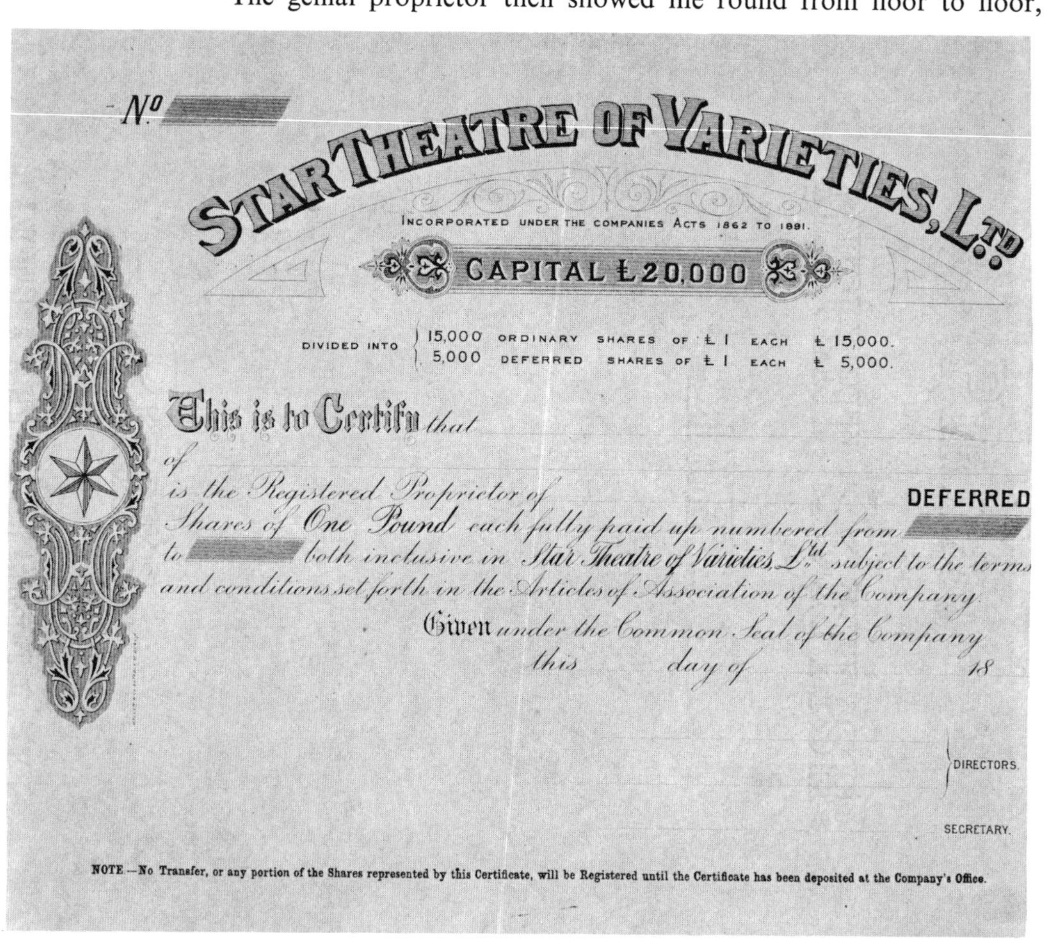

No.

STAR THEATRE OF VARIETIES, LTD.

INCORPORATED UNDER THE COMPANIES ACTS 1862 TO 1891.

CAPITAL £20,000

DIVIDED INTO 15,000 ORDINARY SHARES OF £1 EACH £15,000.
5,000 DEFERRED SHARES OF £1 EACH £5,000.

This is to Certify that
of
is the Registered Proprietor of DEFERRED
Shares of One Pound each fully paid up numbered from
to both inclusive in Star Theatre of Varieties, Ltd. subject to the terms and conditions set forth in the Articles of Association of the Company.

Given under the Common Seal of the Company
this day of 18

DIRECTORS.

SECRETARY.

NOTE.—No Transfer, or any portion of the Shares represented by this Certificate, will be Registered until the Certificate has been deposited at the Company's Office.

Shares Certificate of The Star Theatre Company

surprising me not a little by the spacious corridors and commodious exits, the wide galleries, the elegance and finish of the appointments. My guide paused on one of the lobbies to point out a fine oilpainting of his Father in the character of 'The Whistlin' Thief', and others of him in the roles of 'Emigrant Departing' and 'Emigrant Returned'. After a handshake I turned homeward at the unlit end of a not half-bad cigar.

Adam Seaton Findlater, Chairman of The Star Company

That week the Accountants estimated the total net profits for the current Year as £3,296. The Star as a going concern, including Bar and Theatre fittings, was valued at £20,400.

The prospectus of The Star Theatre of Varieties Company (Limited) was published on Saturday. Board of Directors: Chairman, Adam Seaton Findlater, M.A., J.P., of Alexander Findlater & Co. Wine & Provision Merchants; John J. Farrall, Architect; Thomas Ritchie, Wine Merchant. Managing Director, Daniel Lowrey. The new Company had a capital of £20,000, divided into 15,000 Ordinary Shares of £1 paying a dividend of 12½ per cent, and £5,000 worth of Deferred Shares paying a similar dividend.

Lowrey in effect had sold the Theatre to the Company for £19,000, taking £14,000 in cash, and £5,000 in Deferred Shares, agreeing to accept no interest on these until a dividend had been paid to the buyers of Ordinary Shares. Out of the cash received, he had to pay off all debts and mortgages on the premises (amounting to over £7,000). In addition, he would receive a salary as Managing Director.

The Chairman of the new Board, Adam S. Findlater, was an ambitious young financier, a man of wide reading and intellectual power, square-headed, bearded in the imperial style, a merchant prince of the Nineties, Chairman of the Kingstown Harbour Commissioners, of the Port & Docks Board, of the Dublin Chamber of Commerce, patron of the arts, a firm upholder of the political Union, a genial man in Town. Dan Lowrey, son of the illiterate Whistlin' Thief, was perhaps rather dazzled.

'My Father was a fool in business,' says Norah. Her story is that the Lowrey Family were against the sale to the Syndicate, but that Dan was blinded by the lure of the big money and sold his birthright for a seat on the Syndicate Board.

On the other hand, Dan was now at the peak of his form. He had recently married his third wife, Edith Adams, and was buoyantly planning a new life, private and public. The Syndicate would enable him to expand The Star, move in the direction of his 'National Theatre of Ireland', and send branches out into Belfast and Cork. Yet Norah was probably essentially correct in her view. The Star would remain 'Dan's' while he remained at the helm; but there was no question that the old Family flavour which had been a creative force in Music Hall (indeed as Marie Kendall suggests, it was the breath of life in People's Theatre) began to evaporate from this thirteenth day of June, 1893. The shareholders' eyes were fixed on Profits; they had no real feeling for Theatre.

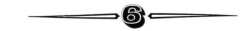

The first sign of the new wind blowing at Dan's was the engagement in

Bessie in Pants, from *Pick-Me-Up*

September of Bessie Bellwood. 'One of the most charming and cultivated women you could meet, on certain occasions, and on others it was positively dangerous to be in her company' – Arthur Roberts. 'The saucy, slangful Serio' – Newton. The Cockney carollings of Vance, Coburn, Rowley, and even of Arthur Lloyd, were fashionable because they were at one remove from the raw life of the London street: the true Cockney character was felt to be too primitive, too close to the knuckle for fashionable consumption, until the growing taste for Naturalism and the 'Folk' brought native speakers like Jenny Hill and the uninhibited Bessie Bellwood into the limelight.

Bessie, of Irish parentage, born Eliza Anna Katherine O'Mahoney, claiming to be descended from Father Prout the Poet, daughter of a rabbit-skinner in the New Cut, was a woman of boundless generosity who often spent the last penny of her earnings on Masses for some soul desperate or dead – often for those 'wot 'ad done 'er a bit of no good'. Once after a charming tête-à-tête with Cardinal Manning to plan a Catholic charity, she was arrested for beating a cabman over the head with an umbrella.

A Cockney Irish Roman Catholic, she brought to the Stage all the sizzling vitality and biting humour of the slum, sang Irish ballads in her early teens at obscure saloons, and knifed her way via The Winchester into the West End with searing Cockney studies – 'Aubrey Plantagenet', 'The Barmaid', 'Whoa, Emma!' and, her most ethnic hit, 'Wot Cheer Ria?' – delivered in a tone and tongue which was half-way between the cheeky chirping of a street sparrow and the cut of a saw.

She had often come to George West's Grafton in the Eighties. 'Bessie Bellwood is the very – beg pardon – draws well. She'd make her fortune on the boards as a low – a very low – comedienne.' – *Pat*. It is notable that Dan never engaged her for The Star until after the Syndicate had taken over.

She went on her tempestuous way, one of the most explosive forces of the Nineties, and died burnt out in 1896, aged thirty-nine.

This time of change also saw the last appearance of Pat Kinsella in The Star. Thence we may track his footsteps in old programmes through the Decade, drolling here, fusiliering there, in Solo, Panto, Burlesque. His last marked appearance was at The Empire Palace in Dame Street in 1899, when he 'encountered a warm reception and demonstrated that, to use his own phrase, he is not played out' – *Times*. Old music hall-goers say they saw him, again at The Empire, one night in the New Century when he stood in for Harry Lauder.

Pat held the little Harp until 1893 when, in a fit of depression following the sudden death of his son, he let the business lapse. The Harp was never used as a Music Hall again; it lay idle for some years and then became The Empire Buffet.

After the whacking comic verve of his Bob Martin songs, Pat's greatest creation was Conn in Boucicault's *The Shaughran*. In the mid-Nineties he is found playing it (quite illegally) in The Mechanics, before it became The Abbey Theatre. An old-timer in the *Evening Telegraph* in 1915 remembers:

The dressing-rooms which were under the stage were of a terrible character.

There were no sanitary arrangements and everything was filthy. The rats – beautiful ones from the Liffey and from the Morgue – used to make short work of the artistes' greasepaint. This dressing emporium was reached by a broken ladder and a small trapdoor through which you would have to squeeze yourself, but if you were after eating a hearty dinner then you would never go through the hole. This was the position in which Pat Kinsella found himself.

Pat was appearing at a Benefit and arrived late. He made a rush for the hole and got stuck. The artistes downstairs couldn't get up and nobody could get down. It was an extraordinary crux – the audience were hissing and booing at being kept waiting – till at last Pat was liberated.

His language at the condition of the stage was strong, yet in his own theatre, The Harp, when the back curtain would be up, to cross from one side of the stage to the other the performer would have to climb to the roof of the theatre and walk across the slates and down a forty-foot ladder to the other side of the stage.

The death of his son took the comic heart out of him. 'He apparently lost all interest in the affairs of life. The strong, hale, hearty man collapsed for a time into a mere shadow of his former self. He relinquished The Harp Theatre and once more sought his fortune on the boards. Success did not exactly smile on him. He manfully struggled against bitter fate and at last resolved to try what was in store for him in Liverpool. In that city on the Mersey he has just breathed his last' – *Telegraph*, 4 May 1906.

'A quick run down to the foots, a roll like a drum with his feet, his leg raised and brought down with a loud clap from the foot.' Leno has arrived.

We see the small strained face, the eyes are infinitely sad, brows quirked up in pained surprise, garments too big, the body is frail and delicate – the face flickers into song, something about a Shop, voice and legs are one interlacing anxious pattern – 'Walk this way!' – if the legs would only cease their contortions we might hear, voice low, husky, flat a's, rolled r's – 'a grraand displaay' – Cockney? no, it's Irish, no, it runs too fast for Dublin ears, until we become attuned to the chorus:

Walk this way! Walk this way!
The Sales are on, we've a grand display.
Upon me word we're giving them away –
Step this way, Madam, walk this way!

Applause polite, puzzled. The wide mouth seems to grin under the superfine hat which keeps engulfing the twinkling tragic eyes. Star packed on an October night and a throng of latecomers disconsolate in the street, for this little man is Leno and Mr Lowrey is paying him £100 a week.

A starched collar and shirtfront causes him trouble all the time and he fights them desperately, worry in his eyes. One can sense the tense spirit of the poor scrap of humanity paid to keep up a shopocracy front, the

Leno in the Dumps, from *Pick-Me-Up*

grim determination to be a go-getter. Stalls and Galleries feel strangely uneasy – if this is a comedian – but he is off again like a demon – 'Never more!' he breathes in hoarse determination, same tone with subtle change of Mask, seems he is not going to the Seaside ever any more, not on your nanny, no, the flickering feet will not stay still, gripped in a frustration on the edge of mania, he is chattering now, a kind of vocal seizure:

> *Fish! Everything was fish, when I left that place I'd scales on me. Y'see I'd no right to go to the seaside, with the family I've got it costs money, had to draw cash – out of the child's moneybox. Y'know a family like mine is no joke, eight childer and two boys. And the Wife . . . she's very much larger than I am, not that I want to say anything against her 'cos whatever my Wife is she's my Wife, oh yes, she's – My – Wife! Sure, I wish she wasn't, but there y'are. She's. My. Wife!*

Light laughter, the Audience is uneasy, unnerved by this fierce compulsion to do the right thing by the Wife, in spite of the flaming hatred he all too clearly reveals. This is not Ashcroft, nor Vance nor Arthur Lloyd; there is some intense hysteria in the fragile figure, some demon driving him.

Born at No. 4 Eve's Court, St Pancras in 1860, the child of Mrs & Irish Johnny Wilde, and christened George, the little bundle was left in a chest-of-drawers to sleep in dim lodgings while the parent pair were playing the boards of oil-lamp saloons. His father died and a new 'Dad' took him out to earn, pale and puny, at the Cosmetheka Hall, Paddington: Little George the Infant Wonder, Contortionist & Posturer. 'Dad' called him Leno, his own itinerant name, and a misprint on a playbill changed 'George' to 'Dan' – nothing would stay still, not even his own name. All his childhood was on the move, shifting landscapes, railway stations, ocean waves. The Leno Family on Tour: 'Dad', Mother, Dan & brother Jack, lodging in box-room after box-room where the child was trained to sing, clog-dance, shuffle in flapshoes, earn, earn.

As a boy he walked the streets of Dublin in a white hat shaped like a basin and a pair of elastic boots which he shared with his Mother – unless he wore his clogs the two of them couldn't walk out together. The tune of the Dublin voice fell on his ears, stirred dim memories of his dead Father; he listened avidly and learned the intonation in a pathetic attempt to identify, and belong somewhere. Made his first solo appearance as Dan Patrick Leno, Descriptive & Irish Character Vocalist . . .

In Belfast, in a hole-and-corner dressing-room, a man from the Audience pushed his way past the curtain calling: 'Where is this boy?' Terrified, greasepaint off, the pale little sparrowface confronted the great beard and authoritative eyes. The man laid a hand on his shoulder, saying: 'Boy, you are going to be a great Artiste.' When he had gone the awed whisper went round: 'Charles Dickens!'

His education proceeded: backstage, the street, the pawnshop, the technique sharpened by poverty, the grinding round.

At twenty-three he won the World Championship & Silver Belt as a Clogdancer, Midland style. Tasting his first success, he married Lydia Reynolds, Serio, and the pair went from their bit of a tavern breakfast to play the little halls together. At the end of two years they had penetrated to the London suburbs. Here no Clogdancers need apply, so Dan turned Comedian, a fiver-a-weeker. In 'Going to Buy Milk for the Twins' he appeared as a scat nurserymaid that might have strayed out of Dickens but came in fact from his own sharp knowledge of a woman's life. With a big bucket on each arm she broke into a chatter of patter, a vocal St Vitus Dance, every now and again recollecting herself she would jerk into the refrain, 'Going to Buy . . .'

At The Pavilion, the Centre of the World, this lean wolf rapidly became the bony embodiment of the timeless English Clown. This is a comic energy which springs again and again from wild roots in English earth (Tarleton in Shakespeare's day, Joe Grimaldi, Leybourne, Leno, Chaplin . . .), subtly different from all other Fools on earth. With him, the Audience identifies with some stark reality behind the clowning. As he wrestles with the Starched Front that continues to spring from its moorings, Stalls and Galleries sense a tragic frustration that is their own frustration. Inadequate Leno drew men and women like a magnet.

At Christmas 1886, Harris, always quick, engaged the pale fellow with the wrinkled brow in the Drury Lane Panto *Babes in the Wood*; as the daft Baroness he drew such crowds to the Lane that the Panto roared on into April. He stepped at once into the shoes of Joe Grimaldi and for fifteen consecutive years played Panto there. Christmas for many meant Dan Leno.

Dan in himself and in his art laid bare the fusty makeshift behind the brave façade of the times. This was the pith and the pinnacle of Music Hall. He gave a glimpse of the grim understructure of life out of which Music Hall as a People's Saturnalia emerged. He was a disruptive force, like Ada Lundberg, too close to the lunacy of actual living for a Dublin Audience innured to the more romantic humours of an Ashcroft or a Pat Kinsella. The English, attuned to the bite of their own tongue, loved him as Clown. 'He not only made you laugh, but broke your heart.' – Ethel Barrymore. The Irish, who often use language and the theatre as an escape from fact, were less enthusiastic. 'Dismally futile,' wrote the Drama Critic of the *Saturday Review*, a Dubliner, one Bernard Shaw.

Leno went through a myriad of incarnations, a whole spectrum of life, from the Recruiting Sergeant and the Shopwalker to the Railway Guard, the Anatomy Professor, the Highland Chief; a gaggle of females, past their girlbloom mostly, each distracted in a subtly different way, all garrulous. And alone on the Stage he surrounded himself with a host of imaginary people, talked to them, answered them back, one would have sworn they were there. Persuasive creation:

Y' See we had a row and it was all through Mrs Kelly.
Y'know Mrs Kelly of course. Mrs Kelly? Ah y'know Mrs Kelly,
you must know Mrs Kelly. Good life-a-night don't look so simple,
she's a cousin of Mrs Niplet's and her husband keeps the what-not
shop in the – ah, y'must know Mrs Kelly. Everybody knows
Mrs Kelly –

She pops up in all sorts of places, he has given her life. A life of babies' nappies, dumbtits, Sunday suits, visits to the Threeball counter, the pewter pint, smells of cabbage on stairways, cheap lodgings, the birdcage, lonely men in shirtsleeves leaning on Summer windowsills, a string of tired children wailing to be carried home from the Sea, a maul at the bargain basement, bumbailiffs come for the three-piece suite, suicide, heartburn, gazing at the Guards at Buckingham Palace, singing the Year out with

Leno in a Manic Mood, from *Pick-Me-Up*

The Clown at Home

'Auld Lang Syne', fill them up again, and what in the name of luv-almighty have we left to pop to pay the Doc for your appendix . . .

He had a modern house with marbles and bronze horses and tiger-rugs for Lydia and the children, but his materials never changed, nor the man either. He never ceased learning, couldn't; the figure of 'Dad' seemed always to be hounding him on. He sketched on the backs of envelopes, anywhere, thumbnail prints of the shifting phantasmagoria of faces life was to him. He never ceased to scribble a kind of compulsive talking nonsense, but a nonsense which betrays a master of the common tongue. Those close to him tell how hard he worked to develop some such germ of a notion into one of his Christmas characters or one of his Music Hall legomaniacs. The little bundle of body in the clothes grew frailer, ethereal almost, consumed by the demon driving it.

He visits America, fails completely, something as yet quite out of their ken. Dublin is attracted, repelled. 'I saw him,' says Norah Lowrey. 'He went down very well, but he was not the draw my Father expected he would be.'

He had one burning ambition: he persistently asked Beerbohm Tree to let him play in Shakespeare. Poor Dan, thought Tree, he doesn't realise that Shakespeare is Literature. Poor brilliant Tree, how dull he was really; Leno as Bottom in the *Dream* would have run forever.

When the dashing Prince of Wales succeeded to the Throne as grave Edward VII one of his first acts was to command Leno to Sandringham. The little man was terrified. Royalty face to face! His Imperial Majesty presented him with a tiepin set in diamonds in the shape of an E, surmounted by the Crown. King. In the same year, 1901, he published *Dan Leno Hys Book*, a collection of his sketches and storyscraps. Thinking of his birthplace, Eve Court, long since swallowed up in the great Terminus, he wrote: 'Here I spent my happy childhood hours. Ah, what is Man? Wherefore does he why? Whence did he whence? Whither is he whithering? – Then the Guard yelled out: "Leicester, Derby, Nottingham, Manchester, Liverpool!" '

The mists began to settle over his mind. Still haunted by his visit to Sandringham, the poor Clown began to confer knighthoods upon all and sundry. He gazed for hours at his Tiepin, and signed his name like a Duke: Leno. He died at Hallowe'en 1904. The funeral of the little bundle of Cockney Irish bones was the Event of the Year. All England mourned. Papers published long lists of the wreaths and the inscriptions. Marie Lloyd: 'Sleep well old pal.'

CHAPTER EIGHTEEN

1894 The Other Eye

1

The required capital for the new Star Theatre had been subscribed almost four times over. The first sign of this new prosperity was the succession of sparkling Serios; Dublin swayed to the dulcet rhythms of Lily Burnand, irresistible in:

Two little girls in blue, lad,
Two little girls in blue.
They were sisters, we were brothers
And learned to love the two.
And one little girl in blue, lad,
Who won your father's heart
Became your mother, I married the other –
But now we have drifted apart.

1894 also saw Kate Carney, raucous and robust as a barrel of apples,

Kate Chard, from *Pearson's Portfolio of Footlight Favourites*

and the exquisitely comic Vesta Victoria, followed by Bonnie Kate Harvey, Lily Marney and Kate Chard. Photos of Kate Chard had a wide sale and were featured in the glossy portfolios. She was something to look at, and worth hearing too; Opera lovers flocked to the Court for she had been with the Carl Rosa Company and had created the role of Lady Psyche in Gilbert & Sullivan's *Princess Ida.*

But all were dwarfed by the tremendous éclat of Marie Lloyd, engaged at £100 a week in June.

Vulgarity, the quality of the common multitude as distinct from the 'cultured' few, is an essential ingredient of People's Theatre. It is a dangerous element; its crude exhibitionist form is the death of Theatre, but in the hands of an Artiste it can be controlled and exploited and made the very lifeblood of the living Stage. That was the achievement of this peculiar woman.

One night at Sheffield Miss Lloyd got the bird from a hostile Gallery. She paused, fixed the House with a scathing eye, pitched her voice perfectly into the silence: 'So this is Sheffield? Where they make the cutlery? Well, you know just what you can do with your knives and forks!'

The prolonged roar of applause testified to her flair for striking just the right note of impudent vulgarity. This was her art in a nutshell. She had none of Leno's gift of motley creation; her amazing dynamic lay in an effortless ease of shocking suggestion. In that age of the ultra-prim she made appalling innuendoes with such apparently harmless ditties as 'Among My Knick-Knacks', 'The Tale of a Skirt', 'A Little of What You Fancy', and (in cycling bloomers, complete with machine) 'Salute My Bicycle'. 'Cycling is all the go,' commented *Ariel*, 'and Miss Lloyd has acquainted us with the gentle art of kissing hers.' She may be said to have invented the Art of the Other Eye.

She was never the Female Clown in tights of the Fanny Leslie type, the funny Frustrated Female *à la* Vesta Victoria, nor the scat figure comically suffering the ironies of life as portrayed by Ada Lundberg. Something much more cutting and insolent spilled out of her, and she exulted in the roar of destructive laughter. 'All her songs are variations on the theme of sexual naughtiness,' notes Arnold Bennett. Where Leno disturbed Audiences to a sense of the essential lunacy of living, Marie Lloyd played on the animal quality hidden under the romantic image of Victorian sex, mocking something which she hated and feared and could never come to terms with in her own life.

This gave the dynamism to her ripe and racy style and made her the dominant figure in the last days of Music Hall. Harold Scott claims that the deep understanding between Marie Lloyd and her Audience was 'rooted in class-consciousness'. This seems doubtful. She certainly spoke the rich suggestive tongue of the working-class, but she was not quite of them: the Cockney tone is tart and subtle, whereas hers was rather an exuberant, hysterical, destructive treatment of the sexual myth.

She was born Matilda Alice Victoria Wood in 1870 in Hoxton where her father made artificial flowers and worked as a waiter at the local Music Hall. The little girl, helping in her mother's dressmaking business, singing uplift songs at Missions, learning to teach in a Sunday School, had a yen for the Theatre, a feeling for the lights and the fame. As Tilly Wood she organised an amateur Concert Party, all girls – The Fairy Bell's Minstrels.

At fifteen, still starry-eyed (and unpaid) she made a first stage appearance at The Grecian Saloon, and as 'Bella Delamere' got a trial engagement at a Hall in Hackney Road at fifteen shillings a week. Here George Ware spotted her possibilities and got her engagements, ending with a year at The Royal Holborn. Dressed in a short-sleeved frock with a large pinafore, doing the leggy madcap romp and singing Ware's own song, 'The Boy I Love is Up in the Gallery', she made a name for herself as a Naughty Songstress and set the tone for her Music Hall career.

In this precocious bit of entertainment, the shock to her Sunday School ideals of life and love must have been severe. From now on she seems to have been unconsciously bent on destroying herself, or at least destroying the image of 'Fairy Bell' and 'Bella Delamere'. In a passion to be common she took a name from a popular paper, *Lloyd's Weekly*, and called herself 'Marie Lloyd'.

At seventeen she married Percy Courteney, a hanger-about-town and a racecourse tout. The wedding was on Saturday 12 November 1887, and on the following Monday, instead of a honeymoon, she opened a week's engagement at Dan Lowrey's and was retained for a second week, singing such early essays in the Art as 'Sure to Fetch Them' and 'When the Leaves Begin to Fall'. Dan may not have liked her style; at least he seems never to have asked her back until Findlater and the Company took over.

In 1891 she played Principal Girl with Leno in the Drury Lane Panto *Humpty Dumpty* and also in the two following Pantos. During these years she developed to the full her style of ripe suggestion – too ripe, perhaps, for the Lane: she was never asked there again. But in Music Hall she was now Comedy Queen, at £20 a week per Hall, working five Halls a night.

The Other Eye, from *Ariel*

Offstage she lived in something of a whirlwind, working off her hysteria in bouts of prodigal generosity (one thinks of Bessie Bellwood), fiercely asserting herself by upholding the unlucky of the world, buying boots for hordes of barefoot urchins who swarmed around her again the following night, minus the boots. She tore through work with the energy of a dozen men. Scenes were frequent, her temper flared, there were nerve-storms at rehearsals, whiskey in the dressing-rooms and choice bits of Hoxtonese and colourful profanities shot from her lips with the speed and precision of a machine-gun. She was happy only on the Stage, exercising her power over packed Houses that resounded to her superb cheek.

In 1894 Dan Lowrey induced her to recross the Irish Sea. Monday, 11 June for six nights only. Salary £100. No 'Miss' in the ads; Marie wouldn't have it – 'damned swank'.

They came from all quarters and from all sections of society, Church-goers and Chapelgoers, the merchant, the academic and the bricklayer's mate. Young things of the 'advanced' set and respectable wives, they all lay helpless with laughter, turned crimson and hid their faces in their hands. The songs were little or nothing; the dire effect lay in the Art of the Other Eye, communicated to the innocuous words by shrugs, stoppages, leers, nods, short laughs, lazy glances, the Marie Lloyd smile. Such was her 'Twiggy Vous?' sung with subtle tone and knowing wink; and such was her 'Almond Rock', on the surface nothing but a ditty of a girl hungering for her first ball:

Only fancy if Gladstone's there
And falls in love with me . . .

If I run across Labouchère
I'll ask him . . . home to tea!
I shall say to a young man gay
If he . . . treads upon my frock
Randy pandy, sugary candy,
Buy me some Almond Rock!

'Almond Rock' became a byword. The blue eyes, the cosy little figure, five feet two, the knee coquettishly leaning to knee, the girly voice asking for the sugarstick, filled the imagination of the Town for years. Those who saw Marie Lloyd felt that they had been in touch with no mere Idol but with the very Goddess of the Rite.

Not one single bit of newsprint raised an eyebrow, all kow-towed to the Venus Vulgaris of the New People. It is curious to see the serious papers canonising the lady: 'Last night Miss Marie Lloyd appeared with great success. She met with a reception such as is accorded to an old favourite, or to one who comes with the best credentials in her line as a vocalist and a comedienne. She sings lively songs, comic songs and dances with great spirit and with so much success that again and again she received the hearty applause of the audience.' – *Irish Times*. No one reading that could imagine what had gone on in The Star.

The details of her private life added spice to her appearance. While she was at Dan's, her husband, Percy Courteney, was charged at Marylebone Police Court on a warrant issued on her behalf: that she went in fear of her life of him. The case was reported in all the Irish morning papers on the Wednesday of that week; that night prolonged roars of acclamation greeted her 'Madame du Van', 'When you Wink the Other Eye', 'She Sits Among the Cabbages', and her delicious bit of 'Almond Rock'.

The reign of the Goddess still had three decades to run. On stage her suggestiveness became ever more outrageous; it became a debauch of personality, often passing the limits of artistic restraint, and reflected the growing social anarchy of the *fin de siècle*. Popular Theatre had passed its pinnacle with Leno; personal control and personal flavour had gone with the Syndicates. The Age of the anti-Drama, the anti-Theatre, the anti-Everything, was at hand. 'Like it,' said Marie, 'or lump it.'

She was ageing quickly, becoming ever more unhappy in her emotional life. In 1905 her marriage with Courteney was dissolved; he cited her adultery with Coster Comedian Alec Hurley, whom she married the following year. Then, pathetically, she fell for a jockey, Bernard Dillon of Tralee, eighteen years her junior. In 1910 Dillon rode the Derby winner and cocked the walk about Town. Alec Hurley applied for a divorce and got it. On her fourth visit to America in 1913 she took Dillon with her, and they were married the following year at the British Consulate in Portland, Oregon. Dillon, who fancied himself on the accordion singing soothery Irish songs, turned out to be even more of a brute than Percy had ever been; he was in and out of Court for drunkenness and assault, deserted from the Western Front in 1917, lost his riding licence for malpractices, beat his wife up and spoiled her famous smile by knocking out one of her teeth.

Alec Hurley, from *Pick-Me-Up*

And still she was Goddess to millions of devotees, creating the tone and the essence of what remained of Music Hall in the New Century. Towards the end there was a strange and unexpected flowering. The Artiste re-asserted herself and gave a display of restrained and comic vulgarity which

The Goddess offstage

drew admiring comment from Sarah Bernhardt, Ellen Terry and T. S. Eliot. 'Genius' was their word for it.

At The Palladium, just before her last tour of the Provinces, she sang of the alcoholic wanderings of an ageing bleary-eyed female during a 'removal':

My old man said, Follow the van
And don't dilly dally on the way.
Off went the cart with the home packed in it,
I walked behind with my old cock linnet,
But I dillied and dallied, dallied and dillied,
Lost the van and don't know where to roam.
I stopped on the way to have the old half-quartern –
And I can't find my way home!

No, poor Tilly Wood in real life could never find her way; but the Artiste had found the perfect piece to which she brought the comic technique and the tragic experience of a lifetime.

In 1922 she sang her last song of all – 'I'm One of the Ruins that Cromwell Knocked Abaht a Bit' – superb in its serio-comic pathos. Already in the grip of a fatal illness, she staggered on the Stage, fell in agony, the Audience not realising that the poor old Ruin was really in the throes. She died in the dusk of her shuttered villa at Golder's Green, and Tavern Theatre died with her. 50,000 Londoners wept at her funeral.

The Company money ensured a galaxy of Comics on this Year's Bill: The Two Macs, Charles Bignell, Horace Wheatley, George Beauchamp, Charles Coburn, T. E. Dunville, Chirgwin, Harry Lauder, Tom Costello, Little Tich.

The Original Macs, from the *Idler*.

The Little Man

The cracks and the whacks of The Two Macs resounded for the last time through the House. The original Pair (English MacCabe & Irish McNally) had broken up into two Pairs. MacCabe had gone off with his brother, McNally had gone on tour with a new twin and each Pair called themselves The Two Macs. They went to law over the title, the Court decided that the McNally Pair had the proper claim to it, so they came to the Halls in triumph as 'The Men Who Won the Verdict'.

George Beauchamp, dandy in tophat and draughtboard checks, knocked on the knuckles in earlier years for exceeding the limit in 'blue', sailed merrily on. His 'Get Y'r Hair Cut!' became a catchphrase, his 'One of the Early Birds' a classic:

She was a sweet little dicky bird,
Chip, chip, chip, she went.
Sweetly she sang to me
Till all my money was spent.
Then she went off song,
We parted on fighting terms –
She was one of the early birds
And I was one of the worms.

'Dear old Horace Wheatley' had been on the go since the Sixties. He was from Lancashire, renowned for his Irish brogue, his breezy patter and infectious laugh. He was an immense favourite, a figure from the early days, his hulk immobile while his slippered feet wove intricate patterns to a lilting air. His style lacked the finesse and breadth of such men as Ashcroft and the gusto of Pat Kinsella, yet he made a niche for himself with a strain of Irish comic sentiment, an irresistible naïveté – 'The Incombustible Duck', 'Bonny Kate of Sweet Mayo', 'The Ball of Whirligig Magee'. 'Dear old Horace' always brought with him a flavour of the Gaslight Era and of the dim taverns from which the vast and glittering auditoriums of World Variety had sprung. It was a mark of the Audience that they loved a touch of that bygone time. It made them feel at home.

One evening during the following month a low-sized bandylegged fellow dressed as an Irish navvy with moleskins and the ritual clay pipe sang:

Said I to Calligan, You'll have to call again.
Call again? said Calligan – not I!

Connoisseurs noted the beautifully clear diction, the rich baritone voice, the Scots intonation. He was new to Ireland, seeking a grip on the first rungs of the ladder – a young man of twenty-four named Harry Lauder.

In September Mr Lowrey was given a well-earned Benefit, and presented by the Lord Mayor of Dublin, on behalf of the Committee, with a silver salver with kettle to match, two silver punchbowls, a meerschaum pipe and a cigar case.

Among the players on this occasion was the Ghost of Paganini. The costume was now wearing thin, the face and figure were haggard with advancing years and with neglect, yet his playing had all the old hypnosis. He rendered piece after piece but still the Audience would not let him go.

Then he drew the bow across the strings again, a hush fell on the House, the violin spoke a Gaelic melody – the *Coulin*, a love-song of long ago. It was his thirteenth visit to Dan Lowrey's, and his last.

A note in one of Dan's Engagement Books is eloquent: 'Won't keep sober.' His death is recorded in 1904, but the Ghost lingered long in Dublin memory; 1919: 'he is believed to be still living' – W. H. Grattan Flood.

11 November. 'Long looked for, Come at last! The Great Little Tich!' The House was packed out at 7.30 and the most puzzling of all Music Hall men appeared.

When Harry Ralph was born near Sevenoaks in Kent in 1868, his parents were shocked to find that he had an extra finger on each hand and an extra toe on each foot. As the child grew the legs remained tiny. He was an intelligent little fellow, quite furious to find himself different from the rest of his kind, but determined to make the best of it. At twelve, he earned coppers playing a tin whistle outside a local Theatre, and the shortlegged urchin drew such attention that the Manager invited him on stage at £1 a week.

The legends are many and conflicting, but it seems he made his first appearance at Rosherville Gardens, Gravesend, in 1880, as a blacked-up comic. In contrast to Sir Roger the Tichborne Claimant, an elephant of a man, Harry billed himself as 'Little Tichborne' which was soon cut down to 'Little Tich'. For years he tramped the provincial round, dancing and pattering blackface, at times overcome by bitterness and depression as his body grew to manhood and his legs remained those of a midget. He studied feverishly, pored over books, languages, philosophy, world religions, mathematics, mastered the theory of music, became adept at painting in oils and watercolours – but none of these subjects was for him. No prospect but the weird existence of a Human Freak. So be it.

Tich as a Soldier

He designed for himself a freak pair of boots, nearly thirty inches from heel to toe, soled with wood. When he flap-danced in these the ambitious length of the boots emphasised the pathetic brevity of the body, barely four feet high. People's hearts went out to him – the figure of the Little Man comically overcoming his handicap and 'playing such fantastic tricks before high heaven as make the angels weep'.

He toured America in 1887, first with Tony Pastor's Company, then with the Chicago Opera House Company who taught him to drop the black-up and paint his face white: the pathetic White Man proved a much more vibrant figure. With the Opera House Company he also learned the art of burlesque, the comic parody of the serious, the highfalutin' or the eminently respectable. Statesmen, romantic heroes, warlords, the mandarins of science and of the arts – all were cut down to the size of Little Tich. The dwarf derived a personal satisfaction from this derisory send-up of the civilised and the intellectual world from which his handicap had excluded him.

After two years of intensive American training, he came back and scored a resounding success as Buttons in *The Babes in the Wood* at The Princess, Manchester. Thence to The Gaiety and Drury Lane – Quasimodo, Humpty Dumpty, Man Friday, Hop-o'-my-thumb (delicious in draggy

Mr Tich offstage

skirt and pantalettes). World fame followed. He toured the Colonies and the Continent, sang in French, German, Spanish, Italian. Paris, quick to discern *le type*, went wild for him; a cry in the street, 'Le Petit Tich!' and crowds would gather. Hating notoriety, loathing his public image, he went about in a closed cab, trembling and infuriated.

He gave his private time to philosophy, music, painting, and had a refined taste in women. His first wife was an American girl, his second a Spanish dancer, his third a beautiful young soprano. Little Tich to the public, but Mr Tich to Music Hall Managers: call him Tich and he would simply pack his bag and disappear from the scene.

At Dan Lowrey's he was treated like Royalty. Everyone held their breath and kept their fingers crossed lest the slightest mishap should throw Little Man into a fit of nervous depression. All went well. Jacket bunched, hands pushed into trouser pockets, the toes of his boots sticking out a yard in front of him, all the distilled drollery of the ages seemed to have dropped onto the Stage. A puckish smile creased his features; he had a habit of turning his eyes up till the whites showed; people were convulsed with laughter just to look at him. He was in the best of humour, burlesqued the Jockey, the Police Inspector, the sultry Spanish Dancer. Deeper still went the stabs of pity and humour when he broke into his pethetic hungering refrain:

I could do, could do, could do,
Could do wiv a bit.

To show he was pleased he did his famous flap-boot dance, and he was cheered to the echo. His salary was £95.

Monday 3 December. The Empire Theatre of Varieties was opened in Victoria Square, Belfast. Chairman, Adam S. Findlater. Managing Director, Daniel Lowrey. Share Capital, £30,000. Seating, 2,000. A special excursion train, first-class only, was run from Dublin for the occasion. In addition to his shares in the venture, Lowrey was to receive a salary of £300 a year for his managerial know-how.

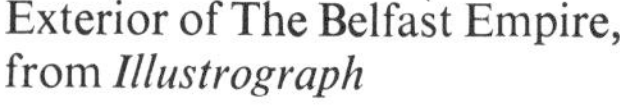

Exterior of The Belfast Empire, from *Illustrograph*

CHAPTER NINETEEN

1895 The Insubstantial Pageant

1

Saturday 12 January. Grand Fashionable Illuminated Matinée at 2.30 in aid of 'Ierne' Bazaar Funds for St Patrick Dun's Hospital, under the Distinguished Patronage of The Lady Mayoress, The Marchioness of Ormonde, Countess Fitzwilliam, Lady Victoria Hamilton, Countess of Wicklow, Lady Iveagh, Lady Inchiquin, Lady Talbot de Malahide, Lady Muskerry, Hon. Mrs Henniker, Lady Ball-Green, Lady Harrel, Lady Grubb, Lady Jackson, Lady Reed, Countess of Bandon. Entire Star Company. Carriages at 5. 'Dan's is coming on.' – Diarist Joe Holloway.

Monday 11 February. The Renowned Comedian of the Legitimate Stage, Charles Collette. Famed as Micawber in *David Copperfield*, and world-famed in the title-role of *The Colonel*. In song and monologue, and with Miss Roma in Comedy Sketch. 'An entertainment not altogether in touch with the traditional sympathies of a Star audience' – *Independent*. 'Collette will best be remembered in the part of 'The Colonel' which attracted such attention ten or twelve years ago, when sensible people deemed it advisable to check that wave of Aestheticism connected with Oscar Wilde which threatened to flood Society, by some wholesome satire' – *Times*. 'Spent a pleasant afternoon at The Star. Collette sang "Gilhooley's Supper Party" with great clearness and neat articulation, also "Baa Baa" and "Phil the Fluter's Ball". The Sketch was nicely staged and naturally played. Mr Collette however made a big mistake in singing Irish, or so-called Irish, songs to an Irish audience.' – Joe Holloway. Salary £20. Miss Roma, £2. 10*s*.

Kate Carney Coster Queen

3

Monday 18 March. Kate Carney making her third and final visit was recalled again and again. Broad as she was long, a great-hearted little woman, she did her coster number with a melodious power of lung to shake the stanchions of the Galleries. She wept for a wanderer returning to 'The Old Village Home in the East', and delivered 'Janey Delaney' in London–Irish tones of rich and raucous sentiment – 'on fire, she's my desire, heart, never to part, tarry, marry, how happy we'll be, Janey Delaney, that you'll belong to me' – her short and robust torso trembled, the feather quivered on the brim of her hat, her choruses rang resonant through the happily roaring House. £12.

Kate went on to become the Coster Queen, and made an all-time hit with 'When the Summer Comes Again'. In a Command Performance before King George V, a recording machine was present and captured the nostalgia of one of the most vibrant voices in the Halls for the times to come:

Oh, won't we have some money, Nell,
When the Summer comes again.
Life will be all honey, gel,
When the Summer comes again.

Minnie Cunningham

We shall roam all round the country
With pretty flowers, sunshine or rain –
Strite! we'll buy up Covent Garden
When the Summer comes again.

April. Easter Monday. Charles Bignell Character Comic. Cheeky and irrepressible, with facial expression and suggestive quirks, he played to the Gallery with some very brash lyrics:

My wife one night I took for a blow,
Our thirteenth little 'un went also.
Just hold the pet half a tick, she said,
While I put Fanny and Jimmy to bed.
(Facial gestures – he hands the baby back)
I've 'ad some! – thanks – don't want any more!
You take me for a jay I'm sure.
Wot say? Nurse that kid? Oh lor!
Take him away – I've 'ad some!

This was the note of uncreative crudity which was to invade the Halls when they became centres of Fashion. Salary £27. 10*s*.

Monday 29 April. Star Serio Minnie Cunningham. Salary £18. Pretty as a picture, eyes sparkling out of a cloud of light brown hair, Minnie piped her jaunty little 'fables', like –

You never saw a feather, a pretty little feather,
Black or white, red or green, yellow, pink or pale –
No matter what the colour, as well the one as t' other –
You never saw a feather on a Tom Cat's Tail!

Monday 20 May. First time for the Burlesque Actress, Connie Ediss. There was humour in her waddle in front of the footlights, humour in her rich Cockney voice, the most infectious good humour in her sallies. Despite her bulk she was a splendid dancer, and delivered 'Rosie, or I Ride to Win' with point and gusto. The only sense of strain one might observe was her incessant smoking of cigars, even in the wings, where Dan did not normally allow it. The Lowreyites expecting a buxom Cockney girl to be a Marie Lloyd, a Kate Carney or a Bessie Bellwood, were slow to tune in to her subtler sense of poking fun at the socialites. Salary £12.

Later, Dan found she was not available for a return visit, for she had been teamed up by George Edwardes in the Gaiety series of *Girl* Musicals. Her name conjures up a mental picture of acres of white satin rucked to the rotundities of her considerable figure, a lowcut lace corsage, an immense black matinée hat with plumes and taffeta frills perched at an angle of forty-five degrees on a froth of flaxen wig, framing a face to grace the Duchess of the Crème de la Crème. Her perfected art was to gag the new vulgarian aping of the *bon ton*:

In the West End I've taken a flat –
Well, you talk about swingin' a cat!

Vesta Victoria

When I go home, before I can get through the door
I've to take off my matinée hat.
And the Bath – well, can't get into that.
Chorus:
But it's class, class, class.
I can see all Society pass –
That is, at a distance, and with the assistance
Of a powerful binocular glass.
There's a lift, I should state,
But it won't bear a weight,
And when folks on the stairs I've to pass
It often results in most deadly insults –
But it's Class, Class, Class!

Monday 27 May. Vesta Victoria. Top of the Bill. £25. Up to all the tricks of the trade, ready to skirt-dance, to be quaint, to be pathetic, this little Leeds girl had made her modest way through Halls and hideouts all over Britain. Then unexpectedly she found herself famous, thanks to a song 'Good for Nothing Nan' in which she found her personal style.

Vesta Victoria was rather sharp-featured, yet had a generous mouth, a bit gap-toothed, and bright eyes that might be innocent, might be naughty, one couldn't be sure which. In 'Nan' she discovered herself, the eccentric comedienne, the mannish girlish figure, long-legged, half serious, half mocking. The sharpness and piquancy of her tone sauced the pathos, and Audiences flocked to hear this rarest of all Artistes, the true female Comic.

'Nan' was followed quickly by the finest cry of female frustration of the entire Century, 'Daddy Wouldn't Buy Me a Bow-Wow-Ow'. She sang it holding a cat, the quaint voice childishly, plaintively, roguishly asking that she be given a dog instead. That yearning for something with a bite in it became the theme-song of the Nineties and the erstwhile Baby Victoria joined the Idols of the Halls. Babies learning to speak lisped the famous words, duchesses intoned them at the pianoforte, drovers from their taverns near the cattle-marts carried them to the remotest cabins of the hinterland:

Daddy wouldn't buy me a bow-wow (wow-wow)
Daddy wouldn't buy me a bow-wow (wow-wow).
I have a little cat, I'm very fond of that –
But I'd rather have a bow-wow wow-wow wow-wow!

'A first-class artiste. Knows how to act. Her coster and doll songs were admirable.' – Joe Holloway.

Connie Ediss, from *Pearson's Portfolio*

Monday 10 June. Star packed to receive Katie Lawrence, in man's cap, trews, Norfolk jacket, delivering the song which had lifted her at last to fame:

Daisy, Daisy, give me your answer do.
I'm half crazy all for the love of you.
It won't be a stylish marriage,
I can't afford a carriage,

But you'll look sweet upon the seat
Of a bicycle made for two.

'The Best Music Hall song I ever heard' – Vesta Tilley. Joe Holloway 'didn't think great things of her. All her songs are poor affairs with catchy choruses. She hadn't much idea of characterisation, sings all her songs in the same manner.' £35.

Monday 17 June. Welcome Back to Marie Loftus, known as the Hibernian Hebe. The taste of Albert Edward Prince of Wales for wide-hipped women with fruitful bodices had set the fashion for the full feminine look. Marie was the kind of Hebe that Dublin loved. Yet she had far more to offer than the lure of the eye. Her humour was quick and infectious, and Dan hardly exaggerated in billing her as 'the biggest-salaried Serio-Comic travelling'.

Young men swooned to hear her sing 'That is Love'. But her choicest bit was perhaps 'Sister Mary', the ditty of a pretty country bumpkin just come to Town:

What is she to say? What is she to do?
If a swell should want to treat her
To a diamond ring or two?
Should he offer her his chestnut mare
To canter in the Row
Is it etiquette to take it?
Sister Mary wants to know.

The eyes of the arch comedienne peeking through the gaze of mousey Mary, and the sexual undertones gave a *richesse* to her act which put her among the most delectable of Dan's Dolls. £70.

29 July. Return of Charles Coburn, dapper and debonair. £40.

The most refined and many-languaged of all the older humorists, Coburn had received a new lease of Music Hall life. It happened one day, he tells, on a train between Aldgate and Shepherd's Bush, when an American sentimental song 'Sweet Nellie's Blue Eyes' was drifting through his mind. In a flash words formed to the tune, 'Two Lovely . . .' – ha-ha, this would be good, and well-bred ladies would find the slang delightfully daring. He had the great Chorus worked out before the train reached the Bush, tried the number out in The Paragon in the Mile End Road, yes, he had arrived. Engaged at The Trocadero for a fortnight he caused a roaring rapturous riot, shoals of costerboys and girls went arm-in-arm chanting the Chorus through the evening streets, the song spread like influenza and London succumbed. 'Two Lovely Black Eyes' ran round the world. Coburn sang it in nine languages, Aristocracy flocked to The Troc and his engagement lasted fourteen months, a record.

Then late in 1891 the modest Scotsman had another lucky strike. Fred Gilbert wrote and composed him a character-narrative which in his own delightful *tempo moderato* he sent cruising the world in the wake of the Lovely Black Eyes:

As I walk along the Bois Boulong
With an independent air

Among the Novelties this Month, the Kellinos, from *Pick-Me-Up*

The Incomparable Harriet Vernon

You can hear the girls declare
He must be a millionaire.
You can hear them sigh and wish to die,
You can see them wink the other eye
At the Man who Broke the Bank at Monte Carlo!

At The Star he received a tremendous acclamation. The Band played the Chorus of 'The Man who Broke the Bank' over and over again while the Dubliners, who had always had a soft spot for Coburn, clapped and cheered; the shy Comedian blushed, smiled, bowed, waved. Groups on the way home went chanting the great Chorus into the night:

Two lovely black eyes.
Oooh, what a surprise!
See what I got for kissing my mot –
Two lovely black eyes!

On this same night the veteran Scot, Tom Maclagan, Tenor of Opera Bouffe and Character Comic, made his last appearance, bringing a taste of the now legendary Old Dan Lowrey days. Once Top of the Bill, now in his Caledonian twilight. £5.

Vesta in Feminine Costume

August. Topping the Bill for Horse Show Week, 'England's Incomparable Harriet Vernon.' £50.

If Katie Lawrence had voice and Vesta Victoria vivacity, Harriet Vernon had configuration. Tall, torsoed and plenteous, she had come a long way up since her first visit eleven years earlier. A deal of her success was due to the fact that, even in her male parts, she conformed to the contemporary ideal of all-round woman. After many opulent Principal Boys in the Lane, she had discovered a series of peachy personations of a 'cultivated' kind to suit the plentitude of her powers – 'Cleopatra', 'Mark Antony', 'Nelson', lesbic 'Sappho', the nymphophiliac 'Don Giovanni', and 'Joan of Arc'. In this way she too distilled something of the doomed aristocratic culture into Dan's. Her act combined the charm of Poses Plastiques with the art of serio-singing, and the crowds came to luxuriate in her presence as much as to hear her. Less exotic was her song of the Spanish mandoline girl who 'only answered Ting-a-ling to all that I could say'; this flavoured the opulence with a comic piquancy, for even as Sappho Harriet was 'incomparably English'.

2 September. Vesta Tilley, recently returned from a highly successful American tour, was still her bright little vibrant self. She had married Walter de Freece, of a solid Liverpool Theatre firm, who formed his own big circuit of Halls, the Variety Theatre Controlling Company, becoming a magnate of the Music Hall world in time to be knighted. De Freece nurtured her career, even wrote some of her songs.

With marriage the Boy–Girl Vesta had undergone a subtle change. Dan who loved her best of all his Idols noted the difference in her tone:

'The pathos is become beautifully sympathetic and womanly'. At his Benefit this month she graced the occasion with two specially chosen songs: 'Mary and John' and 'The Shamrock's Appeal to the Rose'. There were few dry eyes under the Venetian Gothic roof.

Her many metamorphoses of male attire and attitude – military, naval, the flash young man – were as meticulously studied and as fetching as ever. Her voice had gained in crisp effectiveness and in emotive overtone; she still sounded her r's with a pleasing Midland burr ('the Tilley touch'), and her new song 'After the Ball' awakened a yearning in every heart. The carriage trade was brisk. All Dublin adored her. £100.

That was her seventh appearance in The Star. She never came again. The day of the Syndicates was in full swing, de Freece was knighted and Vesta, late Tilley Ball, appeared as Lady de Freece among the new Aristocracy of the Variety Theatre. In the years before the Great War she was drawn into the escapist fantasy of the *Jeunesse Dorée*. In the Summer of 1914, aboard the *Aquitania*, Vesta was singing 'Monty from Monte Carlo' to the champagne and pearls of Good King George's Golden Days on the very brink of the holocaust. After the War she retired from a changed Stage. At the Farewell Performance given her by Music Hall magnate, Sir Oswald Stoll, she wept before a thronged and weeping Coliseum. She died in 1952, aged eighty-eight.

Her memory endures as one of the most telling images in the Drame. Her life story is an epitome of that flimsy, florid, fermenting, fascinating Age, both in the Theatre and in Society as a whole.

Monday 14 October. Alec Hurley Coster Comic and his (first) wife appeared in a Sketch, *He & She*. Hurley had a splendid tenor voice and his album of songs included 'His Old Man's Hat Won't Fit Him', 'The 'Addick-Smoker's Daughter', 'The Lambeth Walk'. £10.

Monday 11 November. The ancient Arena lives again. The Imperial Turkish Wrestlers Omer & Hussman, with Masteo of Bordeaux, Alphonso of Madrid, Wolff the Champion of Belgium, and with special addition of Irish Champion J. Carroll, appear in nightly bouts and feats of the Gladiatorial Art. 'Spendid fellows, worthy of the éclat with which they have been heralded. The big audience went simply wild over their extraordinary feats. Mr Lowrey has outstripped himself.' – *Independent*.

Monday 9 December. Return of T. E. Dunville the Famous Distiller of Furious Fun. £30. VVVVG. (Dan's code for 'good', 'very good', 'very very good', etc.)

A tall, black-and-white figure with sticklike limbs and a limewhite face harlequins onto the Stage. This dangling Marionette with his homely tone and pistolshot delivery is quite a new thing in Comics. Refreshing.

Dunville's rise to fame from the backroom of a Bicycle Factory to be English Prankman *par excellence* is one of the most unusual stories in Music Hall history. Born among the spires of Coventry, son of a tailor, fond of physical jerks, he played a backstreet turn at sixteen as an Acrobat, amused the boys and girls of the Bicycle Works with gags and homemade song-snippets. Then amateur busking – song, dance and tumble – at fairgrounds and on holiday sands, with two other lads of his Town, all on the long side – The Three Spires. He always retained this local touch, grew up tall, thin, wiry, and chanced his arm as a professional in an acrobatic duo, The Merry Men, clowning the cartwheels in Coventry and thereabouts.

He got his first break in 1889. W. J. Ashcroft on a six-month tour of the Provinces noted the fluent plastique and natural tone of the thin young man, liked both, and had him taken on in a touring *Cinderella* which was then at The Victoria, Bolton. Playing to large provincial Audiences Dunville found he could stand on his own comical feet, singing his own songs in his own quaint style, and discard the acrobatics. Yet in a sense the ghost of the Acrobat always remained with him: his arms and legs jerked, he worked like a Puppet on strings.

Next an American engagement: booked to play in an open-air Spectacle, a costume-and-choreography piece, *The Fall of Pompeii*. This opened his eyes. He glimpsed the stylisation of 'Art Theatre' as distinct from local gags with the gods back home. The Coventry boy discovered (as Chirgwin had discovered it) the distinctive quality of Clown: the Mask.

1890. London. A triple début on the one night, at Forrester's, The Middlesex and Gatte's-in-the-Road. His numbskull jerks, flat accent and rapier delivery sent the Houses into wild applause.

Among the first of his hits was 'Lively On and Lively Off!' English to the quick, this song had the same dialect directness and much the same offbeat rhythm as 'Pleese One and Pleese All' as sung by Tarleton, one of Shakespeare's male Comics. Followed by the even more laconic and staccato 'Verdict':

Little Boy –
Pair of skates –
Broken ice –
Pearly Gates.

Next came a crackling bit of Old English nonsense, 'Bunka-doodle-ido'. After 'Bunka' he harlequinned a whole kaleidoscope of characters, Butcher,

Roslyn Park

Dan Lowrey, Managing Director, Dublin and Belfast, from *Illustrograph*

Baker, Soldier, Quaker, Policeman, Postman, Taxman, Sweep, but all in the same Costume, all in the one rigorous face make-up.

Soon after his London début, Lowrey was quick to sign him up for The Star. He was something quite new to Dubliners, a cross between a human Marionette, a male Comic and a Parisian Clown. His dress was one long piece of black material, big buttons, large white Quaker collar, black skin-tights, bulging boots. And a Face that might have come out of the Cirque Médrano, ghostwhite in the gaslight, eyebrows like big black antennae on an immense forehead. He seemed to dangle and the words shot from the deadpan Face:

When Spring cum Mick stole a plum
But the plum was green –
Just below the belt what a pain he felt –
Oooh! God save the Queen!
And the Verdict was:
Farmer's lad –
Stolen plum –
Belly bad –
Kingdom Come!

13

The Star and Dan Lowrey were now in the final phase of their long career. By now he had moved with his young wife and family to Roslyn Park, a handsome house standing in its own grounds at Sandymount in the fashionable south suburbs. He had set up his carriage and was often to be seen driving along the pleasant road to Dublin among the merchant princes of the Town.

Yet of leisure he had little or none. Travelling incessantly in search of fresh material and ideas, keeping the Accounts and the Engagement Books, meticulously noting the quality of each Stage item for future reference, he had little time for the family festivities at Roslyn Park this Christmas. The affairs of the Lowrey Kingdom – Belfast, Cork (where work on a new Palace of Varieties had already begun), and Crampton Court – were multitudinous, and coming to a tricky pass.

He had sold the pretty little Bijou in Anne Street; it was too small and intimate for these times, and besides he needed the money. It was bought by a Company who opened it as the Savoy Theatre of Varieties with plans to acquire adjoining property and extend. They failed, and the place closed for the last time as a Theatre early in 1898.

Dan was feeling the strain. That ferocious dynamic of his which had driven George West out of business at The Grafton, queered the pitch for Michael Gunn, and possibly helped to drive Ashcroft to near-suicide in the dusk of the Belfast Alhambra, was having its effect on him. He had to keep right there at the heart of affairs, lest the Theatre in these get-rich-quick days should run completely out of theatrical control. The Star Company were businessmen, if it seemed to suit their pockets they would deal with him and his family in the same merciless way as long ago he had dealt with George West. He was in the same position as many of his Artistes, and well he knew it – a Leybourne, a Maclagan, a Barney Ferguson doing dime-stands down-at-heel: only as long as the name 'Dan Lowrey' remained a spellbinder with the public was he safe.

CHAPTER TWENTY

1896 The Philm Pholk

It was Ta-ra-ra time. From coast to coast, town to town, hamlet to hamlet, the epidemic spread; streetorgans churned it; German Bands came stepping down village streets drumming and trumpetting it; armies marched to it; old ladies beat it out with their umbrellas; it voiced the seismographic centre in the Pandemonium of the Age, and from cockcrow to midnight the cry was – *Ta-ra-ra-boom-de-ay!*

Lottie Collins, a waif of the Theatre, orphaned at five and with two sisters left to make a living, had done her song-and-dance act on the boards of many a Tavern Music Room. At fifteen she grew too tall and awkward for her sisters' liking so they went their own way and she went hers, all over Queen Victoria's kingdom, an obscure little performer with a skipping-rope. Her face rounded and grew pretty, her voice was sweet, and she packed uncanny tension in her gangling legs.

One October night in 1890, at The Tivoli in the Strand, the bomb burst. The demure Artiste took a deep breath, suddenly released that amazing sforzando, 'Ta-ra-ra-BOOM-de-ay!' A tumult of brass, drums, cymbals walloped the 'BOOM'; the Girl kicked high in a frenzied, wild delirium of whirling words and legs and the Audience, intoxicated, threw their heads back, let their hair down, saw the red flame and danced round mythical midnight fires. 'It had an unspeakable origin in America' – Hibbert. The tom-tom pulse invaded London; crowds in the night streets, both sexes, wearing each other's hats, stamped, kicked, yelled, 'Ta-ra-ra-Boom-de-ay!' It spread all over the Globe.

The shock was soon felt in Dublin. At Dan's the feet stamped, the Band banged and bucketted, Ventriloquists' Dolls, Marionettes, Mimics, in Lottie Collins contortions, in Lottie Collins clothes, all jerked to the rhythm.

Lottie, provided with a luxury suite on the liner, had crossed the Ocean and was received in New York like European Royalty. She ta-ra-ra'd in salmon-pink and black to tumultuous Houses, appearing between the acts of Fashionable Legit. Back in England, the erstwhile skipping-rope waif was now a Personage. True Artiste, she did not rest on her success, but evolved the Boom style into a brilliant set of dance-characters – 'The Widow', 'The Girl on the Ran-Dan', 'A Leader of Society', 'The Coalman's Wife' – a one-girl Surrealist Ballet in herself, well before Cocteau and *Parade*.

29 June 1896. 'Mr Lowrey delights to inform the Public that Miss Lottie Collins has Arrived!' 'The audience were only half-hearted in their enthusiasm. Her peculiarity is being sedateness itself one minute and the next kicking up her heels all over the place.' – Joe Holloway.

What disgruntled the Audience was that she refused repeated calls for 'Ta-ra-ra'. She was tired of it, had heart only for her newer dance-dramatics. She was hissed by the spirits who wanted at all costs to 'Boom'. Overcoming the catcalls and counter-cries she went on with her repertoire, the Band ably abetting. Just before her last bit of polished ballymania, Dan Lowrey himself came on Stage and led her forward firmly to the footlights to receive the acclamation which was overdue. Salary £100. VVVVVG.

Neither Joe Holloway nor the Dublin Press of the day was able to get to grips with the artistry of this later Lottie. In fact we have to go to Australia, where her tour was riotously successful, to get a close-up of this last great Serio in the Drame:

Knowles reincarnate as Traveller and Lecturer after the Music Hall Slump

She whirls on to the Stage in a riding-habit and hat of brilliant scarlet, as the Girl on the Ran-Dan. She almost whispers her song, the pace grows swifter, the scarlet riding-habit flicks with increasing devilry till the sudden explosion of utter abandon – a dance of jagged angles in which the red skirt flashes about with pointed jerks reminiscent of forked lightning, and she ricochets off the Stage amid thunders of applause. Back again, in short skirts of purple plush glimmering with spangles, the brazen, hardfaced Wife of the Coalman. . . . Afterwards, as the packed, sweltering house composes itself, a plump, pleasing Widow glides on. She trails her weeds across the brilliant garden scene, weeps softly for the two departed dears, then, with a world of desire in her glance, whispers of a third. A sudden swoop, the black skirt is whirled up and as the Widow spins round the Stage there is a lurid glare from the glowing underskirts of ruby-coloured Liberty silk. Above, in the centre of the circling lingerie, the Widow's face with light brown hair appears. Swift, clever and brilliant. It is the World, the Flesh, and a very strong Devil. Lottie is going to boom. – *The Sydney Bulletin.*

She died in 1910, aged forty-four. From heart failure.

Another voice of the disintegrating days was that of R. G. Knowles who appeared with his wife in April – £70. 'Took the house by storm' – *Independent.* Knowles came from Ontario and brought a breath of the Prairies into The Star. A shock. A hoarse voice gargling the r's – 'Gurrly', 'Gurrly', 'Ea-rr-uly', and 'Ah'll Nevurr Go t' Brright'n Anamo-urr!' Hypnotised, the Audience found themselves gargling the chorus in the same raw tones up to the louvres of the roof:

To Brighton, to Brighton
Where they do such things
And say such things
In Brighton, in Brighton –
But I'll never go there anymore!

The outsize gnome of a man, battered topper, drab white trews, gaping boots, took a jerky jogtrot round the Stage, spattered rather than pattered a shower of wisecracks like hail, spat out bits of anecdote through a carking medium of chronic bronchitis, shot into his 'Gurrly Gurrly' girlie theme. He rasped as if he was being strangled. Sheer nonsense, exhilarating in its raw lack of common sense. The voice of a new Continent. Full of a mock violence, a send-up of the Old World mystery of sex. Billed 'this very peculiar American Comedian'. And no wonder.

The Audience was at first aghast, not geared to this crackling speed, the jigsaw style, knifelike cuts of anecdote, the metallic voice, the American cheek of it; but once it dawned on them that this was the new thing – a strident sham satire, sham virulence, sham passion, sham everything – the Anti-Comic – the House went gargling with him.

His image remains, oddly one of the most haunting from the last days of The Star. We seem to see the sad eyes that have looked upon desolate

Cissie Loftus, from *Lady's Realm*

places in a heavy face darkened with the gloom of the eternal Joker, and the voice crackles out at us from an old cylinder recording, 'Nevurr Anamo-urr!'

One of the signs of the times was the increasing amount of Mimicry. It was a debunking spirit, a restlessness of the masses and classes refusing to take the Victorian solemnities seriously, even if they were their own Idols. Tich, Leno, Stratton, Marie Lloyd – all were endlessly mimicked in the Saturnalia.

The prime exponent of the spirit was Cissie Loftus. American Theatre Manager Augustin Daly sums her up: 'As a mimic, she is a genius; as an actress, she is nil.' Slim, svelte, she had an intense and poignant personality. Born in Glasgow in 1876, daughter of Marie Loftus the Hebe of the Halls and Dan Brown of the Coon Trio, Brown, Newland & Wallace, she was given an exclusive education at the Convent of the Holy Child, Blackpool, and the Royal Academy of Music. Acutely intelligent, boyishly beautiful, not quite of the Stage and not quite of the cultured class for which her education had groomed her, Cissie at seventeen had nothing to do but begin at the beginning. She appeared first on the Stage of the Belfast Alhambra under Ashcroft's tutelage, then drifted into Musical Comedy. At eighteen she made a runaway marriage to Justin Huntly McCarthy, author of sophisticated novels and clever verse. The story made all the papers and the glossy magazines, for her mother Marie Loftus was news, and this young McCarthy was the son of the Irish Nationalist M.P. who had chaired the Anti-Parnellite faction after the fall of the Chief. They got to America where she scintillated on the social scene, developed an uncanny skill as a mimic but failed in drama. Returning to England, concentrating on her personations, she was eagerly snapped up as a leading attraction. Lowrey calculated the cost.

It was February, foggy weather, flagging Houses. He offered her £150 for six nights plus a matinée – a record figure for The Star.

Though she drew flattering Houses, Dublin was not all that impressed. The *Independent* critic notes:

> It will we think strike many of her hearers that, clever though she is, she is slightly over-rated across the Channel. Take just a single instance – Florence St John – the beauty of St John's singing and acting is the animation and perfect naturalness she invests them with; now in Cissie Loftus' imitation of St John the qualities defined above are lacking, and if we regard it as a caricature it is a feeble one, for there is little humour in it, unless that be humour which reproduces merest weaknesses apart from strength. . . . Both Eugene Stratton and Dan Leno she treats cleverly, that is, as cleverly as any woman dressed in regulation female costume can well treat male character. She has their mannerisms and their style and gives a lively picture of them. Of Letty Lind, too, she makes capital and has a neat revenge in what she styles 'My imitation of Miss Letty Lind's imitation of me in my imitation of her!' . . . In short, while she is not just all we may have fancied her, Cissie Loftus is exceptionally brilliant for her years, is worth hearing, and will no doubt draw good houses during her engagement.

The coolness of her reception may in part be due to the fact that she had married on the anti-Parnellite side of the political fence. Subsequently, she flashed like a meteor through cosmopolitan Theatre, mimicking *à merveille* in the Companies of Madame Modjeska, Sir Henry Irving and E. H. Sothern. Yet she too was an unhappy girl; her marriage with McCarthy was dissolved in the last year of that Fantasy Decade. Later she married a Dr Waterman of Chicago and lived until 1943.

Nothing is stranger in this story than the unfailing impact of the Blacked-up Act. Next to the Irish Comic (and for much the same reasons) the Black Jester with banjo and plantation drawl, with pathetic white eyes and the quick humour of the underprivileged, solo or in a troupe of Christy Minstrels, was the most enduring figure in the whole of English-speaking Music Hall.

The dynamic figure of Chirgwin, the Devil in the Drame, topped the Bill again in 1896, rating £50, but all the blacked-up boys paled before Eugene Stratton. His following was enormous, his 'Coon' on everybody's lips:

Why, it's John James Ebenezer
Hezekiah Peter Hennery Zachary
John James Brown!
Don't yuh know me? – Garn! yuh will very soon
For I'm John James Brown the Dandy Coloured Coon!

He came in June, drawing huge summer-evening crowds, and rated £62.10*s*. Compared with Chirgwin and other exploiters of the coloured man, his voice had little range; he never threw it out to resound in the timbers of the House, preferring a more restrained style, seductively cooing and broken with an odd staccato jerk; his whistling was dulcet and there were endless patterns of movement in his shuffling feet. He was a good actor, lived the song he sang, whether in the plaintive 'Is Yer Mammy Always with Yer?' or in the exuberant

My gal's a highborn lady,
She's black but not too shady,
Feathered like a peacock, just as gay,
She is not coloured, she was born that way.

Stratton crooned and shuffled on into the New Age, appearing in Joyce's Bloomsday of 1904 where the huge Dark Face with blub lips on the posters round Town strike a disturbing chord in the theme of the story.

Gallery Manners Old Style, from *Pick-Me-Up*

The Star, sailing now on the high seas of Fashion, was Dan Lowrey's still. The Audience was lively and criticism was frequent and free from all floors. Tom Costello says: 'It was a byword in the profession that to pass muster of the Audience at Dan Lowrey's was a passport to success in any

other part of the English-speaking world.' The Gallery was the life and soul of Music Hall, but it needed Dan's constant curb else the place would explode into a 'free-and-easy'. 'I can picture him now standing at the foot of the stairs leading from the Gallery, all the coalmen were running down as hard as they could when the Show was over, and my Father saying: "Steady, gentlemen!" Then their hands would go out to shake his hand and they would say: "All your own boys, Sir!" ' – Norah.

The Magistrates in Cork now granted a licence for his proposed Music Hall there. The premises acquired extended from Patrick's Quay to King Street. The new Theatre, it was urged, would revitalise a disreputable site, consisting of ramshackle sheds and coalstores opposite a disused quarry, a favourite pitch for merrygorounds and reputedly haunted by the Fairies. Mr Lowrey stated that his Cork Palace Theatre of Varieties would be in the most modern style, eclipsing The Star. Share Capital £13,000. Debenture Trustees in this extension of the Ta-ra-ra Boom to the haunt of the Cork Fairies were mostly leading Wine & Provision Merchants of Dublin and Cork. Managing Director, Daniel Lowrey.

In November the Directors of The Star Theatre are happy to state that the dividend paid, 17½ per cent, is the highest paid by any Variety Theatre outside London. It is agreed to issue 10,000 new Shares of £1 at 6 per cent to provide for a reconstruction of the Theatre. The new Theatre will have an entrance on Dame Street, the premises have been very quietly acquired and without any fuss. Mr Lowrey: 'It took fourteen years to acquire them!'

In the same month The Gaiety Theatre celebrated its silver jubilee, and Michael Gunn gave up active connection with it. Thus ended one of the great reigns in the Theatre.

Monday 20 April. 'The World's Most Scientific Invention. The Greatest, most Amazing & Grandest Novelty ever presented in Dublin. THE CINÉMATOGRAPHE. Living People brought (in Animation) from all parts of the Globe and presented with every Action of Real Life on the Stage of The Star.' This was the first flicker of the flicks.

After many haphazard and fumbling attempts, the Motion Picture had become a reality when Auguste Lumière of Lyons patented his first Projection Machine for the large public showing of celluloid film on 15 February 1895. He called the whole contraption *Le Cinématographe*. On 20 February 1896 Trewey, a French Conjuror, gave the first public exhibition of the Lumière Cinématographe in England at The London Polytechnic. It attracted widespread attention and moved next month to The Empire Palace Music Hall. Two months after they were first seen in England the Films were at Dan's.

Great pains were taken. Intense secrecy was maintained as to how this miracle worked. Stage hands and staff were under orders not to tell. A boxlike shelter was built to hide the Conjuror-Operator (it wasn't Trewey) and his machinery. Box-office was excellent; the other items on the Bill were barely attended to since all were agog to see the new Novelty.

For a long time nothing happened. Then fitful points of light were seen to glimmer on the Screen. People were mystified. All the flicks and flashes

Among the Male Comics this final Year, Tom Leamore, from *Pick-Me-Up*

sparking on and off did not seem to add up to anything. They were prepared however to give it a chance to 'warm up'. Sure enough, for a brief moment what appeared to be the Phantom of a Prizefighter – in fact a Pair of Prizefighters – came up on the dusky Screen; eyes watching closely saw the Pair actually swiping and swaying in slow motion like the ghosts of outsize Ballet Girls. A wave of laughter ripped across the House. But the whole thing dissolved in darkness, and though the Band played manfully it could not hide the commotion in the Conjuror's Box where the Magic Machine had broken down.

The audience grew impatient, groaned, wisecracked. They could not know they were sitting in on an historic moment; all they were aware of was that The Star of Erin was in pitch darkness, and that there was the devil of a row going on in the Secret Box.

Suddenly the light flashed on again and was greeted with a cheer. Splotches appeared, here a glimmering arm, there a leg; a figure formed, moving beautifully and with a gasp the House recognised an Acrobat somersaulting at speed in flickering jerks. The more accustomed they became to the flickering light the better they were able to imagine what they were supposed to see on the Screen, and each new bit of the quivering jigsaw to be solved was greeted with cries – 'Look, Highlanders!' 'Dragoons!' 'Tigers!' 'No, Cats!' And Cats they were, apparently boxing. Things happened either too fast or too slow. A Scots Dancer lifted a kilted knee in ponderous deliberation, a Drummer beat his Drum – the drummer in the Orchestra whacked his own instrument – too late, too soon – it was impossible to anticipate the fragmented movement of the Phantom Philm Pholk.

'The Cinématographe was exhibited, but the character of the exhibition would perhaps be more correctly conveyed by a not unfamiliar word and one which has a recognised place in respectable dictionaries – Kaleidoscope – which is defined as an optical instrument in which we see an endless variety of beautiful colours and forms.' – *Irish Times.*

'£60. Not enough light on the pictures.' – Dan Lowrey's Engagement Book.

Dissatisfied with the experiment, Dan went to London to seek out the real thing, taking Jeannie with him to discuss the business with the agents of the Lumière Brothers and their Operator, Felicien Trewey. Satisfied that this time he was getting the proper celluloid he booked *Le Cinématographe* for the first week in October at £70.

This time there was no hitch. Seven thousand people thronged through the doors at Crampton Court and Sycamore Street for the first week of the Pictures.

> Chief item of attraction on a particularly good programme is the exhibition of the original Cinématographe under the direction of Mons. Trewey, from The Empire Palace London, where it ran six months. This very wonderful instrument produces with absolute correctness in every detail animated representations of scenes and incidents which are witnessed in everyday life. To those who witness the exhibition for the first time the effect is startling. The figures are thrown upon a screen erected in front of the audience and, taking one of the scenes depicted – that of a very busy Railway Terminus into which the locomotive and a number of carriages dash with great rapidity – the effect is so realistic that for the moment one is almost apt to forget that the representation is

artificial. When the train comes to a standstill the passengers are seen hurrying out of the carriages, bearing their luggage, the greetings between themselves and their friends are all represented perfectly true to life and the scene is an exact reproduction of the life and bustle and tumult to be witnessed at the great Railway depots of the world.

The representation of Westminster Bridge was equally attractive. A representation of a Cavalry charge, in which every action of the galloping horses in the advancing line was distinctly marked, was a grand picture. The Wedding of H.R.H. Princess Maude of Wales and the Procession in St James's Street after the ceremony were magnificent and impressive spectacles, second only to the actual scenes themselves. The representation of the Sea-bathing was also wonderfully true to life. The audience witnessed the bathers jumping into the water and the spray caused by the plunge rose into the air and descended again in fleecy showers. – *Freeman's Journal.*

Among the Operatic Singers, Lucy Clarke, Welsh mezzo-soprano, from *Pick-Me-Up*

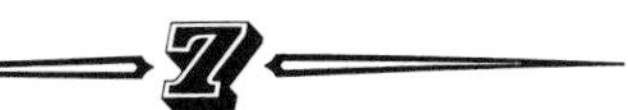

Revels ending, we take our leave this Year of many old friends. Marie Loftus. VVVG. Tom-Cat Minnie Cunningham. VVG. Billie Barlow. VVVVG. Harriet Vernon. VVVVG. Katie ('Daisy') Lawrence. VVG. The Tiller Girls, rating £30. Harry Lauder. £5. 10*s*. Coster Alec Hurley. £22. 10*s*. VVVVVG. Grand old man Charles Coburn, steadfast Artiste, refusing repeated calls for 'The Man who Broke the Bank' and the 'Eyes'. 'Over' Rowley. £25. Millie Hylton Male Impersonator. The Bohee Bros Banjoists to the Royal Family. £40. The Craggs Family of Seven, immaculate Acrobats ('as babes unable to talk we performed with Father in the bed'). T. E. Dunville (during the Music Hall Slump his body was taken from the Thames. Verdict: suicide).

CHAPTER TWENTY-ONE

1897 Curtains

1

From his Office at Sycamore Street, Mr Lowrey issued, on 1 January, his last Address to the Public:

Another rapid Revolution of the Wheel of Time. Another
New Year's Morn is ushered in upon us and welcomed
amid the peal of many bells. Before the Curtain
then ascends upon the Great Drama of Life
MR DANIEL LOWREY
steps in front again to wish you all a Bright and
Happy New Year.
Look on This Picture – to recapitulate the Battles
& Victories achieved by
THE STAR THEATRE OF VARIETIES
since the time when, seventeen years ago, I took possession of
its site and year by year have striven – and Succeeded Too –
in raising it from the Slough in which it then in the eyes of the
Public stood, to the proud position it now occupies –
A FINANCIAL COLOSSUS
Patronised by the Elite
standing in the Very Front Rank of the Foremost Theatres
of Great Britain.
and Now on This! – It has been a matter of notoriety that the
accommodation of the Theatre is now inadequate for the
Enormous Patronage, and in my previous communications
to the Public I intimated my intention of having it enlarged
to double its present capacity and having a
GRAND MAIN ENTRANCE FROM DAME STREET.
I trust I may be spared to see that promise faithfully
fulfilled. Already the work of rebuilding is greatly
advanced, and if my determination be fulfilled I venture
to state that when The Star Theatre is re-opened, the
eyes of the Public will also be opened, to the
FINEST AMUSEMENT PALACE
INSIDE OR OUTSIDE LONDON
a structure of beauty worthy of the City of Dublin and of the
generous support with which its Citizens have always upheld
my efforts in catering for their healthy enjoyment.
I remain
Faithfully yours
DANIEL LOWREY.

While the external construction at the Dame Street front was in progress, all through January and February the nightly shows went on within. But all were eclipsed by that new Lowrey Novelty, the Cinématographe. The Lumière Pictures topped the Bill for a fortnight, the House 'crammed to suffocation'. They were followed by Professor Jolly's Cinématographe which went on for six weeks with a new series of Animated Photographs each week – 'a whole new world revealed', everything from Scenes in the Streets of Belfast to the Czar of All the Russias making his State Entry into Paris with an animated crowd of 40,000 people on the Screen. £30. VVVVVG.

Saturday 27 February. The last Bill of all:

Programme Cover from the Carefree Nineties: this worried the Canon in Cork

1 OVERTURE BY THE BAND. *Leader, E. J. Taylor. LA DIADÈME*

2 VISCOUNT WALTER MUNROE, '*the Man that Struck O'Hara*'

3 JESSE BURTON, *Actor Vocalist*

4 ELLIOTT TROUPE OF COSTER ACROBATS

5 *Selection by the Band, from* THE SHOP GIRL

6 LILY MARNEY, *Serio Comic*

7 PROFESSOR HOWLETT'S MARIONETTES

8 ST JOHN & DWIGHT, *Duettists & Dancers*

9 THE THREE CASTLES, TYROLEANS, *in a new Pantomime Statuesque Act: THE MISER*

(*Unnumbered, a late booking*) BONNIE KATE HARVEY

10 PROFESSOR JOLLY'S ANIMATED PHOTOGRAPHS. *Views of Dublin. People walking in Sackville Street. Traffic on Carlisle Bridge. The 13th Hussars marching through the City*

The crowd moved out into the night, still in a trance after the flickering images, and The Star closed for the last time.

The breakdown gang moved in. Lowrey reached a pitch of nervous exhaustion in his anxiety to speed things up; there was a huge construction programme ahead and less than six months to go until Horse Show Week when he hoped to open. The outer walls were retained but raised to bring the roof up to a height of seventy feet; bars and Auditorium were stripped; the Galleries were taken down; O'Callaghan's exposed beams and Gothic bearing-timbers were knocked out; the elegant Proscenium which had framed so many faces was broken up; the medallion of Tom Moore disappeared in the stucco dust.

The new design was by R. H. Brunton, a noted Theatre architect. The change was to be thorough – more thorough perhaps than Dan himself was aware – for the Company, behind the scenes, was already flirting with one of the biggest Music Hall Syndicates in the British Isles. The House was to be turned round, the Stage was to be at the Dame Street end instead of at the Sycamore Street end where it had always been and the entrance to the private Boxes and Stalls from Dame Street was to pass under the Stage as in the London Opera Comique. Capacity: 3,000, of which 1,000 would be seated. For lighting the Company had two dynamos of their own installed. Décor to be in opulent neo-baroque with touches of Louis Quinze in satin and gold. The Fashion Theatre had arrived.

Of the oil-paintings which had been part of the colour and the Family atmosphere of The Star, Lowrey took two home to Roslyn Park for safe-keeping. The others, showing Old Dan as 'Exile', as 'Whistlin' Thief', as 'Exile Returned', he sent to Dockrell's to be cleaned and retouched for his new Theatre . . .

In the event, the Company had no time for the paintings. In the new 'Dame Street' atmosphere, they felt, all trace of 'Dan Lowrey's' and its demotic overtones were best eradicated. The paintings lay neglected in Dockrell's yard until 1908, when they perished in a fire which gutted a large part of the premises.

Easter Monday 1897. Opening Night of The Palace Theatre of Varieties, King Street, Cork. The portico in coloured glass shone out prettily on the street and crowds in Bank Holiday mood thronged the entrances. Inside the dreaded 'Music Hall' they looked in delight at the brilliant electric illumination, the gilt and colour of the richly dressed interior. The Orchestra played the Overture, *Semiramide* (Rossini), after which the reverent hush was broken by the gods who, as if to the Music Hall manner born, cheered a dropscene representing Cork's own Pope's Quay, gave ovations to Wellknown Men as they appeared in their seats below, and delivered 'badinages and choruses between whiffs of the weed in all its forms'.

Mr Lowrey made a brief appearance on the Stage and stammered his appreciation of the friendly reception he had met with in Cork. Highlights on the Bill were the Australian F. J. Millis ventriloquising his Dolls with Corkonian drolleries, Madame Alma on the Electric Globe which flashed many colours richly lighting her costume and acrobatic limbs, Minnie Cunningham whose dulcet tones were a surprise and a delight to that songful City, and Professor Jolly's Cinématographe. The last Lowrey Chicks, the Tiller Girls, danced amid rousing cheers and sang 'Killarney'.

The venture was successful. But it was difficult enough, and close Lowrey supervision would be required for a time. Since it was hard to attract women and girls (the very notion of Music Hall in Cork being nextdoor to damnation), 'Ladies' Nights' were instituted and each lady was presented with a cup of tea on a tray during the interval. The local Canon was actually won round to the idea that Variety Theatre was respectable, that it had the blessing of His Royal Highness, that the 'shewing of limbs' was no longer an object, and that men consumed less drink there than they would in a common tavern. But when he saw the Chorus Girl on the cover of the Programme he was scandalised.

On May Day the Artistes appearing at The Palace came on Stage in a body and presented Mr Lowrey with an Illuminated Address as a mark of appreciation of his energy and enterprise. Dan was deeply moved: it was the first time that Artistes anywhere had given him a present.

He was worried. He could concentrate neither on Cork nor on Belfast; all his care and anxiety was for The Star. Work there seemed to hang fire. His nervous tension increased. He began to be haunted by the spectre of Horse Show Week and the importance of having the Theatre ready in time. He could think or talk of nothing else.

Her Majesty and H.R.H. the Prince of Wales (in kilts) thank the Artistes after a performance at Abergeldie. From the *Theatre*

Financially his affairs were in an impossible tangle. To finance Cork, Belfast and his share of the new Star, he had mortgaged all his leases and properties including Roslyn Park. Everything depended on the success of the new Theatre. He began to have sleepless nights, bouts of intense irritability, stretches of stupor and exhaustion. In May the papers announced that he was confined to his home at Roslyn Park suffering from an acute illness brought on by overstrain. At the end of the month it was learned that he had gone with his wife Edith to a health resort in Derbyshire.

The change soon did him good. In July the papers were glad to announce that he was recovering. In August his son Daniel came from Belfast. Dan's only question was for The Star: would it be open in time for Horse Show Week? – No. He turned his face to the wall.

Sir Edward Moss, from *The Green-Room Book*

In September Adam S. Findlater announces that H. E. Moss of the Moss & Thornton Group of Provincial Empires has joined the Board of The Star Theatre Company Ltd. The new Theatre will be part of the Moss Circuit, Artistes to be booked by the Moss assistant-Manager. It is planned, under Moss guidance, that the 'free-and-easy rowdyism of sing-songs which has lingered in certain sections of Music Hall' will be toned down. Queues will be organised to avoid crushing at the doors.

In November Oswald Stoll who, with his string of Provincial Halls, is co-operating with the Moss Circuit of Empires, enters the picture. Scaffolding removed from the Dame Street Entrance. Coloured portico carried on

Sir Oswald Stoll, from *The Green-Room Book*

The New Look at Crampton Court: The Empire Palace, showing the ornate interior, the well-bred Audience, the Galleryites tucked away under the ceiling. From *Illustrograph*

thin pillars across the sidewalk, style vaguely Italianate. Tympanum of ecclesiastical glass, stained and leaded, carries the new title: The EMPIRE PALACE. There is a feeling that something has altered in the City.

Monday 13 November. Queues at The Empire Palace for Opening Night. Interior brilliant under electric chandeliers. Auditorium opulent in curves of neo-baroque, immense Proscenium, mirrors, 'a palace of satin and gold' – *Irish Society*. Charles Coburn reads the Prologue, welcoming the Audience to their new Theatre. The night ends with the Lumière Pictures. Groans from the Gallery whose occupants are packed away too high and too far from the scene to be able to take part in the Show with the old intimacy.

The weeks tick by, Bills roll along, the new crowds throng to Dublin's new Theatre. Nice people who would not have been found dead in Dan Lowrey's now flock to the glittering and innocuous fun. The Century turns. Variety booms. Moss & Stoll become Sir Edward & Sir Oswald, amalgamate, form their Empire of Empires, Capital £2,086,000. A serious falling-off in standards is felt. The Combine is geared for the competent, not for the genius; they have no time for the highly-flavoured personality, the creative vulgarity, the destructive humour. Mockery of the Dingy Old Days and their Idols is encouraged. The *Irish Playgoer* laments the

Dan Lowrey the Third

scarcity of first-class Artistes and leading Comics and says: 'The Hall should be renamed The Empire Palace of Monotonies'.

The Years roll along. The Empire Palace survives the Rebellion, the War and the dissolution of the Moss–Stoll Empire in the Music Hall Slump. In January 1923 it is reopened under a new name: The OLYMPIA. Presenting Drama, Opera, Ballet, Films, Oratorio, Pantomime, with a mainstay of Revue and Variety, The Olympia weathered the Second World War and survives to the present day. In the meantime 'Dan Lowrey's' has faded to a name and a nostalgia, a time and an experience impossible to recreate.

At Buxton in Derbyshire, high up among the peaks of flint where Dan Lowrey lay dying, all these developments belonged to the Shadowgraph of the Times to come. He was never to draft a poster, never to mark the Engagement Book again. On Monday 16 August, he died. A postmortem disclosed a malignant tumour of the brain.

Friday 20 August. Torrential morning rain blotted out the whole of Dublin bay and hills and fell on the black slates, made rivulets in the streets and drenched the flags, the banks of flowers, the bunting, which decked the City for the Royal Visit. Their Highnesses the Duke & Duchess of York arrived in Kingstown. Among the Reception Committee on the quayside, silk-hatted and umbrella'd against the rain and the driving spray, stood the Chairman of the Township Commissioners, Adam S. Findlater. He delivered an Address of Welcome to the Royal Pair who then drove into Town and up a beflagged and dripping Dame Street to be received by the Lord Lieutenant at Dublin Castle. The Chairman stepped into his carriage and was driven at speed to Sandymount for the Lowrey funeral.

The coffin, massive and heavily mounted in silver, was laid in the hearse with wreaths and floral tributes from many parts heaped upon it. A large crowd had gathered under the downpour at the gates of Roslyn Park to see the start of the cortège, to pay their last respects to The Guv'nor, and to look at the notabilities as they went by in carriage and cab. Daniel Lowrey, son. William Lowrey, grandson. J. H. Harris, son-in-law. Thomas Dunbar, nephew. John Gunn, nephew of Michael. J. J. Whitbread, lessee of The Queen's Theatre. The Editor of *Sport*. J. J. & Alec Powderley, Printers. Oscar May. Adam S. Findlater. W. J. Ashcroft. Four representatives from the journal *Era*. H. Glenville, Mechanics' Theatre. Justin McCarthy, Author. William West. Sir Henry Cochrane. Sir R. W. Jackson, Commander of the Bath. Pat Kinsella . . .

The burial and graveside services took place in Mount Jerome, not far from the grave of Artois.

'It is generally agreed that he was the father of the profession.' – *Era*.

'The craze for Limited Liability Companies which has worked so much mischief did not leave Mr Lowrey untouched. . . . There can be no doubt that the worry and cares of big adventure had no small part in prostrating him. He will leave a blank in Dublin, for where shall we find another like him? – *Irish Figaro*.

Charles Davis as 'The Leprechaun'

Opting for union with the Moss–Stoll Empire of Empires, The Star Theatre Company seems to have been anxious to erase the Lowrey image. There was a backstreet flavour about the name 'Dan Lowrey's', a whiff of male tavern delights, and the tone was a bit too 'common' for the respectable new regime. The month The Empire Palace opened in Dame Street they dispensed with Daniel, son of the great Showman, as Manager of The Belfast Empire. For a time he leased a public-house; later he became a tram-driver in London.

Jeannie had managed The Palace Theatre, Cork, for a time during her father's illness. She too found herself unwanted and retired into obscurity. At her death in 1959 it was found that she had kept an ostrich feather from the hat of Vesta Victoria all through the years.

Hannah, the eldest girl, had married John Harris in Belfast. They had six daughters, one of whom, Ann, became the mother of Charles Davis. With Davis the old Lowrey flair for Theatre recurs. Having begun with Radio Eireann Repertory, he took over the part of Leprechaun in the Broadway production of *Finian's Rainbow*, became a Hollywood actor, then director, appeared constantly on television, and produced the documentary *Kennedy's Ireland.*

Norah married W. R. Sargeant, an engineer at Jacobs Biscuits. After his retirement they decided to emigrate to Woking in Surrey, and before she left Norah presented the two oil-paintings which she had rescued during the demolition of The Star – the one of Old Dan in evening-dress and the one of Barry Sullivan's *Hamlet* – to the Old Dublin Society. She never lost her love of the little Theatre in which she had been born, and retained vivid memories of it right up to her death in 1967 at the age of eighty-five.

Edith Lowrey, Dan's widow, and the remaining children departed from the scene. Two years after his death all the premises which Dan had acquired in Crampton Court passed from Edith Lowrey to Adam S. Findlater the mortgagee. Later Adam S. Findlater applied before the Master of the Rolls for leave to value and sell the property known as Roslyn Park which Mr Lowrey had mortgaged to him. Leave granted. Valued at £1,500 and sold. In time it became a Convent of the Sisters of the Sacred Heart.

Final item: Autumn 1897. The workmen chipped away the old name which had been cut into the stonework: DAN LOWREY'S STAR OF ERIN MUSIC HALL.

General Index

Index of Songs